# lose weight
## the *Smart*
# low-carb way

**200** **HIGH-FLAVOR RECIPES** and a 7-step plan
to stay slim **FOREVER**

bettina newman, r.d., and david joachim

RODALE

recipes by leslie revsin

**Notice**

This book is intended as a reference volume only, not as a medical manual. It is not intended as a substitute for any treatment that may have been prescribed by your doctor. Keep in mind that nutritional needs vary from person to person, depending upon age, sex, health status, and total diet. The foods discussed and recipes given here are designed to help you make informed decisions about your diet and health. If you suspect that you have a medical problem, we urge you to seek competent medical help.

Cover and Interior Designer: Joanna Williams
Cover and Interior Photographer: Mitch Mandel/Rodale Images
Cover and Interior Food Stylist: Diane Vezza
Cover recipe: Whole Grain Pancakes with Berry Cream Syrup (page 97)
The recipe for Janet's Roasted Eggplant and Chickpeas (page 291) is adapted from *Higher Choices: Life-Enhancing Recipes*, by Janet Lasky. © 1997 by Janet Lasky. Reprinted with permission of Higher Choices Alternative Food Concepts, L.L.C.

**Library of Congress Cataloging-in-Publication Data**

Newman, Bettina.
    Lose weight the smart low-carb way : 200 high-flavor recipes and a 7-step plan to stay slim forever / Bettina Newman and David Joachim ; recipes by Leslie Revsin.
        p.   cm.
    Includes index.
    ISBN 1–57954–438–X   hardcover
    1. Low-carbohydrate diet—Recipes.   I. Joachim, David.   II. Revsin, Leslie.   III. Title.
RM237.73 .N493   2002
613.2'5—dc21                                                              2001005550

**Distributed to the book trade by St. Martin's Press**

2   4   6   8   10   9   7   5   3   1   hardcover

Visit us on the Web at www.rodalestore.com, or call us toll-free at (800) 848-4735.

**RODALE**

WE **INSPIRE** AND **ENABLE** PEOPLE TO IMPROVE
THEIR LIVES AND THE WORLD AROUND THEM

# acknowledgments

After 3 decades of working with a lower-carbohydrate approach to weight loss, there are many people to thank for this book. Numerous friends, colleagues, researchers, and clients have contributed, directly and indirectly, to what you now hold in your hands. In particular, we would like to extend our thanks and warmth to:

Dr. Robert C. Atkins, a mentor and good friend who provided a foundation of knowledge and inspired in us a different approach to weight loss.

Leslie Revsin and Carol Munson, who worked magic in the kitchen by translating the principles of smart low-carb eating into truly fabulous recipes.

All of the people who generously shared their weight-loss stories, tips, and recipes with us. Special thanks to Jeanne Bennett, Betty Carlucci, Becky Cleveland, Alice Cooper, Amanda Di Pietro, Lindsay Dooley, Norma Gates, Janet Lasky, Joan Lawson, Lynne Peters, and Howard Lee Whitehorne.

The wonderful staff at Rodale for their talent, creativity, thoroughness, and dedication, especially Neil Wertheimer, Janine Slaughter, Anne Egan, Sindy Berner, Holly McCord, Regina Ragone, Joanna Williams, Mitch Mandel, Jim Gallucci, Jennifer Kushnier, Barbara Thomas Fexa, Kathy Dvorsky, JoAnn Brader, Cindy Ratzlaff, and Kathy Hanuschak.

Nancy Hancock for her tireless support.

Jeff Coombs and Mike Napier for patiently tracking down the nutrition information on whole, natural foods.

The Chesapeake General Hospital's Lifestyle Fitness Center for bringing to life the people who are profiled in these pages.

Gene Newman and Christine Bucher, two extraordinary spouses, whose unflagging encouragement and support allowed us to take on the challenges of writing this book. Thanks also to Leonard and Marie Montalbano.

And a big thank you to Rose Marino, who has waited nearly a century to read her granddaughter's book!

—Bettina Newman, R.D.,
   and David Joachim

# contents

# introduction:
# why low-carb?

No one can pinpoint the one thing that causes weight gain. For most people, a variety of factors are to blame, including genetics, family history, eating and exercise habits, and lifestyle choices that influence everything from how much sleep you get to how stressed you feel. Fortunately, diet is one of the factors that you can control. Even so, there is great debate about the best dietary changes to make. Eat less fat? Eat fewer calories? Or simply eat less food? Any of these approaches would be better than doing nothing. But years of clinical experience and research make us believe that reducing carbohydrates gets closer to the underlying metabolic problems in weight control than any other dietary modification.

This book is the result of more than 30 years of working with a lower-carbohydrate approach to weight loss. We have talked with and counseled hundreds of people, all of whom have lost weight, kept it off, and improved their health by using the simple plan presented in this book. Most family doctors have been surprised to see that these people—their patients—have reduced their

risk of heart disease, diabetes, and cancer while dropping pounds, boosting their energy levels, and getting a new outlook on life.

Becky Cleveland lost 63 pounds and has kept it off for 3 years and counting. She started with one simple change: She switched from eating refined grains like white flour to eating whole grains like whole wheat flour and oatmeal.

Lindsay Dooley had been called a chunky girl since she entered kindergarten. In her teens, she adopted a smart low-carb approach and dropped four dress sizes. She has stayed slim ever since.

These and many more people share their real-life weight struggles, best slimming strategies, and favorite recipes in this book. We also brought in the expert advice of weight-loss professionals who have studied the health benefits of eating fewer carbohydrate-rich foods. This is a fairly new area of weight-loss research, and the results are exciting. They show that a low-carb approach, when planned wisely, may be one of the most effective and satisfying ways to lose weight and keep it off long term.

If you're familiar with low-carb eating, you'll notice that our plan is a little different. This book should not be roped into the current stable of low-carb, high-fat diet books and dismissed. When you read it, you'll see that we're not saying you should eliminate carbohydrates altogether. We're not saying that the only starch you can eat is oatmeal. And we're not saying that you can eat all the bacon and cream you want. What we're saying is that the majority of your calories—your daily diet—should come from lean protein foods such as chicken, healthy fats like olive oil, and yes, good-for-you carbohydrates like vegetables and whole grains.

The idea of smart low-carb eating is simple: Minimize refined-grain foods and sweets. Replace them with protein-rich, high-fiber meals. And eat sensible portions. For most people, this approach helps to normalize blood sugar levels and curb the impulse to binge eat.

Of course, occasional treats are a key component of long-term success. So we've built a few indulgences right into the book. You may notice that a few recipes are slightly higher in carbohydrates (20 to 30 grams of carbohydrate for a main dish or dessert). These recipes are meant for those times when you want to indulge—every other week or so. You might also see that some recipes are slightly higher in fat than what you might expect (15 to 20 grams of fat for a main dish or dessert). Don't be scared off. A little bit of fat in your diet can actually help you lose weight. Fat carries flavor and leaves you feeling full and satisfied (because it is slowly digested) so you're less

tempted to overeat. Also, if you look closely at the recipes, you'll see that most of the fat used here is the healthy monounsaturated or polyunsaturated kind, which has been shown to help reduce heart disease risk. The less-healthy saturated fats are kept to a minimum.

After working with hundreds of people trying to lose weight, we've learned that most people want delicious, healthy meals for themselves and their families. Yet almost everyone says they can't spend lots of time in the kitchen. So we've made sure that every recipe in this book comes together easily. Time-Savers and Flavor Tips have been sprinkled throughout so you can take preparation shortcuts when you're busy, or change ingredients to appeal to finicky eaters. And every recipe has been taste-tested at least twice; in some cases, three times. We know that great-tasting food is absolutely critical to reaching your weight goals, so we made sure that every recipe tastes fabulous. In fact, that was the best part of the writing! Flip through the recipes and you'll see that nothing here even remotely resembles diet food. Chocolate Hazelnut Flourless Cake (page 338) is a slice of decadence at its finest. Pesto Chicken Sandwich with Roasted Peppers (page 156) is pure eating satisfaction. And Whole Grain Pancakes with Berry Cream Syrup (page 97)? Grab the forks!

We hope that you will truly enjoy the food in this book. We believe that, when combined with the simple seven-step plan, these smart low-carb recipes are your quickest route to long-term weight-loss success.

# the science behind low-carb success

If you could ask a caveman what he ate yesterday, you'd quickly find out that a low-carbohydrate diet is nothing new. There is little doubt that the Paleolithic diet consisted primarily of meat, vegetables, nuts, fruits, and berries. It's true that we don't have records showing how these foods were balanced, but common sense tells us that once an animal was caught and cooked, it yielded a greater number of servings than cavemen could possibly have gathered and consumed from locally available and seasonal vegetables and fruits. Add to this the fact that refined grains, soft drinks, and candy bars were unavailable, and we can safely assume that the invention of the low-carb diet took place long before people began to read about it.

Doctors began to pay formal attention to the effect of carbohydrate restriction in the 1920s, when this diet was used as a treatment option for people with intractable epilepsy. Another 30 to 40 years later, the first public hype about the health benefits of higher-protein, lower-carbohydrate meals hit the United States. In the 1960s, Dr. Irwin Stillman touted this eating plan in a widely read book and on late night TV. In the 1970s, Dr. Robert Atkins popularized this eating plan when he publicly defied conventional medical wisdom with his "diet revolution."

The 1980s and 1990s brought several variations on the low-carb theme, including the Scarsdale Diet, The Zone, Sugar Busters, Protein Power, and the Carbohydrate Addict's Diet. Technically, all of these low-carb diets work. People lose weight on them. They might even be able to keep the weight off for a time. However, many of these diets are impractical because they require you to suddenly eliminate your favorite foods—even some of the healthy ones. And some of these low-carb diets are nutritionally inadequate or nearly impossible to sustain over a lifetime.

Our plan takes a whole new approach by starting with your current eating patterns and your degree of motivation for change. Unlike a strict diet that forces you to empty your fridge and cupboards into the trash, smart low-carb eating includes many of your favorite foods such as pasta, grains, and even potatoes. No food is completely off-limits. The plan can be started immediately or gradually adopted over time. It is a plan that you can live with for good.

Our approach also incorporates new research that helps explain why low-carb eating reduces weight. We take into account all the beneficial aspects of the carbohydrate-controlled plans that have come before. But more important, we include the key elements of calorie control; glycemic index; unsaturated versus saturated fat; the nutritional benefits of whole, natural foods; and the flexibility to choose from each of the major food groups.

Another unique part of the smart low-carb approach is that it addresses food triggers. Regardless of how nutritious and/or low in carbohydrates a food may be, if it somehow triggers you to overeat, reaching a healthy weight and overall good health might be an endless struggle. We show you how to identify and manage potential food triggers so that you can achieve your weight-loss goals and reach optimal health.

## What's a Carbohydrate?

Eating smart does not mean avoiding carbohydrates altogether. We're not about to tell you that carbohydrates are evil. The fact is, you can't live without them. Carbohydrates are one of three basic macronutrients needed to sustain life (the other two are protein and fat). But eating too many carbohydrates—especially refined carbohydrates—can cause you to gain weight and can adversely affect your health. Numerous studies demonstrate the relationship of these less-healthy carbohydrates to type 2 diabetes, heart disease, and some kinds of cancer. It's true that eating too much of any food can cause weight gain and increase disease risk, but there's more to the story when it comes to carbohydrates.

Carbohydrates encompass a broad range of sugars, starches, and fibers. There are two general classes of carbs—refined and unrefined. Refined carbohydrates are essentially refined sugars and refined flours. Unrefined carbohydrates are the kind found in whole grains, beans, fruits, and many vegetables. Generally speaking, refined carbohydrates are less healthy for our bodies and unrefined carbohydrates are more healthy. Here's a list of foods classified as refined or unrefined carbohydrates.

### Refined Carbohydrates

| | |
|---|---|
| Table sugar | Maple syrup |
| Soft drinks | Sweetened yogurt |
| Any ingredient ending in "-ol," such as sorbitol | Any ingredient ending in "-ose," such as dextrose |

### Unrefined Carbohydrates

| | |
|---|---|
| Vegetables | Buckwheat |
| Beans | Quinoa |

| | |
|---|---|
| Peas | Tapioca |
| Milk | Plain yogurt |
| Fruit | Fruit juice |
| Amaranth | Whole grains (wheat, |
| Arrowroot | oats, barley, rye) |
| Potatoes | Whole-grain breads, |
| Sweet potatoes | cereals, and pastas |

Unrefined carbohydrates are usually more healthy because they include two kinds of fiber, soluble and insoluble. Fiber is extremely important for weight management because it makes you feel full so you don't overeat, and it helps to slow down your body's absorption of carbohydrate foods. Good sources of soluble fiber include citrus fruits, apples, dried peas, beans, oatmeal, and oat bran. It helps to stabilize blood sugar levels and may help reduce the risk of heart disease. Good sources of insoluble fiber are whole grains, wheat bran, broccoli, carrots, asparagus, and pears. Combined with soluble fiber, insoluble fiber helps maintain good bowel function. Because these fiber-rich foods are so important to a satisfying weight-loss plan, we've included a wide variety of them in this book.

## CARB METABOLISM: THE GLYCEMIC INDEX

If you want to lose weight and keep it off, it's important to know how various foods will affect your energy levels and your waistline. Here's how it works: All carbohydrates, including the lactose in milk, the starch in a bagel, and the sucrose in table sugar, are eventually converted by your body into glucose (blood sugar), which is our primary source of energy. One hundred percent of the carbohydrate you eat turns into glucose, but only 58 percent of the protein and about 10 percent of the fat you eat is converted to glucose. For this reason, carbohydrate-containing foods are often regarded as energy foods. It also takes your body longer to convert protein into glucose and still longer to convert fat into glucose. Carbohydrates take a fraction of the time. That's why people with diabetes carry sugar pills or drink orange juice if they begin to feel weak. That's also why if you are feeling hungry and pop a piece of gum or candy into your mouth, the hunger quickly disappears for a while. You are raising your blood sugar (glucose).

Now it gets really interesting. Although all carbohydrates are converted to glucose and raise your blood sugar, not all are converted at the same rate. In the early 1980s, researchers began to study this phenomenon. You might think that all refined carbohydrate foods raise blood sugar quickly and all unrefined carbohydrate foods raise it more slowly. However, researchers demonstrated that this isn't always the case. They developed a number system called the glycemic index (GI), which ranks carbohydrate-containing foods according to how quickly they raise your blood sugar within a 2- to 3-hour period after eating. The glycemic index goes from 1 to 100, with the highest ranking of 100 assigned to pure glucose. The higher the GI, the

(continued on page 6)

# I Did It!

## Jeanne Bennett

Jeanne had a bicycle accident that led to years of medical problems and weight gain. None of the diets she tried worked very well, until she started reducing her intake of sugar and flour. Then she lost 44 pounds and kept it off for 4 years and counting.

before

"I was always thin and healthy. I could eat anything I wanted without ever gaining weight. That was my life before age 30. Then a bicycle accident marked the beginning of several physical and medical problems. I also had two children and was a stay-at-home mom.

"After recovering from the accident, I sent my second child off to kindergarten, and I was ready to return to the workplace. When I started assembling my wardrobe, I realized that I had gained almost 50 pounds! My life was loaded with stress and constant change

**Weight lost:** 44 pounds
**Time kept off:** 4 years
**Weight-loss strategies:** Reduced carbohydrate intake, ate smaller portions
**Weight-maintenance strategies:** Avoids foods containing sugar, eats whole grains instead of refined, does aerobic and strength-training exercises 3 times a week

around this time. I completed my master's degree in speech/language pathology, went through a divorce, remarried, moved to a different town, and started a new job. Food was the only constant in my life! It was my comfort—and most likely my downfall because I usually ate quick, unhealthy meals on the run.

"My weight-loss efforts were always thwarted by medical problems, too. I was diabetic, had high cholesterol, could not get a good night's sleep, and suffered with arthritic pain. By the time I reached my fifties, I was desperate. As my doctor put it, 'You have dodged a lot of bullets!' I was motivated to do more than dodge bullets. But I had no idea how to help myself. I only knew that all of the diets, sleep aids, and pain relievers that I tried were merely temporary bandages on the symptoms rather than a cure for the underlying problems.

"I had managed to lose about 10 pounds on my own when my doctor referred me to a dietitian to develop a sound eating plan. That was when I really began to lose weight and keep it off. During my very first visit, the dietitian carefully listened to me, took a complete health and diet history, and gave me a plan of action. First, we had to know what I was eating every day. I soon realized that I had been eating way too much food (about 2,500 calories a day) and far too many foods high in white sugar, white flour, and other refined carbohydrates. Best of all, I learned that even though several physical and medical problems had resulted in my present health profile, I could take control. I could get healthy and I could lose weight.

"Over the next several months, I avoided eating foods high in refined sugar and refined flour. Instead, I began to eat more vegetables, lots of lean protein foods like fish, chicken, lean cuts of beef and pork, beans, and some fresh fruit. My quality of life changed dramatically. I lost another 34 pounds in 4 months and my blood sugar levels normalized, my cholesterol came down, my arthritis pain was gone, and I got more sleep. I was so much happier! I had accomplished a significant lifestyle change—not a diet, but a way of eating and living that was right for me.

"Now I'm in my late fifties and I no longer feel like I am 'dodging bullets.' It's more like I have been armed with understanding and the tools that I need to live a more healthy life. I watch my carbohydrate intake, eat the foods that are healthy for my body, and exercise three times a week. I know I still have progress to make. But I'm much more motivated now that I've found a plan that works."

quicker the food breaks down and increases blood sugar after you eat it. The lower the GI, the more gradually the food is absorbed and the more slowly it raises your blood sugar. Foods ranked 55 or below are considered low GI because they only cause a little blip in blood sugar. Foods ranked 56 and over are considered high GI because they can spike your blood sugar, or send it soaring.

As a rule of thumb, choose more low-GI foods to help you lose weight. But don't avoid all high-GI foods. For instance, oatmeal has a "high" GI of 59, but its soluble fiber makes it a healthy food, so there's no reason to avoid it. Likewise, a chocolate bar has a "low" GI of 49, but that doesn't mean you should load up on chocolate—the extra calories and saturated fat will sabotage your weight-loss efforts.

To tell whether a high-GI or low-GI food is a healthy choice, take into account the other nutrients in the food. For example, whole wheat bread and white bread have similar GIs. But whole wheat bread is the healthier choice because it contains extra fiber and other important nutrients that white bread lacks. By the same token, brown rice is more nutritious than white, and whole wheat pasta is more healthy than white pasta. Surprisingly, potato chips have a somewhat low GI, but they're not the healthiest snack choice due to their high calorie and low nutrient content. Peanuts or a plum would make a more nutritious snack.

## Smart-Carb Insider Tip

### STAY FOCUSED

Keep your eye on the big picture. When you can, look at your eating plan for the week. Will you be going out to eat? Do you have a special luncheon to attend? A reception of some sort? Will you be traveling? Decide when you will be able to make smart choices and when you're likely to throw caution to the wind. Some foods may be more important than others to your enjoyment of life. For instance, if you have lunch planned at your favorite restaurant, avoid carbohydrates that morning and indulge in that deep-dish pizza you dream about come lunchtime. Or if there's a cake you simply must have for dessert one night, plan on eating just a salad, protein, and vegetables for that evening's dinner. Then enjoy your dessert. These occasional indulgences are crucial to maintaining a smart eating plan.

If you *do* choose to eat a high-GI food, try combining it with a low-GI food in the same meal or combining it with foods higher in protein or fat. This will slow down the rate at which the high-GI food raises your blood sugar. For instance, high-GI oatmeal could be balanced with a topping of low-GI milk and/or nuts. Again, no foods should be completely avoided. Variety, balance, and moderation are the keys to a smart eating plan. Occasional indulgences are important, too.

Here's a snapshot of low-GI and high-GI foods. See "The Glycemic Index" on page 8 for a detailed ranking of foods and their GI scores.

**Low-GI Foods**

**Breads:** Pumpernickel, sourdough

**Grains:** Barley, parboiled rice, bulgur, kasha

**Pasta:** Angel hair, linguine, and other thin strands; bean threads (cellophane noodles); whole grain spaghetti

**Cereals:** Rice bran, unsweetened high-fiber (all bran) cereals

**Vegetables:** All, except those listed as high GI

**Fruits:** Cherries, grapes, apples, peaches, pears, plums, strawberries, oranges, dried apricots

**Snacks:** Cheese, nuts, olives

**Protein foods:** Unsweetened peanut butter, beans, eggs, unsweetened soy milk

**Miscellaneous:** Low-fat yogurt, foods sweetened with sucralose, saccharin, fructose, or aspartame

**High-GI Foods**

**Breads:** Whole wheat bread, corn bread, all baked goods made with white flour

**Cereals:** Old-fashioned oats, corn and most corn products, some rice products, millet, some dry cereals

**Pasta:** All thick shapes such as ziti, penne, and rigatoni

**Fruits:** Watermelon, raisins, pineapple, cantaloupe, very ripe banana

**Vegetables:** Parsnips; potatoes (especially instant mashed potatoes), including French fries, fresh mashed potato, baked russet potato; corn, beets, carrots

**Snacks:** Corn chips, tortilla chips, pretzels, rice cakes

**Alcohol:** All beer, all liquors and wine, except red wine

**Miscellaneous:** Foods sweetened with a lot of sugar, honey, molasses, corn syrup, glucose, or dextrose

## KEEP INSULIN IN CHECK

So what's the real problem with eating lots of high-GI foods? A little hormone called insulin, which is a good guy in moderation, but not in excess. Whenever carbohydrate foods are broken down into glucose in your body, glucose stimulates the release of insulin by the pancreas. The function of insulin is to grab the glucose and deliver it to your body's cells. Then your cells convert the glucose to energy or store the glucose as fat if there is already more than enough glucose to meet current energy requirements.

More important, though, are your insulin levels. When your blood sugar soars, so does your insulin. Eating high-GI foods causes your insulin levels to go up or spike, which researchers say may increase your risk of diabetes, heart disease, and possibly cancer. Your body has a very precise means of regulating how much sugar stays in your bloodstream and how much gets into your cells. If you eat excessive amounts of quickly absorbed carbohydrates, you upset your body's precise bal-

(continued on page 10)

# THE GLYCEMIC INDEX

Choosing foods with a low glycemic index (GI) can help you lose weight. That's because low-GI foods are slowly digested and help prevent the spikes in blood sugar that can cause food cravings and lead to weight gain. Low-GI foods have a ranking of 55 or lower. High-GI foods have a ranking of 56 or higher. If you choose a high-GI food, try to combine it with a low-GI food or a food that is high in protein or fat. This will slow the absorption of the high-GI food and prevent your blood sugar from rising rapidly. Foods printed in green are high-GI foods that you need not avoid; these foods, such as carrots and watermelon, contain important nutrients besides carbohydrates. Foods printed in red are low-GI foods that are best eaten sparingly; these foods, such as potato chips, are high in fat or calories—and don't offer much else nutritionally. See page 3 for more details on the glycemic index.

| Food | GI | Food | GI | Food | GI |
|------|----|------|----|------|----|
| **Baked Goods** | | **Cereals** | | **Pastas** | |
| French bread | 95 | Puffed rice | 88 | Brown rice pasta | 92 |
| Waffle | 76 | Corn flakes | 84 | Gnocchi | 68 |
| Graham cracker | 74 | Puffed wheat | 74 | Boxed macaroni | 64 |
| Kaiser roll | 73 | Cream of Wheat | 70 | and cheese | |
| Bagel | 72 | Shredded wheat | 69 | Rice vermicelli | 58 |
| Melba toast | 70 | Quick-cooking oats | 66 | Durum spaghetti | 55 |
| White bread | 70 | Old-fashioned oats | 59 | Cheese tortellini | 50 |
| Corn tortilla | 70 | Oat bran | 55 | Linguine | 46 |
| Whole wheat bread | 69 | All-Bran | 42 | White spaghetti | 41 |
| Taco shell | 68 | **Grains** | | Meat-filled ravioli | 39 |
| Angel food cake | 67 | Instant rice | 91 | Whole grain | 37 |
| Croissant | 67 | Millet | 71 | spaghetti | |
| Stoned wheat thins | 67 | White rice | 68 | Vermicelli | 35 |
| 100 percent whole rye | 65 | Cornmeal | 68 | Fettuccine | 32 |
| bread | | Couscous | 65 | Bean threads | 26 |
| Rye crispbread | 65 | Brown rice | 55 | **Legumes** | |
| Bran muffin | 60 | Buckwheat | 54 | Fava beans | 79 |
| Whole wheat pita | 57 | Bulgur | 48 | Canned kidney | 52 |
| Oatmeal cookie | 55 | Parboiled rice | 47 | beans | |
| Pumpernickel bread | 41 | Pearled barley | 26 | Canned baked beans | 48 |

| Food | GI | Food | GI | Food | GI |
|------|----|------|----|------|----|
| Canned pinto beans | 45 | Orange juice | 57 | Beet | 64 |
| Black-eyed peas | 42 | Mango | 55 | Boiled new potato | 62 |
| Canned chickpeas | 42 | Banana | 53 | Fresh corn | 59 |
| Chickpeas | 33 | Kiwifruit | 52 | Sweet potato | 54 |
| Lima beans | 32 | Grapefruit juice | 48 | Yam | 51 |
| Yellow split peas | 32 | Pineapple juice | 46 | Green peas | 48 |
| Butter beans | 31 | Orange | 43 | Tomato | 38 |
| Green lentils | 30 | Grapes | 43 | **Snacks and Misc** | |
| Kidney beans | 27 | Apple juice | 41 | Pretzel | 83 |
| Red lentils | 26 | Apple | 36 | Rice cake | 82 |
| Soybeans | 18 | Pear | 36 | Vanilla wafers | 77 |
| **Dairy and Ice Creams** | | Strawberries | 32 | Tortilla chips | 74 |
| Tofu frozen dessert | 115 | Dried apricots | 31 | Corn chips | 72 |
| Ice cream | 61 | Peach | 28 | Table sugar | 65 |
| Sweetened, | | Grapefruit | 25 | (sucrose) | |
|   fruited yogurt | 33 | Plum | 24 | Popcorn | 55 |
| Skim milk | 32 | Cherries | 22 | Potato chips | 54 |
| Whole milk | 27 | **Vegetables** | | Chocolate | 49 |
| Artificially sweetened, | 14 | Parsnip | 97 | Chocolate-covered | 32 |
|   fruit-flavored | | Baked potato | 85 |   peanuts | |
|   yogurt | | Instant mashed | 83 | Soy milk | 31 |
| **Fruits** | |   potato | | Peanuts | 14 |
| Watermelon | 72 | French-fried potato | 75 | | |
| Pineapple | 66 | Pumpkin | 75 | | |
| Cantaloupe | 65 | Carrot | 71 | | |
| Raisins | 64 | Fresh mashed potato | 70 | | |

NOTE: Vegetables not appearing in this table are all low-GI foods.

SOURCE: "International Table of Glycemic Index," as it appears in *American Journal of Clinical Nutrition* and *The Glucose Revolution* by Thomas Wolever, M.D., Ph.D.

ance of blood sugar, which puts you at risk for these diseases.

By eating less of the quickly absorbed carbohydrates, keeping moderate amounts of lean proteins and healthy fats in your diet, and getting a reasonable amount of physical activity, you set the stage for safe and effective weight loss. These strategies form the basis of the smart low-carb approach in this book. Put the emphasis on unrefined carbohydrate foods, and you will get more fiber, vitamins, and minerals to help slow the absorption of carbohydrates into your bloodstream. Slow, gradual absorption will prevent your body from producing excess insulin and prevent sudden or excessive drops in blood sugar. As a result, you experience less hunger and are less likely to get sudden urges for sweets or extra portions.

We've talked with hundreds of people who found that this type of eating satisfaction is what really helped them to keep the weight off and stay healthy. Janet Lasky lost more than 155 pounds and has kept it off for 8 years. "I feel wonderful now!" she explains. "My doctor discontinued my blood pressure medication; my blood sugars are within normal range despite my being diagnosed with diabetes years ago; and unlike earlier readings, my cholesterol now stays well below 200. What I like best about this approach is that I don't ever feel deprived or like I am on a diet."

Alice Cooper adopted the smart low-carb approach, dropped 30 pounds, and has kept it off for 4 years. "'Happy' does not describe how I feel these days," she says. "I don't have nearly as many cravings. My desire for foods has changed."

## WHY DOES LOW-CARB WORK?

As in so many areas of nutrition, some controversy surrounds the low-carb approach. Most health professionals agree that this eating strategy results in sustainable weight loss, but the reasons why are hotly contested. To the person who loses weight, keeps it off, and stays healthy in the long run, it may not matter what the reason is. Invariably, though, once you begin shedding pounds, an inquisitive relative, friend, or coworker is going to ask why you think it works.

Proponents of the low-carb approach usually base their reasoning upon a comparison between how the body metabolizes carbohydrates and how it breaks down proteins and fats, as explained above. Simply put, eating too many carbohydrate grams may increase insulin to such a high level in overweight people that more glucose becomes available to the cells than the body needs for energy. The excess glucose gets turned into fat. Consequently, blood sugar goes down because the glucose is going into the body's cells as fat. And when your blood sugar begins to drop, you feel hungry. If, like many Americans, you eat a lot of refined carbohydrates such as soft drinks and candy bars—or even pretzels and crackers—you are feeding a vicious cycle in your body that never really satisfies your hunger because you get only short-term re-

## SUGAR ADDICTION: IS IT POSSIBLE?

Science hasn't found that sugar is addictive in the way that nicotine or even alcohol can be. However, many people claim to be addicted to sugar (and carbohydrates). Here's some support for the theory. Sugar and alcohol do have something in common. They both release a brain chemical called serotonin, which makes you feel calm and relaxed. In our frenzied world, who wouldn't want to eat more of something that relieves stress? It's extremely interesting, too, that there is frequently alcoholism in the families of people who claim to be addicted to sugar. A study done in the Addiction Program at the Royal Ottawa Hospital in Ontario even found a distinct subgroup of alcohol-dependent subjects who craved carbohydrates during sobriety.

Here's another possible explanation: When refined carbohydrates raise your blood sugar levels, these carbohydrates can stimulate the release of feel-good brain chemicals called endorphins. As with serotonin, it's natural for the body to want more and more endorphins to continue that good feeling. These explanations of sugar addiction are far from clear. The point is that some researchers believe that psychological processes are at the heart of both food cravings and addiction.

Recent research suggests that there may be a genetic explanation for your sweet tooth. Using data from the Human Genome Project, two separate research teams identified a gene that appears to regulate a sweet receptor on the nerves in your taste buds. Decreasing this gene's activity may help people control cravings for sweets.

What can you do today to stop cravings? Try replacing sugary foods or refined-carbohydrate foods with higher-protein foods for a few days. You may experience some fatigue early on, like many of the people we talked with who tried this trick. They described this temporary fatigue as sugar withdrawal. If you stick with the protein foods for more than a week, you may find, like they did, that you can break your sugar "addiction."

lief. Plus, most refined carbohydrate foods are low in fiber. As mentioned earlier, eating fiber-rich foods gives you a sense of fullness. On the other hand, eating low-fiber simple carbohydrate foods leaves you feeling constantly hungry. This cycle may help to explain why sugar seems to have an addictive quality and how carbohydrate-rich meals may lead to excess weight.

As much sense as this explanation may make to you, skeptics of reduced-carbohy-drate plans claim that this is not the whole story. They agree that reducing carbohydrates reduces insulin levels; however, they argue that the only reason low-carb eating works is that it diminishes hunger for some people, and they eat less. They remind us that the extra protein and fats in these diets also help satisfy hunger longer. The bottom line, according to skeptics, is that people lose weight on low-carb diets *not* because carbohydrates are reduced, but because protein

(continued on page 14)

# I D★id It!

## Lindsay Dooley

Lindsay was overweight for as long as she can remember. After adopting a low-carbohydrate diet in her teens, she got active in sports and dropped four dress sizes.

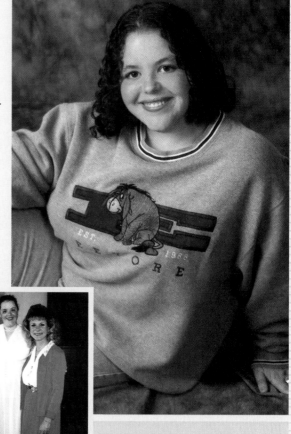

before

"From the time I entered kindergarten, I was always called a chunky girl. When I hit puberty around age 13, I mysteriously gained 30 pounds. It was a mystery because I didn't change the types or amounts of foods I was eating, nor the amount of exercise I was doing. I just gained weight. My mother tried her best to help me shed the excess pounds. She put me on a low-fat diet that limited my intake to 20 fat grams a day. When that approach failed, she took me to a doctor. He told her not to worry about my size (a women's 20!) and to quit focusing on diets. He warned her that she could cause me to have an eating disorder. For the next year, I went back to eating what I wanted to. I can

**Weight lost:** 40 pounds
**Time kept off:** 4 years
**Weight-loss strategies:** Avoided refined carbohydrates and trigger foods, strength trained, played volleyball
**Weight-maintenance strategies:** Controls carbohydrate intake, swims, stays active

*the science behind low-carb success*

remember having tremendous cravings for pasta with butter and salt. I rarely, if ever, ate sweets because I had been diagnosed with hypoglycemia (abnormal blood sugar) at age 4. My mom told me that when I was a toddler, she could give me an ice cream cone and I would be sound asleep in less than half an hour. To this day, sugar puts me right to sleep—usually for a 10-hour stint!

"Between the ages of 14 and 15, I gained another 50 pounds. Yes, 80 extra pounds in just 2 years! You can imagine what that did to my self-esteem at that critical time in my life. I became extremely depressed. Sometimes I sought solace in front of the television with any kind of food. Sometimes I would be so upset that I'd go without eating for 1 to 2 days. My depression worsened and my waistline spread as my mother searched for a doctor who could understand the weight problem.

"Finally, a doctor gave me antidepressants, which made me feel better, and identified that I had insulin resistance and several trigger foods. He advised me to eat a lower-carbohydrate diet and avoid my trigger foods, including wheat, milk, beef, and eggs. Within 2 weeks of this new eating plan, I lost 8 pounds and immediately began feeling better. After avoiding my trigger foods for 3 months, I was able to reintroduce beef and milk into my diet every 4 days. (If I eat beef 2 days in a row, I have terrible insomnia.) I admit, the plan was somewhat difficult to follow at first. But that's only because it was different from what I was used to. I soon began to adore vegetables in salads and stir-fries. Any time I had a food craving or felt deprived, I reminded myself about how much better I was feeling by not eating those foods. I also realized that if I ate the foods that weren't right for my body, I would be depriving myself of feeling and looking my best. I steadily lost about 32 more pounds and felt better and better. My energy was so great that I joined the volleyball team at school.

"I am graduating high school this year. I can't wait to pick out my graduation dress—especially since it will be at least four sizes smaller than the size I once wore!"

and fat are increased and total calories are reduced.

There's no doubt that total calories and portion control are key factors in any long-term weight-loss plan. Here's some very basic weight-loss science: One pound of fat equals 3,500 calories. For every 3,500 calories you cut out of your diet or burn off through physical activity, you will lose 1 pound. Seems simple. But if you've ever tried a rapid weight-loss diet, you know there's more to it than that. Cutting too many calories too quickly makes your body go into starvation mode, and then your body hangs on to every calorie and bit of stored fat it can. That's why rapid weight-loss diets don't work. People regain weight on them.

A few studies provide insight into why "calories in versus calories out" may oversimplify the route to successful weight loss—especially with regard to carbohydrates. Researchers at the Albert Einstein College of Medicine in the Bronx, New York, looked at caloric intake of overweight teenagers following a low-carbohydrate plan compared to that of teens on a low-fat plan over a period of 12 weeks. Although the teenagers on the low-carb plan ate an average of 600 calories more per day than the other teens, they lost an average of 11 pounds more. The teens on the low-fat plan ate fewer calories but lost an average of only 10 pounds, while those on the low-carb plan ate more calories and lost around 20 pounds. This study suggests that calories are not the only deciding factor in weight loss.

Another study found that a low-carb diet may lead to more sustainable weight loss and better health in the long run. Researchers at the University of Illinois compared the widely recommended United States Department of Agriculture (USDA) diet (high carbohydrate) to a lower-carbohydrate diet that is very similar to the one recommended in this book. Interestingly, both diets had the same number of calories. In the study, 24 midlife women above ideal weight ate 1,700 calories a day for 10

## HIDDEN ROADBLOCK to weight loss

### ALCOHOL

Carbohydrate foods form the basis of most alcoholic beverages, including the grains in beer and whiskey and the fruit in wine. Alcohol supplies mostly empty calories, and it can cause spikes in blood sugar levels. So it could be holding you back from losing the weight you'd like to lose. Surprisingly, the morning after having a drink with dinner, the scale may show that you lost up to a pound. But within a day or two, most folks regain the weight—and sometimes extra. If you drink alcoholic beverages, try slowly decreasing the amount to see if a little less alcohol might help you lose a little more weight. Or choose drinks lower in carbohydrates. One ounce of hard liquor has only trace carbs; 1 glass of table wine has about 2 grams of carbs; and one 12-ounce bottle of beer has 13 grams of carbs. The worst choice is rum and cola, which has nearly 40 grams of carbs.

weeks. One group ate according to the USDA food guide pyramid (55 percent carbohydrates, 15 percent protein, and 30 percent fat). The other group ate a lower-carbohydrate, higher-protein diet (40 percent carbohydrates, 30 percent protein, and 30 percent fat). After 10 weeks, the women in both groups lost about 16 pounds. But the women on the lower-carbohydrate diet had a more healthy weight loss. They lost about 12 pounds of body fat and just over 1 pound of muscle mass. Those who followed the USDA diet lost only 10 pounds of body fat and a surprising 3 pounds of much-needed muscle mass. Muscle mass is important because once you lose it, your body is less able to burn calories. The women on the low-carb diet lost very little muscle mass compared to the women on the USDA diet. This means that the low-carb, high-protein diet was almost twice as effective for long-term weight loss because the women who followed this diet were more efficient at burning calories. The women on the low-carb diet also had increased levels of beneficial thyroid hormones at the end of the study, suggesting that their metabolisms went up—another plus for burning calories. One more bonus for the low-carb diet: The women following this plan experienced a sharp reduction in triglycerides (fat in the blood) and a slight increase in high-density lipoprotein (HDL, the beneficial type of cholesterol), which improved their overall heart health.

These studies coincide with our clinical observations of hundreds of low-carb clients over the years. Norma Gates was steadily gaining 10 pounds a year for over a decade. She cut back on refined sugar and refined flour—all junk food—lost 44 pounds, and has kept it off for 3½ years so far. "Within a few weeks of eating fewer refined carbs, I felt like I had broken my carbohydrate addiction. The food cravings finally subsided," she says. "I no longer put my head on the kitchen table right after dinner or make my way to the den to lie on the couch, and I have newfound pleasures in life besides just food."

## HOW IT CAME TO THIS

There's no doubt that eating lower-carbohydrate foods—and especially reducing refined carbohydrates—can help you lose weight and stay healthy. Maybe this phenomenon can be explained simply. Perhaps our bodies are just not used to metabolizing so many *refined* carbohydrate foods.

Data from the USDA show that per capita soft-drink consumption has increased by almost 500 percent over the past 50 years. According to USDA reports, 74 percent of adolescent boys and 65 percent of adolescent girls now drink at least one sugar-sweetened soft drink every day. In fact, nondiet soft drinks are the number-one source of added sugars in the American diet. According to government statistics, the average woman consumes 19 teaspoons of added sugar each day, while the average man eats 28 added teaspoons, or roughly 68.5 pounds of sugar per year. How much should we be eating? Experts recommend that people who eat the average 2,000-calorie daily diet get no more than 10 teaspoons of added sugar a day. But USDA surveys show that the average American in 1998 was consuming about 20 teaspoons of added sugar every day—twice the amount.

This liberal consumption would be of no concern if sugar had a nutrient value similar to that of vegetables, protein foods, or other nutrient-dense foods. The problem is that sugar is not endowed with significant amounts of any nutrients. It provides you with only empty calories. The following chart shows just how many foods are loaded with teaspoon upon teaspoon of refined sugars. Keep in mind that many low-fat foods are sky-high in sugar because sugar is often added to these foods to replace the flavor lost when fat is removed. Overconsumption of these low-fat products helps to explain why low-fat dieting is not necessarily the answer for everyone.

| FOOD | SUGAR (TSP) |
|---|---|
| Orange soda, 12 oz | 13 |
| Cinnamon bun, large | 12 |
| Brownie, 2.5–3.5 oz | 10 |
| Cola, regular, sweetened, 12 oz | 10 |
| Ice cream, 1 cup (not fat-free, with milk sugars) | 10 |
| Cheesecake, plain, 4 oz | 9 |
| Chocolate shake, 10 oz | 9 |
| Ginger ale, 12 oz | 8 |
| Chocolate bar, 2 oz | 7 |

| FOOD | SUGAR (TSP) |
|---|---|
| Pastry, bun-type | 7 |
| Pie, fruit, double crust, 4 oz | 7 |
| Cake, frosted, $\frac{1}{16}$ of 13" x 9" cake | 6 |
| Doughnut, yeast, glazed | 6 |
| Iced tea, sweetened, 16 oz | 6 |
| Angel food cake, $\frac{1}{12}$ tube cake | 5 |
| Chocolate chip cookie, 2 medium | 5 |
| Muffin | 5 |
| Canned fruit, heavy syrup, $\frac{1}{2}$ cup | 4 |
| Croissant | 4 |
| Dry cereal, frosted, $\frac{3}{4}$ cup | 4 |
| Chocolate milk, 1 cup | 3 |
| Gingersnap cookie, 4 medium | 3 |
| Jam, 1 level tablespoon | 3 |
| Toaster pastry, frosted | 3 |
| Jelly, 1 level tablespoon | 2.5 |
| Canned fruit, clarified juice, $\frac{1}{2}$ c | 2 |
| Bread, 1 slice | 0 |
| Canned fruit, water-packed, $\frac{1}{2}$ c | 0 |
| Oatmeal, plain, 1 cup | 0 |

Some more stats: According to the Bureau of the Census and the U. S. Department of Commerce, the per capita consumption of wheat flour increased by 34 pounds within a 27-year period from the early 1970s to the late 1990s. In that time period, wheat consumption reached a peak of 150 pounds per person in the United States.

Refined wheat consumption is of some concern because refined wheat lacks fiber and has a high glycemic index. For instance, white bread and pure table sugar each have a high GI of 65 to 70, and both are quickly turned into glucose and quickly raise your blood sugar.

These statistics shed some light on the continually rising obesity rates in the United States and worldwide. In 1999, 61 percent of Americans aged 20 and older were overweight. Ten years earlier, 56 percent of American adults were overweight. Ten years before that, only 47 percent were overweight. The number of overweight or obese American adults, teens, and children has been steadily increasing for 30 years, concurrently with our increased consumption of refined-carbohydrate foods like soda, white bread, cookies, and cakes.

If, like many Americans, you eat a lot of foods containing white flour or added sugars, you may have found one of the keys to lasting weight loss: Eat fewer refined-carbohydrate foods. Instead, eat more unrefined-carbohydrate foods like whole grains, beans, vegetables, and fruits; more lean protein foods; some fruits; and some healthy fats. Yes, fats. Don't be scared off by them. Dietary fats may not be as bad for you as you think. In 1998, researchers from the Harvard School of Public Health concluded that dietary fat does not appear to be the primary cause of the prevalence of excess body fat in our society and that a

reduction in fat will not solve the problem. The fact is, fats make up most of the structure of the body's cell membranes. They play a vital role in the process of cellular communication. Fats also contain essential fatty acids that are important for the body's formation of eicosanoids, which regulate blood pressure, assist in blood clotting, help regulate body temperature, control pain and inflammation, and manufacture hormonelike substances. The fatty acids are called essential because all but two cannot be made in our bodies. We have to get them from the foods we eat. If you want to lose weight, it's important to include enough fat in your diet. See page 25 for more details on the healthy fats that help to promote weight loss and peak physical condition.

## COUNTERING THE LOW-CARB CONCERNS

Research and clinical observations have convinced us that a smart low-carb eating plan can help you lose weight and prevent disease. But you may still have some concerns. Here are the answers to the health questions that have been raised by doctors, nutritionists, and other skeptics of lower-carbohydrate diets.

**Q: Does restricting carbohydrates reduce energy and cause fatigue?**

*A: Not likely. Only two out of several hundred people we spoke with complained about* fatigue after the first few days of changing their diets. Some folks experience fatigue during the first 1 to 3 days. This may be the result of withdrawal from refined sugar, refined wheat, or other foods that the body may have been accustomed to digesting frequently. Yes, energy production is the main function of carbohydrates. However, you will get plenty of energy from the carbohydrates you do include on this plan as well as from the proteins and fats. Fatigue and energy loss are often signs of low blood sugar, and the smart low-carb approach keeps your blood sugar levels stable.

**Q: Will eating more protein and fewer carbohydrates damage my kidneys?**

A: Probably not. If you've never had a kidney problem, you probably don't need to worry about the warnings that eating more protein and fewer carbohydrates will wear out your kidneys. There is no research confirming this potential danger—even in people who consume three times the recommended amount of protein. Do pay attention to the warning if you already have kidney disease. A higher protein intake may be dangerous if your kidneys are not functioning properly. If you're unsure whether your kidneys are healthy, consult your doctor before changing your diet.

**Q: Won't eating more fat raise my cholesterol and triglycerides and increase my risk of heart disease?**

A: Quite the opposite. We have all been brainwashed into believing that eating foods with any type of fat will cause elevated cholesterol in everyone who eats them. However, saturated fat is the real culprit in increased heart disease risk. We've talked with several people who regularly ate foods high in mono- and polyunsaturated fats while reducing their carbohydrate intake—and their total cholesterol has actually come down. Most people who eat fewer carbohydrates find that their triglyceride levels go down and their good HDL cholesterol goes up. Here's a possible explanation: Fat is stored in our bodies in the form of triglycerides. It's known that excess insulin causes excess triglycerides. A high carbohydrate intake requires lots of insulin to metabolize the extra carbohydrates. As the insulin goes up, so do triglycerides. Likewise, as insulin levels come down on a reduced-carbohydrate plan, so do triglycerides. The bottom line is that a reduced-carbohydrate eating plan may help reduce your risk of heart disease because it brings down your insulin levels and your triglycerides. Just to be sure, the smart low-carb approach in this book recommends limiting saturated fat and instead focusing on foods such as oils, nuts, and olives that are rich in healthy fats.

**Q: Will everyone's blood lipids respond the same way to reducing carbohydrates and increasing protein and fat?**

A: Most likely. Almost everyone who has followed the smart low-carb eating plan has witnessed dramatic reductions in triglycerides and significant increases in good HDL cholesterol. Of course, everyone is a little different. There may be a very small percentage of the population whose *lipid levels respond negatively to the moderate increase in dietary fat that accompanies this reduced-carbohydrate plan. If you're concerned that this may be you, talk with your doctor before you begin, then ask her to check your blood fats 8 weeks later.*

### Q: Will eating more protein increase my risk of heart disease?

*A: On the contrary—the science says otherwise. A study at the Harvard School of Public Health looked at 80,082 women aged 34 to 59 without any previous indication of heart disease. When all other risks for heart disease were controlled for, and irrespective of whether the women were on high- or low-fat diets, the results showed that both animal and vegetable proteins contributed to lower risk of heart disease. Researchers concluded that replacing refined carbohydrates with protein may reduce heart-disease risk.*

### Q: Can a reduced-carbohydrate/higher-protein plan lead to osteoporosis?

*A: This is one warning we may need to heed. Increased protein makes the blood more acidic. The body responds by releasing calcium from the bones in an effort to bring the pH to a more alkaline level. However, if you eat lots of vegetables, you will minimize this problem because vegetables make the body more alkaline. Keep in mind that too little protein (which may be the case for people following a low-fat diet) can also be harmful to the skeleton. To safeguard against osteoporosis risk, the eating plans in this book set an upper limit on protein*

*intake and boost vegetable consumption considerably.*

### Q: Does the plan in this book contain all the nutrients I need to protect my bones?

*A: Yes. These eating plans are high in calcium-rich foods like cheese, dark green leafy vegetables, almonds, Brazil nuts, salmon, sardines, and calcium-fortified soy products. Plus, we recommend that you eat a wide variety of foods and take a daily multivitamin. There are many other nutrients that play a role in bone health, including magnesium, vitamin D, vitamin C, vitamin K, zinc, boron, lysine, potassium, and silicon. Hormonal balance and physical activity are important factors, too. If you're in doubt, ask your doctor whether a supplement is right for you.*

### Q: I have heard that you can eat more meat on a reduced-carbohydrate plan. I am concerned about eating more meat than I am used to eating because I've also heard that there is a link between meat and cancer. Is this true?

*A: We have read similar studies! Just keep this motto in mind: Moderation in all things. Scientists still do not fully understand all of the causes of cancer. Some of the facts we have are that 1) toxins that might cause cancer are stored in fat; 2) nitrates and nitrites usually found in smoked, cured, or pickled meats or fish form cancer-causing nitrosamines; 3) blackened or charred meats, fish, or poultry contain substances known to cause cancer; 4) there may be estrogens in the fat portions of meat that may raise estrogen levels in the body and contribute to estrogen-dominance-type cancers.*

*These are all valid concerns. However, we recommend several steps to minimize their impact. Eating lots of vegetables and some fruits will supply important antioxidants that help protect us from cancer. Also, remember that the body has a wonderful built-in detoxification system in the liver. Eating a wide variety of whole foods as this plan encourages will supply nutrients that support liver function. Cruciferous vegetables such as broccoli, cauliflower, brussels sprouts, kale, cabbage, and others are particularly helpful. Keep in mind, too, that this book recommends eating more protein, but not necessarily more meat. If you prefer not to get your protein from meat, there are plenty of recipes and suggestions in this book for getting protein from beans, nuts, and other nonanimal sources. See also the cancer-reducing cooking tips on page 56.*

**Q: Is my breath going to smell funny on this diet, and should I expect to be constipated?**

*A: No. The ketone breath associated with low-carbohydrate diets is not a problem on this plan because the carbohydrates are not as restricted. This book advocates a smart lower-carbohydrate approach avoiding refined carbohydrates, but not the severe carbohydrate restriction that triggers ketosis. Also, the liberal use of high-fiber vegetables in our plan as well as high-fiber whole grains and fruits will ensure that you are not constipated. On the contrary, most people have found that the extra fiber improves regularity. It also reduces hunger because it makes them feel more full.*

# 7 steps to smart weight loss

Are you a bread eater? Pasta lover? Ice cream binger? Crazy about candy? Chocoholic? Cereal muncher? Beer guzzler? Dessert person? If so, there's good news. You don't need to eliminate these foods to lose weight. However, it may help to choose a different type of bread, a different type of pasta, or a different type of cereal.

Losing weight is really a matter of making smart choices. What follows are seven choices that you can make to start shedding pounds today. Together, these seven choices or steps make up the basis of the smart low-carbohydrate approach. You'll also find several detailed menu plans that put these steps into practice in your everyday life.

Whichever path you choose, the general steps or the detailed menu plans, remember the cardinal rule of successful weight loss: Stick with it! The eating approach and recipes in this book include many of your favorite foods because it's nearly impossible to stick with a plan that doesn't include them. Who wants to go through life without enjoying it? That's the whole purpose of losing weight in the first place. So enjoy your favorite foods. Enjoy the fabulous recipes in this book. And read on to see how you can make great-tasting food work for you instead of against you.

## STEP 1: EAT MORE WHOLE GRAINS

Take a minute to think about the grain foods you typically eat, such as cereals, muffins, breads, rolls, crackers, bagels, tortillas, pitas, pasta, and rice. If any of these foods are mostly white in color or contain enriched white flour, try substituting them with whole grain foods. Today's supermarkets are chock-full of whole grain cereals, whole grain breads, whole wheat tortillas, whole wheat pitas, whole wheat pasta, whole grain pastry flour, and brown rice. These whole grain foods have a more complex taste and texture than refined foods—and many people end up liking them better. If you bake at home, replace all-purpose flour with whole grain pastry flour, which makes excellent muffins, breads, and cakes.

**Make the switch.** The switch to whole grains is one of the most important you can make for weight loss. The main reason: Refined grains are so prevalent in the American diet that switching to whole grains will impact the majority of your food choices.

Gene Newman discovered this principle as his waistline expanded throughout his thirties. In addition to reducing his total carbohydrate intake, switching to whole grains helped Gene lose 40 pounds. He's kept it off for 15 years. One reason is that replacing refined grain products with whole grain products instantly boosts your fiber intake, which satisfies your hunger longer so you don't overeat. Fiber-rich foods come packed with vitamins, minerals, and other nutrients that strengthen your immune system so you can ward off illness and also help reduce heart disease risk.

**Read labels.** When buying breads, cereals, pasta, and other grain-based foods, look for the words "whole grain" on the label. At least one whole grain should appear first on the ingredient list, indicating that it is the largest ingredient in the food.

Some examples of whole, unrefined grains include whole wheat, brown rice, rye, oats, unpearled barley, corn, quinoa, buckwheat, and whole wheat couscous. Limit foods that contain enriched flour, which is essentially refined, low-fiber flour with some vitamins and minerals added. See page 68 for more tips on buying and cooking with whole grain foods.

**Look for low-GI grains.** Foods with a low glycemic index (GI) can help you lose weight. They won't raise your blood sugar as quickly as foods with a high glycemic index and may keep you satisfied longer. To step up your weight loss, put the emphasis on whole grains with a low glycemic index. For instance, a slice of whole grain pumpernickel (1 ounce) has a lower glycemic index than most other breads. Surprisingly, pumpernickel and sourdough breads both have a lower glycemic index than 100 percent whole wheat bread. Oats are another good choice among whole grains because they are high in fiber. Whenever you do eat a food with a higher GI, try to include some protein and fat in the same meal. For instance, if you must eat white bread, try eating it with peanut butter. The protein and fat in the peanut butter will lower the GI of the entire meal. See "The Glycemic Index" on page 8 for a thorough list of low-GI foods.

**Reduce your total intake of starches.** Switching from refined grain foods like white bread, white pasta, and white rice to low-GI whole grains should help you lose weight and stay satisfied. If you make these changes and still want to lose more weight, try reducing the total servings of starches in your diet, including unrefined grains, rice, pasta, and beans. Aim to eat no more than four servings of starches per day. See page 38 to see what counts as a serving.

**Count starchy vegetables as starches.** Although they might not be grains, some starchy vegetables and plant foods really belong in the same food category because of their high starch content. These include corn, potatoes, sweet potatoes, lima beans, black-eyed peas, lentils, and other dried or canned beans. When monitoring your carbohydrate intake, count one serving (½ cup) of these foods as a serving of starch. There's no need to omit or even limit starchy vegetables because they supply key nutrients, particularly fiber. However, when eating starchy vegetables, you may want to reduce your intake of bread, cereal, crackers, or other grains to compensate.

**Make smart restaurant choices.** Most restaurant menus offer only refined grain foods. If that's the case, try to keep the portions minimal. For instance, have an open-face sandwich instead of a sandwich with two slices of bread. Or go for a salad instead of a sandwich. If the meal comes with a side dish of noodles or pasta, ask for a second vegetable instead. When ordering breakfast, choose an egg dish such as an omelette and skip the toast. And if your server brings a bread basket to your table, resist the temptation by asking that it either be left in the kitchen or placed at the other end of the table. Order a glass of tomato juice instead. You will reap the wonderful benefits of the phytonutrient lycopene rather than taking in the nutrient-poor starch of refined grains.

## STEP 2: EAT MORE VEGETABLES AND FRUITS

We've known all along that they're good for us, but now science can explain why vegetables and fruits help prevent cancer,

## HIDDEN ROADBLOCK to weight loss

### OVEREATING

Portion control is a key component of any weight-loss plan. Many of us simply eat too much! Carbohydrates are often the most overeaten type of food, so keep an eye on serving sizes. If you feel you have a good grip on how much you eat but you are still not losing weight, try omitting one or two servings of the carbohydrate-containing foods in your diet for several days. This should help you start losing again. As always, if you have a medical condition or take medications, check with your health care provider before adjusting the carbohydrates to an extremely low level.

heart disease, and numerous other maladies. A University of California scientist reviewed 156 studies on the relationship between eating fruits and vegetables and cancer risk and found that more than 80 percent of those studies supported the cancer-protective effect of beta-carotene-rich foods. The American Institute for Cancer Research says that Americans would reduce their cancer risk by 20 percent just by increasing fruit and vegetable intake to 5 servings a day.

Eating more produce may reduce your risk of stroke, too. In 1999, the *Journal of the American Medical Association* looked at data from two large studies that followed 75,596 women for 14 years and 38,683 men for 8 years. The incidence of stroke was directly related to the number of servings of fruits and vegetables consumed by these women and men. The addition of just one daily serving of fruit or vegetable decreased stroke risk by 6 percent. The produce with the most protective effects includes cruciferous vegetables such as cabbage, broccoli, cauliflower, collards, and brussels sprouts; dark green, leafy vegetables; citrus fruits; and other vitamin C-rich fruits and vegetables.

If you're concerned about osteoporosis, vegetables may be just what you need. According to Katherine Tucker, Ph.D., associate professor of nutritional epidemiology at Tufts University in Boston, "Fruits and vegetables are associated with bone mineral density and may help protect against osteoporosis." With all these health benefits, including reduced risk of cancer, stroke, and osteoporosis, it makes sense to trade in a serving of pasta or rice for a serving of vegetables.

**Get fresh or get frozen.** Choose a wide variety of fresh or frozen vegetables. Canned vegetables work in a pinch, too—especially canned tomato products. Avoid frozen vegetables with breading or sauce; these tend to be high in carbohydrates, sodium, and hydrogenated fats.

**Eat mostly fresh, low-carb, low-GI vegetables.** All green vegetables, such as broccoli, celery, leafy greens, and cucumbers are smart choices for low-carb eating. So are mushrooms, radishes, and cauliflower. These vegetables are low in carbs and have a low glycemic index (they don't spike your blood sugar). See "The Glycemic Index" on page 8 for more low-GI vegetables. These are the ones you should eat most often. But don't completely eliminate higher-carb, higher-GI vegetables such as potatoes—especially if they help you stick with the low-carb approach in the long run. Many high-carb or high-GI vegetables provide important nutrients. These include beets, carrots, onions, peas, turnips, pumpkin, and winter squash. Keep in mind, too, that you'll probably eat most of your vegetables with a meal that also contains protein and fat, which will lower the overall glycemic index of the meal. Low-GI choices are more crucial when you eat the vegetable by itself as a snack. For instance, if you like to snack on raw carrots, dip them in cottage cheese dip or tahini, or eat a few nuts along with them. Each of these accompaniments will lower the overall glycemic index.

**Strive for five to nine.** Needless to say, Americans are currently falling short of the recommended number of servings of fruits and vegetables. We should be getting at least five—and preferably nine—servings a day, but at the close of the 1990s, we were getting little more than three. It's not as hard as it might seem to get five a day. Three-quarters of a cup of orange juice at breakfast counts as one. A cup of salad at lunch makes two. Have some celery or carrot sticks for a snack, a vegetable side dish with dinner, and some fruit with dessert and you're there. Toss more vegetables into the next casserole that you make. Choose vegetable juice instead of soft drinks. Even ¼ cup of dried fruit such as raisins or apricots counts as a serving of fruit. Try to get five to six servings of vegetables and two to three servings of fruit each day. Check out some of the recipes in this book to see other easy ways of incorporating fruits and vegetables into your meals. To get the most nutrients and health benefits, eat a wide variety of richly colored fruits and vegetables.

## STEP 3: FOCUS ON LEAN PROTEINS AND HEALTHY FATS

Some of the popular low-carb diets suggest eating as much protein and fat as you want, as long as you keep carbohydrates low. This may not be a healthy approach for every-

### HIDDEN CARBS IN SEAFOOD

Generally, fish is a healthy choice. But some types of seafood are higher in carbs than others. Here's a ranking of fresh and prepared fish and shellfish to help you make smart choices.

| SEAFOOD | CARB (G) |
| --- | --- |
| Deviled crab, 1 cup | 32 |
| Breaded, fried scallops, 12 | 20 |
| Shrimp cocktail, 4 oz (1 jar) | 20 |
| Imitation crab, ½ cup | 8 |
| Tuna salad (with celery, pickle, onion, egg, and mayonnaise), 1 cup | 7 |
| Fish sticks, 3 | 5 |
| Oysters, raw, ½ cup | 4.1 |
| Scallops, 4 oz. | 4 |
| Clams, raw, each | 1 |
| Lobster meat, 1 cup | 0.4 |
| Crabmeat, ½ cup | 0.4 |
| Shrimp, cooked, 1 cup | 0 |

one. Numerous studies show that diets high in saturated fat (the kind found in butter, cheese, and fattier cuts of meat) can lead to heart disease. The key to smart low-carb eating is to replace refined carbs with moderate portions of lean protein foods and unsaturated fats. That means choosing mostly poultry, fish, seafood, eggs, some lean cuts of red meat, reduced-fat cheeses, nuts, liquid cooking oils, and maybe a few soy foods.

**Go for lean cuts of meat.** Red meat is rich in iron, zinc, and B vitamins and adds variety to your diet. There's no need to swear off it, but try to limit red meats to two or three meals per week. Lean cuts are the smartest choice. If beef is on your menu or shopping list, choose tenderloin, top loin, sirloin, top round, eye of round, tip, or flank steak. For lamb, choose whole leg, loin chop, blade chops, foreshank, or sirloin roast. When choosing pork, look to tenderloin, sirloin, rib chops, lean boneless ham, or Canadian bacon. If you eat veal, any cut except commercially ground will be fairly lean. Game meats such as venison and buffalo are quite lean as well.

**Buy the best ground beef.** Extra-lean ground beef is the best choice for health. Try mixing it with ground turkey breast for juicy hamburgers, meat loaf, meatballs, or chili. If you're a beef purist, mix ground chuck with lean ground sirloin.

**Pick a higher grade.** Reach for meat labeled "select." It will be leaner than meat graded "choice" or "prime." If you can't find select, go for choice.

**Make it natural.** If you eat cold cuts, try to use those without fillers. Use only a minimal amount of smoked and cured meats such as ham, bacon, and hot dogs. If you eat these foods, try to have a tomato product at the same meal. It may help protect you from the possible cancer-causing effects of the nitrates and nitrites.

**Choose poultry wisely.** Most poultry is lean if you avoid the skin. Chicken breasts and legs make good choices. Read labels when buying ground turkey or chicken. Ground turkey breast has the least fat. Seven percent low-fat ground turkey is another good choice. It contains a little more fat that helps keep the ground meat moist. Packages labeled simply "ground turkey" include the greatest proportion of fatty parts.

**Take another look at eggs.** Most health experts have put eggs back on the menu as a good source of protein. Eggs contain important nutrients in both the yolk and the white. If you're a fan, eat up to six eggs a week.

**Eat more fish.** Fish is a terrific source of important healthy fats. Our bodies require two types of dietary fats: omega-6 and omega-3 fatty acids. Research shows that these fats help protect your heart. And they can only be obtained from food because our bodies do not make them. Omega-3 fatty acids are abundant in salmon, tuna, mackerel, herring, sardines, trout, halibut, cod, and bluefish. To boost your heart health, try to eat some type of fish at least twice a week. When you can, choose fresh fish—the flavor beats frozen and canned hands down. But canned tuna and salmon also count as fish meals. If you stock frozen seafood, look for varieties without breading.

**Go nuts.** If you don't like fish, look to walnuts and flaxseed for omega-3 fatty acids. Nuts, seeds, nut butters, and nut oils also contain omega-6 fatty acids. Data from a long-term, large-scale research project called the Nurses' Health Study showed that both of these fats can help reduce blood cholesterol levels, blood pressure, and heart disease risk. That's why these essential fatty acids are referred to as healthy fats. The beneficial amount of nuts consumed in the Nurses' Health Study was 5 to 7 ounces per week—which translates to a little less than 1 ounce of nuts a day. Finally, a snack food that has health benefits!

**Focus on unsaturated fats.** Most unsaturated fats come from plant foods rather than animal foods. Both monounsaturated and polyunsaturated fats are considered healthy fats. Both kinds of unsaturated fat are liquid at room temperature as well as in your body. For this reason, they keep cell membranes flexible and fluid. They regulate blood cholesterol and reduce heart disease risk by helping to lower "bad" LDL cholesterol and maintain "good" HDL cholesterol. Use mostly liquid oils such as olive oil and canola oil for cooking and salads. See page 61 for more tips on using liquid oils.

**The less saturated fat, the better.** Saturated fats—the fats that clog your arteries—are solid at room temperature. Saturated fat is found mostly in animal fats such as butter, full-fat dairy products, meats, and poultry skin. Try to limit saturated fat to no more than two servings a day (about 2 slices of bacon or 2 tablespoons of cream cheese). Less is even better.

**Avoid hydrogenated fats.** Food manufacturers do amazing things to once-healthy liquid oils. They transform them into solid fats. These trans fats are made by heating liquid oils to very high temperatures for 6 to 8 hours, then chemically introducing hydrogen molecules. This results in hydrogenated fats that are less expensive, less perishable, and more spreadable than natural fats. A good thing for food manufacturers but not for your body because hydrogenated oils act more like saturated fat in your body; they tend to raise

## WHAT'S A SERVING OF NUTS?

A 1-ounce serving of nuts each day can help reduce your risk of heart attack. See below to find out how many nuts are in 1 ounce. Notice that nuts with fewer calories have more carbohydrates. To get the best balance in low-calorie, low-carb nuts, go for peanuts, pistachios, or pine nuts.

| Nuts | Cal | Carb (g) |
|---|---|---|
| Chestnuts, 3½ | 70 | 15 |
| Cashews, 18 | 163 | 9 |
| Pistachios, 47 | 160 | 8 |
| Peanuts, 20 | 166 | 6 |
| Pine nuts, 155 | 160 | 5 |
| Almonds, 22 | 170 | 5 |
| Hazelnuts, 12 | 183 | 5 |
| Walnut halves, 14 | 185 | 4 |
| Brazil nuts, 8 | 190 | 4 |
| Pecan halves, 15 | 201 | 4 |
| Macadamias, 12 | 200 | 4 |

## THE BIG FIVE

Sugar is added to everything from frozen entrées to commercial salad dressings. But most foods with added sugar are more obvious—such as cookies, doughnuts, and soft drinks. Here's where the majority of the added sugars in the American diet come from.

| | |
|---|---|
| Nondiet soft drinks | 28% |
| Candy and sprinkle-on sugar | 17% |
| Cookies, cakes, sweet baked goods | 16% |
| Ice cream, frozen yogurt, sweetened yogurt | 10% |
| Sweetened fruit drinks and iced tea | 8% |

your blood cholesterol and increase heart disease risk. Hydrogenated or partially hydrogenated fats are found in most commercially made cookies, pastries, chips, chocolates, crackers, and breads. They're also the key ingredient in stick margarine and the oils used for frying foods in fast-food restaurants. If you can avoid these foods, you will be close to omitting all trans fats from your diet and decreasing your risk of heart disease.

**Dip in the tub.** If you use margarine instead of butter, buy it in a tub instead of a stick. Tub margarine contains less than half the amount of trans fatty acids that stick margarine has. Better yet, look for tub margarines that say "no trans fats" right on the label.

**Choose a better butter.** If you use butter, limit saturated fat by choosing light butter when you can. Light butter has half the saturated fat and half the calories of regular butter. It tastes great on toast, muffins, and vegetables. You can use it in baking, too, but reduce the amount of liquid in the recipe to compensate for the added water in light butter. For instance, in muffins or pancakes, reduce the amount of milk or juice by about ¼ cup.

## STEP 4: GO EASY ON ADDED SUGARS

Sweetness, one of the four basic flavors, is tasted right at the tip of your tongue. That helps to explain why both kids and adults favor sweet-tasting foods over other basic flavors such as bitter, sour, or salty. These other flavors are tasted on the sides or at the back of your tongue.

If sugar only had some valuable nutrients, eating it would not be much of a problem. Alas, sugar does not contain significant amounts of any nutrients and supplies merely empty carbohydrates to your diet. And it can really wreak havoc on your cravings for food. Here's how to tame your sugar intake so that you can reach your weight-loss goals.

**Start with small steps.** Take your time and go at your own pace. Whatever amount of sugar you can eliminate now is a move in a positive direction. Take a look at the list of refined carbohydrates found on page 2. Whenever you can, eat less of these foods. Howard Lee Whitehorne used to drink about 84 ounces of sweetened cola soft drink every day. He was shocked when he learned that he was consuming 70 teaspoons of sugar—nearly 1½ cups—each day from this beverage alone. Howard decided to eliminate just 4 ounces per day for 3 weeks. This one move helped him to lose 15 pounds.

Norma Gates started each day with two slices of iced cinnamon raisin toast, had a midmorning can of soda, ate dessert with lunch and supper, and snacked on cookies, candy, or a sweetened drink before bed. Norma switched to mini bagels with bacon (precooked) instead of cinnamon toast at breakfast, and in the evening, she snacked on peanut butter or sugar-free gelatin with whipped cream. Norma made a few other changes and within 8 months, she lost 40 pounds. She has kept the weight off for 3½ years.

Try making one simple switch at a time. If you usually drink soda, switch to water, tea, coffee, or another unsweetened beverage. After a few weeks, try making another switch.

**Beware of low-fat labels.** Many low-fat foods contain added sugar to make up for the flavor lost when fat is taken out. Scan down to the "Sugars" line on the Nutrition Facts label. Divide the grams of sugar by 4 and you will see how many teaspoons of sugar you'll get in each serving of the food. For instance, if the label says "Sugars:

12 grams," divide 12 by 4 and you'll know that each serving contains a full 3 teaspoons of sugar. If you like to read ingredient lists instead, watch out for any of the following: sugar, brown sugar, invert sugar, corn sweetener, corn syrup, high-fructose corn syrup, honey, fruit juice concentrate, molasses, sucrose, dextrose, fructose, maltose, and lactose. Each of these simple sugars bumps up the carbohydrate content of the food.

**Keep tabs on milk.** To your body, the lactose in milk is a simple sugar very similar to table sugar. Of course, milk contains other important nutrients like calcium, vitamin D, niacin, riboflavin, and vitamin A. So you shouldn't avoid milk altogether. But to limit milk's naturally occurring sugar, try to drink no more than 1 cup of milk and eat no more than 1 cup of yogurt a day. Choose reduced-fat dairy products whenever you can; they are not significantly higher in carbohydrates than whole-milk products but are much lower in fat. These are general guidelines. If you end up eating more dairy foods one day, try to balance your intake by eating fewer the next day. To keep up your intake of bone-strengthening calcium, eat more calcium-rich foods like dried figs, collard greens, and calcium-fortified orange juice and soy milk. If you don't regularly eat these foods, you may want to take 500 milligrams of calcium as a daily supplement.

**Eat mostly low-GI fruit.** Fruit is gener-

> ## HOW TO KICK A SUGAR CRAVING
>
> If you have strong, persistent sugar cravings, take a tip from the low-carb pros. Place just a few granules of sugar on the tip of your pinky finger. Tap them into a tall glass of cool water. Drink all of the water. In a few minutes, the sugar craving should disappear.

ally good for you, but the fructose in fruit is a simple sugar. But since it comes packaged with a treasury of fiber and nutrients, try for two or three servings of fruit a day. Again, your body metabolizes this type of sugar much like table sugar. Try to keep your fruit intake to no more than 2 servings a day. Eat low-GI fruits whenever you can. The glycemic index is especially important with fruits because some fruits cause only a steady rise in blood sugar, while others send your blood sugar soaring. For instance, a less ripe banana raises blood sugar more gently than a ripe banana because the starch in the fruit has not yet "ripened" or converted into sugar. Likewise, an apple has a more mild effect on blood sugar than apple juice. That's because apple juice lacks the fiber contained in the pulp and peel of the whole apple. For more low-GI fruit options, see page 7.

If you eat fruit with a high glycemic index, remember the principle of balance.

Eating a high-GI fruit with some nuts will help to balance out the overall GI of the meal. Many of the people we spoke with also found that fruit works best when eaten in the earlier part of the day. And one study supports the notion. British researchers at the University of Surrey found that our body's cells may be more receptive to the insulin rush of simple carbohydrates in the morning rather than later in the day or evening. So you may want to try eating most of your carbs in the morning, especially fruit. Focus on fresh or frozen unsweetened fruits rather than canned fruits packed in syrup.

**Avoid artificial sweeteners.** Many of the people we spoke with had a love-hate relationship with artificial sweeteners. They loved that they could get the sweetness of real sugar, but they said that eating artificial sweeteners made them crave sweets even more. If you use artificial sweeteners, try to use less whenever you can. Try stevia or Splenda instead. Stevia is a natural herb that is 300 times sweeter than sugar, and Splenda is an alternative sweetener that is made from cane sugar but has no carbohydrates. Both are more natural alternatives to artificial products. See page 57 for more tips on using alternative sweeteners.

## STEP 5: EAT REASONABLE PORTION SIZES

When it comes to food, size does matter. The difference between a standard ½-cup serving of pasta and the amount you actually put on your plate could turn a good-for-you meal into a fattening one. Jeanne Bennett took a hard look at her diet and found that her portion sizes were out of control. She had gone through her twenties eating whatever she wanted without gaining weight. Then, as happens with many people, Jeanne hit her thirties, had two kids, and started gaining weight. "I soon realized that I had been eating way too much food (about 2,500 calories a day) and far too many foods high in white sugar, white flour, and other refined carbohydrates." Jeanne started eating sensible portions, cut back on sugar and flour, and lost 44 pounds.

If you need to, at least early on in your weight-loss plan, measure out your food a few times to get used to how a standard serving size looks on the plate. See page 38 for a list of standard serving sizes. Or use the following visual cues:

- 1 cup = closed fist
- ½ cup = tennis ball
- 2 tablespoons = Ping-Pong ball
- 1 teaspoon = top of thumb (from tip to joint)
- 3 ounces of cooked meat, poultry, or fish = deck of cards
- 1 ounce of cheese = top of thumb (from tip to joint)

Once you get used to dishing out standard serving sizes, you'll be able to eyeball them and skip the measuring cups.

## STEP 6: IDENTIFY YOUR TRIGGER FOODS

Some of the foods you eat may be secretly sabotaging your weight-loss efforts. Ask yourself if there are any foods that you feel you can't possibly live without. If you answer yes, make a list of those foods. There is a strong possibility that these are your "trigger" or "addictive" foods. They may actually be preventing you from reaching your weight-loss goals. According to Rudy Rivera, M.D., a weight-loss expert and researcher in Plano, Texas, when people eat a trigger food, their bodies produce more endorphins. These are the same feel-good brain chemicals released when you have sex, get a massage, experience runner's high, or enjoy a good belly laugh. Dr. Rivera says the problem may be that people need to eat more and more of their trigger foods to raise their endorphins to the same level. As a result, people feel like they can never get enough of certain foods and they overeat, leading to weight gain.

**Look at what you eat.** To identify your trigger foods, write down everything you eat and drink for a few days. Or take a look back at what you've eaten over the past few days and jot down those foods. Then, check off your favorite foods on the list. There's a good chance that your trigger foods are lurking among your favorite foods. To narrow down potential trigger foods, group together the foods that belong to a particular food category such as sugary foods (soda, cookies, cakes, and ice cream), refined starchy foods (bagels, white bread, white rice, and white pasta), and snack foods (potato chips, pretzels, and tortilla chips). Keep in mind that the foods that you eat every day or numerous times daily are most suspect. For many people, refined carbohydrates like sugar and wheat products turn out to be their trigger foods because they are so prevalent in our diets. This is another reason why it's so important to eat a wide variety of foods and avoid eating the same food every day.

Once you identify your potential trigger foods, answer the following questions about them:

- Have I ever eaten this food in place of a meal?
- Do I eat this food even when I'm not really hungry?
- Do I get physiological cravings for this food?
- Is this a comfort food?
- Have I ever tried to give up this food before?
- If so, did I begin eating this food again?

If you answered "yes" to these questions, particularly the last two, then you have found your trigger foods. These foods may be responsible for sabotaging your past attempts at losing weight. To be successful at losing weight, these foods should be carefully managed in your overall diet. You may not need to totally eliminate pasta, ice cream, beer, or whatever your "addictive" foods might be. But minimizing or completely avoiding these foods for at least 3 weeks may really facilitate your weight-loss progress. If you feel very addicted to a particular food, such as sugar, you may need to avoid it for up to 3 months before trying to re-introduce it back into your diet.

**Wean yourself away.** Start by eating less of your trigger foods. If you love cookies, set out just one or two instead of your usual portion. Then put the cookies away to avoid being tempted to eat more. As you eat the cookies in front of you, savor every bite so that you really enjoy the experience. If you're someone with good self-control, you may find that you can enjoy your trigger foods now and then in moderate portions.

**Or go cold turkey.** Some people told us it was easier to avoid their trigger foods completely. Joan Lawson swore off her trigger foods and lost 80 pounds in 18 months. She has kept the weight off for 6 years. If you think you won't be able to resist overeating your trigger foods, remove them from your house, desk, car, handbag, or anywhere else they may be stashed. If the food isn't there, you'll be less tempted to eat it. When making a shopping list, avoid writing down any of your trigger foods. Keeping them out of sight is a giant first step toward avoiding them entirely.

**Plan ahead for tempting situations.** Some advance planning can help you avoid

# DRINK MORE WATER

It's extremely important to drink plenty of water every day. The smart low-carb approach to weight loss includes lots of fiber-rich foods like whole grains, vegetables, and fruits. Water helps the fiber in these foods to do its cholesterol-reducing work, which ultimately helps to reduce your heart disease risk. Water also helps to flush out waste products that come from eating protein. And it can prevent fatigue. In fact, dehydration-related fatigue is the underlying cause of food cravings for many people trying to lose weight. The next time you feel hungry, reach for a drink of water instead of food. It may keep you focused so you eat less.

Aim to drink about ½ ounce of water per pound of body weight every day. For example, if you weigh 150 pounds, you should drink 75 ounces or about 9 cups a day. Here's the math: 0.5 ounces × 150 pounds = 75 ounces ÷ 8 ounces (per cup) = about 9 cups. Pure water is best. But green tea, plain or flavored seltzer, or flavored sparkling water without artificial sweeteners will do in a pinch.

the most common times when people get into trouble with "addictive" foods.

- For many people, the first 15 minutes after getting home from work is an especially vulnerable time. If you usually come home hungry, plan to eat a healthy snack or appetizer as soon you walk in the door. This snack will take the edge off your hunger and may help prevent you from overeating at dinner, too. Stock fruits, nuts, or other non-trigger foods especially for this snack time. See the recipes beginning on page 105 for other ideas.
- If you work at home, keep in mind that most people get hungry between 3:00 and 6:00 P.M. It's wise to eat a healthy snack during these vulnerable hours.
- Plan ahead when eating out, going to parties, or attending other social events that involve food. Alcohol, soft drinks, bread, sweets, and other common trigger foods are bound to be offered there. Before you head out, eat a handful of nuts, a piece of fruit, or another nontrigger food, or take these foods with you.
- Whenever you eat, try not to do anything else at the same time. Avoid eating while watching TV, reading, talking on the phone, or even standing up. These other activities distract you from what and how much you're eating. Instead, take the time to sit down and really enjoy your food.

**Stay focused on your weight-loss goals.** Avoiding your trigger foods takes

(continued on page 36)

# I Did It!

## Alice Cooper

Alice was overweight and overcome with lightheadedness. Avoiding her trigger foods resolved her lightheadedness and helped her to lose 30 pounds.

"It wasn't until I visited my doctor for help with another problem that the answer to my dieting failures became clear. I had been feeling lightheaded, so I visited the doctor to find out why.

"In the doctor's office, I tipped the scale at 193 pounds. My doctor's comment, 'You were supposed to lose weight,' only added to my frustration.

"It's not like I wasn't trying. For months, I went through one diet plan after another with absolutely no success. Why did these plans work for everyone else but not for me?

"To help explain the lightheadedness, my doctor and I agreed that I should have some tests done. While waiting for the

before

**Weight lost:** 30 pounds
**Time kept off:** 4 years
**Weight-loss strategies:** Avoided trigger foods, especially sugar and other refined carbohydrates
**Weight-maintenance strategies:** Avoids trigger foods, eats protein with each meal, eats more vegetables, walks, and rides a stationary bike three times a week

*7 steps to smart weight loss*

results, I decided to stop eating foods that I suspected were contributing to my light-headedness. I avoided eating any sugar, flour, wheat, white rice, potatoes, and anything made from these foods. Amazingly, within 1 week, I was no longer lightheaded. My health problem was resolved. But the best news: I was lighter! Finally, I had begun to lose weight just by avoiding my 'trigger foods.'

"I must admit, avoiding these foods was not easy at first. It took me a while to get in the habit of reading food labels while shopping. At times, it felt like there was nothing I could eat. But I had hope because I was losing weight. For the first time in my life, I felt I understood which foods caused me to gain weight. I was optimistic that I would be able to maintain the weight loss this time. Within a few months, my new eating habits became a way of life. I had more energy, and I even started exercising more. My only frustration was that I couldn't convince others to change their diets. It makes me wonder if certain foods are addictive like cigarettes.

"I have been following my new eating plan for 4 years. My weight has come down from 193 pounds to 163 pounds. I fit comfortably into a size 12 and my desire for foods has changed. I don't have nearly as many cravings. 'Happy' does not describe how I feel these days. I can't find a word in the English language to describe my feelings. I only wish I could box up this remedy and give it to everyone I know."

commitment and time—and yes, you may feel a little crabby at first. Just keep in mind that breaking your "addiction" to these foods can help your weight-loss efforts tremendously. Plus, many people have told us that once their trigger foods were gone, they didn't miss them at all. "My desire for foods has changed," says Alice Cooper, who avoided her trigger foods, lost 30 pounds, and has kept it off for 4 years. "I don't have nearly as many food cravings. For the first time in my life, I feel like I understand which foods cause me to gain weight."

**Manage your trigger foods.** Once you have broken the "addictive" behavior, you may be able to eat your trigger foods in moderation. These occasional indulgences may actually help you to be more successful at losing weight and keeping it off in the long run. Experiment with eating your trigger foods now and then to see what works for you. If you fall back into old eating habits, avoid your trigger foods completely.

## STEP 7: KEEP MOVING!

Every day, scientists discover more and more about the health benefits of physical activity. It burns calories, improves your cardiovascular health, and tones up your muscles. Strong muscles are particularly important for weight loss because strong muscles help you burn calories, which helps you lose more weight—and keep it

---

Smart-Carb Insider Tip

### MAKE PLANNED-OVERS

Always pretend you have at least one extra guest for dinner and make extra "planned-overs." Store the additional servings of the entrée so that they're ready to grab on the way out the door the next morning. Some leftover dinners, such as quiche, may even become the next morning's breakfast. Invest in some single-serving storage containers and an insulated lunch bag to make lunchtime easy. This habit saves loads of prep time, sidesteps difficult choices, and provides healthy foods that are ready when you are.

---

off. It doesn't take much exercise to start seeing health benefits. Just 2 hours of walking per week can reduce your risk of heart disease by more than 50 percent. Physical activity often makes people feel more motivated to make wise food choices, too. The key to sticking with it is to make exercise fun. It shouldn't be a chore.

**Start slowly.** If you are a true couch potato, there's no need to get outside right now and run 3 miles. Start with a walk around the block. Then work up to walking the block a few times a week. Then maybe increase the distance and jog it instead of walking. You get the idea.

**Take every opportunity.** Even small bits of activity can add up to a big health payoff. Use the stairs more often. Grab a basket at the grocery store instead of a cart. Visit another office instead of sending an e-mail. Park your car far from your destination and walk the rest of the way. Or do more household chores instead of delegating them. A 190-pound person can burn over 150 calories in 20 minutes just by mowing grass. In fact, three 20-minute periods of exercise burn the same number of calories as one continuous 1-hour workout.

**Do what you like.** For more sustained periods of exercise, choose activities that are fun so you'll actually look forward to them. Do you like to dance, skate, swim, play basketball, ride a bike? Almost any activity that makes you breathe heavily or that works your muscles will help you to lose weight.

**Switch it up.** When you can, do activities that afford different kinds of exercise. Strength-training or weight-bearing exercise such as lifting weights helps prevent osteoporosis and age-related injuries. Aerobic activities support the cardiovascular system. Getting a mix of both types of activity gives you the most benefits for weight loss and long-term health.

**Stick with it.** Try to plan some type of activity every day. It doesn't matter whether you go for a walk, do some gardening, mow the grass, play tennis, take a bike ride, scrub the kitchen floor, or go to the gym. Just keep moving! Twenty to 30 minutes of activity a day may spell the difference between weight-loss success and failure. If your schedule is tight, pencil in your exercise time so you won't skip it.

## HELP! I'M NOT LOSING WEIGHT!

If you follow the general recommendations above, you should notice significant weight loss. Exactly how much weight loss depends upon how *closely* you follow each step as well as your particular genetic makeup and lifestyle. Perhaps you'll lose a few pounds, but want to lose even more. If that's the case, you may need to lower your total carbohydrate intake, possibly by eating even fewer whole grains if necessary. Or you may need to reduce your portion sizes of proteins and fats. Remember that calories do count.

**Take stock.** Look again at the sources of carbohydrates in your diet. You may need to reduce the amount of each carbohydrate-rich food that you eat, especially breads, cereals, flours, grains, and added sugars. Instead of these carb-rich foods, eat more lean protein foods. For example, if you skip one serving of cereal, two slices of bread, and a potato in your daily diet, you will drop your carbohydrates by at least 60 grams and cut about 320 calories—every day. Instead of these foods, eat an extra 2 to 3 ounces of lean protein such as cooked skinless poultry, fish, or lean meat, and for a snack, 2 tablespoons of peanut butter stuffed into some celery stalks. Extra servings of lower-carbohydrate vegetables such as broccoli and zucchini

## WHAT'S A SERVING?

Most Americans have become accustomed to eating more than they should. The average take-out bagel is at least twice as big as it should be. Even the average supermarket potato is bigger than what experts recommend. Here's a guide to smart low-carb serving sizes. Use these to keep track of how much you're eating.

**Vegetable:** ½ cup raw, chopped, or cooked; ¾ cup vegetable juice; 1 cup raw, leafy greens

**Starch:** 1 slice whole wheat bread; ½ whole wheat bagel or muffin; ½ cup cooked whole grain cereal, pasta, brown rice, or other whole grain; ½ cup cooked beans, corn, potatoes, rice, or sweet potatoes

**Nuts:** 1 ounce nuts without shell; 2 tablespoons unsweetened peanut butter

**Protein:** 1 ounce cooked lean beef, pork, lamb, skinless poultry, fish, or shellfish; 1 ounce hard cheese (preferably reduced-fat); 1 egg

**Fat, unsaturated:** 1 teaspoon ghee (clarified butter); 1 teaspoon oil (such as olive, canola, walnut, or flaxseed oil); 1 teaspoon regular mayonnaise; 1 tablespoon low-fat mayonnaise; 1 tablespoon oil-and-vinegar dressing; 5 large olives; ⅛ medium avocado

**Fat, saturated:** 1 teaspoon butter; 1 slice bacon; 1 ounce salt pork; 1 tablespoon heavy cream; 1 tablespoon cream cheese; 2 tablespoons sour cream; 2 tablespoons shredded unsweetened coconut

**Fruit:** 1 small to medium piece; 1 cup whole strawberries or melon cubes; ½ cup canned or cut fruit; ¾ cup fruit juice; ¼ cup dried fruit

**Milk:** 1 cup fat-free milk; 1 cup fat-free or low-fat unsweetened yogurt; ½ cup low-fat ricotta cheese or cottage cheese; ¾ cup unsweetened soy milk

can also fill in any gaps. For a snapshot of what this smart low-carb approach looks like, see the "Smart Low-Carb Food Pyramid" on page 42.

**Be patient.** How true the often-used saying is: You didn't gain it overnight, so don't expect to lose it that quickly. Losing 1 to 2 pounds a week is safe, effective, and significant weight loss. If you are losing that much, hang in there. In just 2 months, you could be 16 pounds slimmer! Remember that truly successful weight loss is measured not by how many pounds you lose, but by how long you keep the weight off and how healthy you are. If you've lost 10 pounds so far, just keeping those 10 pounds from coming back is a big accomplishment. You will most likely have increased energy and reduced risk of cardiovascular disease, diabetes, cancer, gallstones, and other conditions. So relax. Enjoy eating well and feeling great. Your body will find the weight that is most healthy for you.

## PICK YOUR OWN WEIGHT-LOSS PLAN

Some people do better with detailed plans than with general recommendations. If that's you, pick one of the six detailed plans on page 40. Each one shows you what to eat—and how much—each day. The plans include a careful balance of foods containing carbohydrates, proteins, and fats. Follow one of these plans, and you should automatically lose weight and keep your carbohydrate and calorie intake at a healthy level. Whichever plan you choose, keep in mind the seven general recommendations discussed earlier.

**Determine your current calorie intake.** Each of the plans on page 40 is based on choosing the daily calorie and carbohydrate intake levels that are right for you. If you have no idea of your current calorie intake, here's an easy way to find it. Step one is to decide how active you are. **Sedentary** means that you have a job or lifestyle that involves mostly sitting, standing, or light walking. You exercise once a week or less. **Active** means that your job or lifestyle requires more activity than light walking (such as full-time housecleaning or construction work), or you get 45 to 60 minutes of aerobic exercise 3 times a week. **Very active** means that you get aerobic exercise for at least 45 to 60 minutes 4 or more times a week. Choose the description that best fits your current lifestyle, then find your activity factor from the table below.

| IF YOU ARE A . . . | YOUR ACTIVITY FACTOR IS . . . |
|---|---|
| Sedentary woman | 12 |
| Sedentary man | 14 |
| Active woman | 15 |
| Active man | 17 |
| Very active woman | 18 |
| Very active man | 20 |

Multiply your activity factor by your current weight in pounds. The resulting number is the approximate number of calories you currently need to maintain your weight. The math looks like this:

*activity factor $\times$ weight in pounds = current calorie needs*

Here's an example for an active woman who weighs 170 pounds: $15 \times 170 = 2,550$ calories a day.

**Pick a new calorie level.** Rather than choosing a goal weight, simply reduce your current calorie intake by 500 to 1,000 calories a day. This will lead to safe, effective weight loss of 1 to 2 pounds per week. For instance, if you currently take in 2,300

# SIX WEIGHT-LOSS PLANS FOR EVERY NEED

Here are six smart low-carb weight-loss plans to fit your needs—even if those needs change along the way. Simply choose the calorie and carbohydrate levels that are right for you, then eat from the food groups listed below. To choose your calorie and carbohydrate levels, see page 39. Most folks will start to lose weight by following one of the 180-gram plans.

## ▪▪▪ 180 Grams ▪▪▪

| CALORIES Food Group | 1,500–1,800 Serv | Cal | Carb (g) | 1,800–2,200 Serv | Cal | Carb (g) | 2,200–2,500 Serv | Cal | Carb (g) |
|---|---|---|---|---|---|---|---|---|---|
| Protein | 8 | 440 | 0 | 11 | 665 | 0 | 13 | 815 | 0 |
| Fat | 5 | 225 | 0 | 6 | 270 | 0 | 8 | 360 | 0 |
| Nuts | 0.5 | 100 | 2 | 1 | 200 | 4 | 1.5 | 300 | 6 |
| Veggies | 5 | 125 | 25 | 6 | 150 | 30 | 5 | 125 | 25 |
| Starch | 6 | 480 | 90 | 6 | 480 | 90 | 6 | 480 | 90 |
| Fruit | 3 | 180 | 45 | 3 | 180 | 45 | 3 | 180 | 45 |
| Milk | 1 | 90 | 12 | 1 | 90 | 12 | 1 | 90 | 12 |
| **Totals** | | 1,640 | 174 | | 2,035 | 181 | | 2,350 | 178 |

## ▪▪▪ 125 Grams ▪▪▪

| CALORIES Food Group | 1,500–1,800 Serv | Cal | Carb (g) | 1,800–2,200 Serv | Cal | Carb (g) | 2,200–2,500 Serv | Cal | Carb (g) |
|---|---|---|---|---|---|---|---|---|---|
| Protein | 9 | 495 | 0 | 14 | 890 | 0 | 17 | 1,075 | 0 |
| Fat | 6 | 270 | 0 | 8 | 360 | 0 | 10 | 450 | 0 |
| Nuts | 1 | 200 | 4 | 1 | 200 | 4 | 1 | 200 | 4 |
| Veggies | 5 | 125 | 25 | 5 | 125 | 25 | 5 | 125 | 25 |
| Starch | 4 | 320 | 60 | 4 | 320 | 60 | 4 | 320 | 60 |
| Fruit | 2 | 120 | 30 | 2 | 120 | 30 | 2 | 120 | 30 |
| Milk | 0.5 | 45 | 6 | 0.5 | 45 | 6 | 0.5 | 45 | 6 |
| **Totals** | | 1,575 | 125 | | 2,060 | 125 | | 2,335 | 125 |

to 2,500 calories a day, try reducing your daily intake to 1,800 to 2,000 calories. This will be your new daily calorie level. (Remember that as you lose weight or increase physical activity, you will need to recalculate your activity factor and daily calorie needs.)

**Determine your current carbohydrate intake.** Carbohydrates in the average diet supply 50 to 60 percent of total calories. If you calculated your current calorie intake with the formula on page 39, check the table below to find out the approximate grams of carbohydrates in your diet. You might be surprised by how many grams of carbohydrate you actually eat now. This table is based upon 55 percent of the calories from carbohydrate—the average percentage consumed by most Americans. If your diet is more heavily weighted in carbohydrates, the figures may be on the low side.

| Daily Calories | Carbs (g) |
| --- | --- |
| 1,800 | 248 |
| 2,000 | 275 |
| 2,400 | 330 |
| 2,800 | 385 |
| 3,000 | 413 |
| 3,500 | 481 |
| 4,000 | 550 |

**Choose a new carbohydrate level.** Most people who now consume a high-carbohydrate, low-fat diet (the standard American weight-loss diet) will likely lose weight by cutting carbohydrates some and replacing them with protein and fats. That means following the seven general recommendations discussed earlier or keeping your carbohydrate intake to about 180 grams a day. Some people may need to reduce carbohydrates further to approximately 125 grams a day. Both plans—180 and 125 grams of carbohydrate a day—appear on the opposite page. As with any dietary change, if you are pregnant or nursing, or if you have a kidney problem, check with your doctor before starting any of these plans.

**Try the 180-gram plan first.** To get started right away, try the 180-gram plan for about a week. If you don't notice a change in your weight, stick with the same plan for another week, but reduce your protein and fat servings. If you still don't see a change, move down to the 125-gram plan. Keep in mind that losing 1 to 2 pounds per week is great progress.

**Eat from all the food groups.** Once you pick the calorie and carbohydrate levels that are right for you, simply eat the daily number of servings of food listed under that plan. For example, if you follow the 180-gram plan at 1,800 to 2,200 calories, you should eat 11 servings of protein foods, 6 servings of fats, 1 serving of nuts, 6 servings of starches, 3 servings of fruit, and 1 serving of milk-based foods.

**Keep saturated fat to a minium.** Notice that on each plan, as the servings of carbohydrate foods (such as starch, fruit,

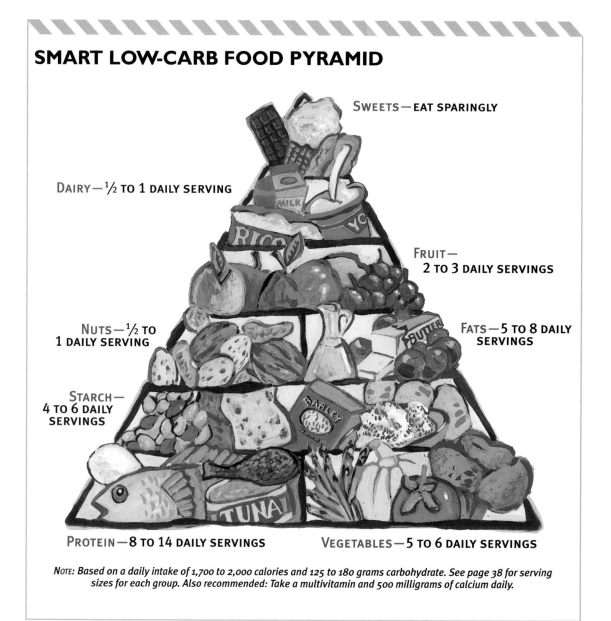

# SMART LOW-CARB FOOD PYRAMID

SWEETS—EAT SPARINGLY

DAIRY—½ TO 1 DAILY SERVING

FRUIT—
2 TO 3 DAILY SERVINGS

NUTS—½ TO
1 DAILY SERVING

FATS—5 TO 8 DAILY
SERVINGS

STARCH—
4 TO 6 DAILY
SERVINGS

PROTEIN—8 TO 14 DAILY SERVINGS

VEGETABLES—5 TO 6 DAILY SERVINGS

*NOTE: Based on a daily intake of 1,700 to 2,000 calories and 125 to 180 grams carbohydrate. See page 38 for serving sizes for each group. Also recommended: Take a multivitamin and 500 milligrams of calcium daily.*

and milk) go down, the servings of protein foods and fat foods go up. Be sure to choose the healthiest protein and fat foods you can find. For protein, that means fish, eggs, poultry, and occasionally lean cuts of beef, pork, and lamb. For fats, focus on mono- and polyunsaturated fats such as olive oil, canola oil, nut oils, and avocados, instead of butter, bacon, and salt pork. These healthier choices will help minimize your intake of saturated fat, thereby helping to prevent heart disease. Try to eat no more than two servings of saturated fat a day. Less is even better. To see what counts as a serving, turn to page 38.

**Keep in mind the carb content of the food groups.** Fats and protein foods have no carbohydrate, but the other food groups contain varying amounts of carbohydrate. Generally, one serving of vegetables contains 5 grams; one serving of milk contains 12 grams; and one serving of starch or fruit contains 15 grams of carbs. Because these food groups all contain carbohydrate, you can make substitutions here and there.

**Substitute other foods if you need to.** If there are certain foods unavailable to you on a particular day, or if you don't care to eat them, you can substitute foods from other food groups. See the suggested substitutions below. The numbers of carbohydrate grams are roughly equivalent.

| FOOD GROUP | SUGGESTED SUBSTITUTION |
|---|---|
| Starch, 1 serving | Milk, ½ serving + Fruit, ½ serving |
| Milk, 1 serving | Starch, 1 serving |
| Fruit, ½ serving | Milk, ½ serving + Vegetable, 1 serving |
| Nuts, 1 serving | Vegetable, 1 serving + Fat, 2 servings |
| Vegetable, 1 serving | Fruit, ½ serving |

**Treat yourself.** Once you start eating the smart low-carb way and enjoying the delicious recipes in this book, chances are that you won't miss some of the foods you once considered special treats. The rich-tasting Chocolate Hazelnut Flourless Cake on page 338 would satisfy almost anyone's food cravings. However, if there are favorite foods that you know you miss—don't go without them for too long. Treat yourself to that special food or meal once a week. Maybe you like a certain ethnic dish that you know is loaded with carbohydrates; perhaps you look forward to a doughnut or ice cream. Go ahead. Enjoy it guilt-free. Then get right back on track at the very next meal. The key is not to deny yourself for too long. If you really have a yen for something high in carbohydrates, eat it. Try to keep the portion small; take your time consuming it and avoid doing anything else at the same time you are eating this favorite food. Before you start eating it, remind yourself of your weight-loss goals. Then dig in and fully savor the food. Stop eating as soon as you are satisfied. You may be surprised to find that a few mouthfuls of your favorite food are sufficient to overcome your urge.

## 7 DAYS TO A SLIMMER YOU

Here's where you can see what smart low-carb eating really looks like. We took the best recipes from the book (and a few other common foods) and organized them into a variety of great-tasting, balanced meals.

Each daily menu includes three main meals and two snacks. Just one look and you'll see that losing weight does not mean depriving yourself.

Each of these menus contains approximately 125 grams of carbohydrate per day (the 125-gram plan outlined on page 40). To choose the calorie level that's right for you, see page 39.

Beverages aren't included here. They're up to you. Remember that water, tea, coffee, seltzer, and club soda are all calorie-free and carbohydrate-free.

These meals offer a great starting place for weight loss. Adjust the foods as needed to fit your personal likes and dislikes. And once you start eating the smart low-carb way, experiment by creating your own delicious menus.

# Day 1

| Menu | Calorie Levels | | |
|---|---|---|---|
| | **1,500–1,800** | **1,800–2,200** | **2,200–2,500** |
| ***Breakfast*** | | | |
| Fried Eggs with Vinegar (page 85) | 1 serving | 1 serving | 1 serving |
| Fat-free milk | ½ cup | ½ cup | ½ cup |
| Apple juice | ½ cup | ½ cup | ½ cup |
| Whole grain bread | 1 slice | 1 slice | 1 slice |
| Butter | 1 tsp | 1 tsp | 2 tsp |
| ***Snack*** | | | |
| Nectarine or pear | 1 | 1 | 1 |
| Cottage cheese | — | — | ½ cup |
| ***Lunch*** | | | |
| Grilled chicken tenders brushed | 4 oz | 5 oz | 6 oz |
|   with Italian dressing | 1 tsp | 1 Tbsp | 1 Tbsp |
| Red leaf lettuce | 1 cup | 1 cup | 1 cup |
| Carrots, shredded | ¼ cup | ¼ cup | ¼ cup |
| Cucumber, sliced | ½ cup | ½ cup | ½ cup |
| Italian dressing | 2 tsp | 2 Tbsp | 2 Tbsp |
| ***Snack*** | | | |
| Walnuts | 1 oz | 1 oz | 1 oz |
| ***Dinner*** | | | |
| London broil | 4 oz | 5 oz | 7 oz |
| Spanish-Style Green Beans (page 322) | 1 serving | 1 serving | 1 serving |
| Couscous | ½ cup | ½ cup | ½ cup |
| ***Snack*** | | | |
| Orange-Walnut Biscotti (page 333) | 2 cookies | 2 cookies | 2 cookies |
| **Total Calories (approx)** | **1,640** | **1,880** | **2,240** |
| **Total Carbs (g)** | **125** | **125** | **125** |

# Day 2

| MENU | CALORIE LEVELS | | |
|---|---|---|---|
| | **1,500–1,800** | **1,800–2,200** | **2,200–2,500** |
| ***BREAKFAST*** | | | |
| Cherry Cream of Rye Cereal (page 104) | 1 serving | 1 serving | 1 serving |
| Fat-free milk | ½ cup | ½ cup | ½ cup |
| Turkey sausage | 1 oz | 1 oz | 1 oz |
| ***SNACK*** | | | |
| Apple | 1 | 1 | 1 |
| ***LUNCH*** | | | |
| Tuna | 3 oz | 4 oz | 5 oz |
| Celery, chopped | ¼ cup | ¼ cup | ¼ cup |
| Onion, chopped | ¼ cup | ¼ cup | ¼ cup |
| Mayonnaise, reduced-fat | 2 Tbsp | ¼ cup | ¼ cup |
| Green olives | 10 small | 10 small | 10 small |
| Green leaf lettuce, torn | 1 cup | 1 cup | 1 cup |
| Sourdough bread | 1 slice | 1 slice | 1 slice |
| ***SNACK*** | | | |
| Pecans | 1 oz | 1 oz | 1½ oz |
| ***DINNER*** | | | |
| Pork Chops Baked with Cabbage and Cream (page 286) | 1 serving | 1 serving | 1½ servings |
| Steamed butternut squash | ½ cup | ½ cup | ½ cup |
| ***SNACK*** | | | |
| Pumpernickel bread | 1 slice | 1 slice | ½ slice |
| Swiss cheese, reduced-fat | 1 oz | 2 oz | 2 oz |
| Butter | 1 tsp | 2 tsp | 2 tsp |
| **TOTAL CALORIES (APPROX)** | **1,670** | **1,960** | **2,240** |
| **TOTAL CARBS (G)** | **127** | **127** | **127** |

# Day 3

| MENU | CALORIE LEVELS | | |
|---|---|---|---|
| | **1,500–1,800** | **1,800–2,200** | **2,200–2,500** |
| ***BREAKFAST*** | | | |
| Scrambled egg | 1 | 2 | 2 |
| Orange juice | ½ cup | ½ cup | ½ cup |
| Rye toast | 1 slice | 1 slice | 1 slice |
| Butter | 1 tsp | 2 tsp | 2 tsp |
| Fat-free milk | ½ cup | ½ cup | ½ cup |
| ***SNACK*** | | | |
| Kiwifruit | 1 | 1 | 1 |
| ***LUNCH*** | | | |
| Salad of lentils, cooked | ½ cup | ½ cup | ½ cup |
| Turkey breast, cooked and cubed | 3 oz | 4 oz | 5 oz |
| Carrots, sliced | ½ cup | ½ cup | ½ cup |
| Peppers, chopped | ½ cup | ½ cup | ½ cup |
| Peas, cooked | ¼ cup | ¼ cup | ½ cup |
| Olive oil | 2 tsp | 1 Tbsp | 4 tsp |
| Cheddar cheese | ½ oz | ½ oz | 1 oz |
| ***SNACK*** | | | |
| Brazil nuts | 1 oz | 1 oz | 1 oz |
| ***DINNER*** | | | |
| Stir-Fried Chicken and Broccoli (page 264) | 1 serving (4 oz chicken) | 1 serving (5 oz chicken) | 1 serving (7 oz chicken) |
| ***SNACK*** | | | |
| Pecan Muffins (page 99) | 1 | 1 | 1 |
| Butter | 1 tsp | 2 tsp | 2 tsp |
| **TOTAL CALORIES** | **1,590** | **1,960** | **2,240** |
| **TOTAL CARBS (G)** | **123** | **123** | **123** |

# Day 4

| MENU | CALORIE LEVELS | | |
| --- | --- | --- | --- |
| | 1,500–1,800 | 1,800–2,200 | 2,200–2,500 |
| **BREAKFAST** | | | |
| Pecan Muffins (page 99) | 1 | 1 | 1 |
| Cottage cheese | 2 Tbsp | 6 Tbsp | 6 Tbsp |
| Peach | 1 | 1 | 1 |
| Fat-free milk | ½ cup | ½ cup | ½ cup |
| **SNACK** | | | |
| Grapefruit | ½ | ½ | ½ |
| **LUNCH** | | | |
| Sandwich of rice cakes topped with (15 g carbohydrate per rice cake) | 2 | 2 | 2 |
| Sardines, boneless, skinless | 4 oz | 5 oz | 6 oz |
| Cream cheese | 2 Tbsp | 2 Tbsp | 3 Tbsp |
| Tomato | 2 slices | 2 slices | 2 slices |
| Zucchini, sticks | ½ cup | ½ cup | ½ cup |
| **SNACK** | | | |
| Almonds | 1 oz | 1 oz | 1 oz |
| **DINNER** | | | |
| Lamb chop, baked with garlic powder | 4 oz ⅛ tsp | 5 oz ⅛ tsp | 7 oz ¼ tsp |
| Mint leaves, chopped | 2 tsp | 1 Tbsp | 1 Tbsp |
| Barley, cooked | ½ cup | ½ cup | ½ cup |
| Stewed tomatoes | 1 cup | 1 cup | 1 cup |
| Green beans, sautéed in olive oil | ½ cup 2 tsp | ½ cup 3 tsp | ½ cup 4 tsp |
| **SNACK** | | | |
| Whole wheat bread | 1 slice | 1 slice | 1 slice |
| Butter | 1 tsp | 2 tsp | 2 tsp |
| Chicken, sliced | 1 oz | 2 oz | 2 oz |
| **TOTAL CALORIES (APPROX)** | **1,700** | **1,950** | **2,210** |
| **TOTAL CARBS (G)** | **122** | **122** | **122** |

# Day 5

| MENU | CALORIE LEVELS | | |
| --- | --- | --- | --- |
| | **1,500–1,800** | **1,800–2,200** | **2,200–2,500** |
| **BREAKFAST** | | | |
| Sweet potato, cooked and topped | ½ cup | ½ cup | ½ cup |
| with walnut oil or canola oil | ½ tsp | 1 tsp | 1 tsp |
| Walnuts, chopped | 1 oz | 1 oz | 1 oz |
| Coconut, shredded | 1 Tbsp | 2 Tbsp | 2 Tbsp |
| Pineapple, crushed | ¼ cup | ¼ cup | ¼ cup |
| Chicken breast, cooked | — | 2 oz | 3 oz |
| Fat-free milk | ½ cup | ½ cup | ½ cup |
| **SNACK** | | | |
| Pear | ½ | ½ | ½ |
| **LUNCH** | | | |
| Salad of spinach | 2 cups | 2 cups | 2 cups |
| Chickpeas | ½ cup | ½ cup | ½ cup |
| Egg, hard-cooked | 1 | 2 | 2 |
| Ham, boiled | — | — | 2 oz |
| Artichoke hearts | ½ cup | ½ cup | ½ cup |
| Olive oil | 2 tsp | 3 tsp | 5 tsp |
| Lemon juice | 1 Tbsp | 1 Tbsp | 1 Tbsp + 2 tsp |
| Whole wheat pita | ½ | ½ | ½ |
| **SNACK** | | | |
| Monterey Jack cheese | 2 oz | 2 oz | 2 oz |
| **DINNER** | | | |
| Breaded Baked Cod with Tartar Sauce | 1 serving | 1 serving | 1½ servings |
| (page 234) | | | |
| Red cabbage, sautéed in | ½ cup | ½ cup | ½ cup |
| sesame oil | 1 tsp | 2 tsp | 1 tsp |
| Yellow squash, steamed | ½ cup | ½ cup | ½ cup |
| Butter | 1 tsp | 1 tsp | 1 tsp |
| Cantaloupe Sorbet (page 349) | 1 serving | 1 serving | 1 serving |
| **SNACK** | | | |
| Popcorn, air-popped | 3 cups | 3 cups | 1½ cups |
| Butter | 1 tsp | 2 tsp | 2 tsp |
| Monterey Jack cheese | 2 oz | 2 oz | 2 oz |
| **TOTAL CALORIES (APPROX)** | **1,640** | **1,980** | **2,310** |
| **TOTAL CARBS (G)** | **124** | **124** | **124** |

# Day 6

| MENU | CALORIE LEVELS | | |
|---|---|---|---|
| | **1,500–1,800** | **1,800–2,200** | **2,200–2,500** |
| ***BREAKFAST*** | | | |
| Cottage cheese | ¼ cup | ½ cup | ¾ cup |
| Blueberries | ¾ cup | ¾ cup | ¾ cup |
| Cinnamon | Pinch | Pinch | Pinch |
| Bacon, nitrate-free, cooked | 1 slice | 2 slices | 2 slices |
| ***SNACK*** | | | |
| Grapes, red | 15 small | 15 small | 15 small |
| ***LUNCH*** | | | |
| Hamburger, lean | 4 oz | 5 oz | 6 oz |
| Hamburger bun, whole wheat | ½ | ½ | ½ |
| Leaf lettuce | 1 leaf | 1 leaf | 1 leaf |
| Tomato | 1 slice | 1 slice | 1 slice |
| Onion, sliced | 1 slice | 1 slice | 1 slice |
| Mustard | 1 tsp | 1 tsp | 1 tsp |
| Mayonnaise | 2 tsp | 3 tsp | 3 tsp |
| French fries | 10 small | 10 small | 10 small |
| Olives, green | — | 5 small | 10 small |
| ***SNACK*** | | | |
| Hazelnuts | 1 oz | 1 oz | 1 oz |
| Cheddar, reduced-fat | — | 1½ oz | 1½ oz |
| ***DINNER*** | | | |
| Mushroom and Kasha Soup (page 136) | 1 serving | 1 serving | 1 serving |
| Turkey breast, cooked | 4 oz | 5 oz | 7 oz |
| Carrots, baby, cooked | ½ cup | ½ cup | ½ cup |
| Peas, cooked | ¼ cup | ¼ cup | ¼ cup |
| Olive oil | 1 tsp | 2 tsp | 2 tsp |
| ***SNACK*** | | | |
| Peanut Butter Cookies (page 330) | 1 cookie | 1 cookie | 1 cookie |
| Fat-free milk | ½ cup | ½ cup | ½ cup |
| **TOTAL CALORIES (APPROX)** | **1,570** | **1,890** | **2,230** |
| **TOTAL CARBS (G)** | **125** | **125** | **125** |

# Day 7

| MENU | CALORIE LEVELS | | |
|---|---|---|---|
| | **1,500–1,800** | **1,800–2,200** | **2,200–2,500** |
| ***BREAKFAST*** | | | |
| Bran cereal, flaked | ½ cup | ½ cup | ½ cup |
| Fat-free milk | ½ cup | ½ cup | ½ cup |
| Banana | ½ | ½ | ½ |
| Cottage cheese | ½ cup | ½ cup | ½ cup |
| ***SNACK*** | | | |
| Cherries, large | 10 | 10 | 10 |
| Protein bar (16 g protein, 2 g carb) | — | ¾ bar | ¾ bar |
| ***LUNCH*** | | | |
| Sausage, Egg, and Vegetable Casserole (page 284) | 1 serving | 1 serving | 2 servings |
| Spinach, steamed | ½ cup | ½ cup | ½ cup |
| Whole wheat bread | 1 slice | 1 slice | 1 slice |
| ***SNACK*** | | | |
| Almonds | 1 oz | 1 oz | 1 oz |
| Swiss cheese, reduced-fat | — | 2 oz | 2 oz |
| ***DINNER*** | | | |
| Scallops in Tarragon Cream (page 259) | 1 serving | 1 serving | 1 serving |
| Asparagus, steamed | ½ cup | ½ cup | ½ cup |
| Tomato, broiled | 1 large | 1 large | — |
| Brown rice, cooked | ½ cup | ½ cup | ½ cup |
| Butter | — | 1 tsp | 1 tsp |
| ***SNACK*** | | | |
| Gingerbread Cake with Peach Whipped Cream (page 334) | 1 serving | 1 serving | 1 serving |
| **TOTAL CALORIES (APPROX)** | **1,530** | **1,950** | **2,350** |
| **TOTAL CARBS (G)** | **128** | **128** | **131** |

# mastering carbs in and out of the kitchen

All of the world's weight-loss science and action plans are useless if they fail to include the most important element of success: great-tasting food. In fact, there's no sense following any eating plan that doesn't include foods that you like to eat.

That's why favorite foods, delicious recipes, and occasional indulgences are built right into this book.

Here's where you'll learn the ins and outs of stocking a smart low-carb pantry, how to cut carbohydrates in your favorite recipes, and how to plan family-pleasing meals.

You'll also find tips on using oat flour in place of all-purpose flour, the best alternatives to sugar, and how to read food labels to decipher the carb content. The following tips cover all of the principles of smart low-carb cooking.

## USE YOUR NOODLE WHEN COOKING MEATS

Eating wisely means reducing simple carbohydrates but not going overboard on saturated fats. Translation: Use oil instead of butter, use reduced-fat cheese, and choose fish, poultry, or lean cuts of meat whenever you can. See page 26 for the best choices of lean meats. Here's how to get the most flavor from meats while reducing any potential health risks.

**Dry off your meats for better browning.** Browning involves quickly cooking meats over high heat until the surface is browned. This cooking method seals in moisture and creates intense flavor, especially in leaner cuts. Before browning beef, pork, poultry, and even fish, pat the food dry to remove excess surface moisture. The dry surface helps the heat of the pan or flame to brown the food and caramelize its natural sugars,

(continued on page 56)

# STOCKING THE SMART LOW-CARB KITCHEN

Keep the items below on hand and you'll minimize last-minute shopping. Here is everything you need to whip up delicious low-carbohydrate meals—a big plus on busy nights when less-healthy take-out options might tempt you. Some of the refrigerator items like parsley and lemons may not last as long as other foods, but they have so many uses and are so inexpensive, it's wise to consider them staples. In addition to the foods below, be sure to stock the foods that your family likes best—even some of the higher-carbohydrate ones. If eating high-carbohydrate foods now and then helps you stick to your overall eating plan, then it's worth keeping them around. Smart tip: Make several photocopies of this list and tack them to your fridge or keep them in a drawer. Each one is a ready-made shopping list that you can tailor to your needs before heading to the store.

### Cool, Dry Place
Bananas
Garlic
Melon (cantaloupe, honeydew, watermelon)
Onions
Oranges
Plums
Sweet potatoes
Winter squash

### Refrigerator
Butter (preferably light)
Cheese (Cheddar, mozzarella, Parmesan, Monterey Jack, cream cheese—preferably reduced-fat)
Eggs
Half-and-half
Milk (1%)
Orange juice
Sour cream (reduced-fat)
Yogurt (low-fat, plain)
Apples
Bell peppers
Broccoli
Cabbage (green or red)
Carrots
Cauliflower
Celery
Cucumbers
Eggplant
Fresh greens
Grapefruit
Grapes
Lemons
Mushrooms
Parsley
Raisins
Scallions
Squash (yellow squash, zucchini)
Nuts (walnuts, pecans, almonds, pine nuts, pistachios, macadamia nuts)
Seeds (sunflower, sesame)

### Freezer
Tortillas (corn and whole wheat)
Whole wheat bread
Broccoli
Corn

Green Beans
Peas
Spinach
Salmon
Shrimp
Veggie burgers
Bacon (pork or turkey)
Beef (lean ground, tenderloin, various steaks)
Chicken (skinless, boneless breasts and bone-in parts)
Lamb (ground, chops)
Pork (chops and tenderloin)
Sausage (pork or turkey)
Turkey (cutlets, tenderloin, ground breast)
Frozen fruit (no sugar added)
Unsweetened coconut

**PANTRY**
Apple juice (or cider in the fridge)
Dried apricots
Dried mushrooms
Canned broth (chicken and beef)
Canned chopped clams
Canned fish (tuna, salmon, sardines, anchovies, trout fillets)
Canned fruit in fruit juice
Canned mild green chiles
Canned tomato products (whole, crushed, sauce, juice)
Dry or canned beans (black, white, pinto, red kidney, chickpeas, brown lentils)
Oats
Oat flour
Soy flour

Whole wheat couscous
Whole wheat flour
Whole wheat pasta
Whole wheat pastry flour
Brown rice
Pearl barley
Quinoa
Hot-pepper sauce
Low-sugar marinara sauce
Mayonnaise (no added sugar)
Mustard
Pesto
Salt
Vinegar (cider, white wine, red wine, balsamic)
Soy sauce
Worcestershire sauce
Brown sugar (or brown sugar substitute)
Splenda
Stevia
All-fruit spread (various flavors)
Maple syrup (low-calorie)
Peanuts, unsalted, dry-roasted (and other nuts)
Peanut butter, natural (and other natural nut butters)
Canola oil
Olive oil
Sesame oil
Olives
Roasted peppers
Tea, herbal teas
Unsweetened cocoa powder
Whole grain crackers

the key to creating flavor. If the surface of the meat is wet, the food will steam rather than brown and release some of its flavors into the air.

**Avoid HCAs.** Scientists have found that when meat is cooked at high temperatures, as in pan frying, broiling, or grilling, it can form potentially carcinogenic compounds called heterocyclic amines (HCAs). That doesn't mean you should stop grilling food. The vegetables and fruits in your diet contain numerous phytonutrients that help protect you from these potential cancer-causing compounds. Here are some other ways to reduce HCAs.

- **Trim the fat.** The fat in meat contributes to the formation of HCAs. Cooking with lean cuts can reduce your cancer risk right off the bat. It's wise to trim any visible fat before cooking. Save the more fat-laden cuts such as Delmonico or skirt steak for special occasions or for when you want to treat yourself.
- **Marinate.** According to the American Institute for Cancer Research, marinating meats can reduce the formation of cancer-causing substances by as much as 92 to 99 percent. See the recipe for London Broil Marinated in Soy Sauce and Mustard on page 205. Even bottled salad dressing or stir-fry sauce works well as marinade.
- **Lower the heat.** The Institute recommends using lower-heat cooking methods such as roasting, braising, baking, microwaving, stir-frying, steaming, and stewing.
- **Microwave first.** Before placing meats on the grill or in the pan, microwave them to get rid of some of the fat that could contribute to HCAs. Microwave burgers for 1 to 2 minutes and steaks for 2 to 3 minutes, then pour off the liquid.
- **Use aluminum foil on the grill.** Place a piece of foil on the grill and poke holes in it. This will minimize the fumes that carry HCAs back into meat.
- **Mix ground beef with beans.** When making burgers, meat loaf, meatballs, or chili, combine the ground beef with mashed black beans, pinto beans, or kidney beans. This will help reduce the fat that contributes to HCAs and boost fiber—plus research shows that eating fiber-rich foods may also lower your risk of colon cancer. You could also use cooked grains such as rice or quinoa.
- **Flip burgers often.** On the grill or in a pan, frequent burger flipping reduces HCAs, kills bacteria, speeds cooking, and makes burgers more moist.
- **Eat veggies and fruits, too.** Don't forget the cancer-preventive importance of phytonutrients in vegetables and fruits. For instance, eating cooked tomato products will increase your intake of lycopene, a phytonutrient that helps fight several types of cancer. No wonder beef-and-tomato dishes like chili and meat sauce have been around so long.

## SWAP SWEETS WHEN YOU CAN

Sugar crops up in so many foods, it's nearly impossible to avoid. Fortunately, when you're the one choosing the food or adding the sweetener, you're in control. Here are some alternatives to popular sweeteners and a few words of caution about using artificial sweeteners. The natural alternatives discussed below either have fewer calories, a lower glycemic index, or the benefit of additional nutrients that are lacking in table sugar. In some cases, these alternatives will help prevent the cravings caused by eating excess sugary foods.

**Use spreadable fruit.** Unlike jelly, which is loaded with sugar and/or corn syrup, spreadable fruit is made with 100 percent fruit. Fruit juice provides the sweetness. Try spreadable fruit on bread and muffins, or use it instead of sugar to sweeten desserts like fruit pies, compotes, and even some snack cakes.

**Go for low-cal syrup.** Instead of pure maple syrup, use low-calorie syrup. You'll save 14 grams of carbohydrate in every 2 tablespoons.

**Try brown sugar.** When it comes to replacing sugar, the bottom line is that nothing tastes or performs quite the same way in cooking. However, you can reduce your carbohydrate intake by using brown sugar instead of white sugar. Brown sugar is a mixture of white sugar and molasses, which gives it a slightly lower carbohydrate content than that of white sugar. If you swap brown for white, you'll save 15 grams of carbohydrate in every ¼ cup you use. Keep in mind that brown sugar is still a refined sugar and is not the lowest-carbohydrate sweetener.

**Don't be fooled by fructose.** You might be wondering if fructose is an option. Sometimes considered a sugar substitute, fructose is really a simple sugar that is refined from corn. Fructose is not the best choice as a sugar substitute not only because it is a refined sugar but also because its effect upon our health is questionable. The potential negative impact of fructose upon the body's levels of cholesterol and triglycerides, platelet clumping in the blood, and status of chromium and copper in the body has made some experts suspicious.

**Try sweetening with stevia.** If you really want to replace sugar or brown sugar, try stevia. The only completely natural alternative sweetener, stevia is an herb that has enormous sweetening power. Look for it in the herbal section of health food stores or large supermarkets in the form of a white powder or a liquid. For cooking, liquid stevia is the most convenient choice because it measures easily and stores in the fridge. But go easy. One-eighth of a teaspoon of liquid stevia is equivalent to ½ cup of sugar. For coffee, just a tiny drop will do the trick. If you add too much stevia, your food may have a somewhat bitter, licorice-like taste. Start out with less than you think you will need, and gradually increase the amount. Remember that stevia only adds sweetness. Unlike sugar, it doesn't aid in browning or provide textural lightening in baked goods. Yet it still works well in everything from pancakes to puddings. See the recipes for

(continued on page 60)

*mastering carbs in and out of the kitchen*

# I Did It!

## Amanda Di Pietro

A lifetime of weight problems didn't keep Amanda from finding a successful approach. She identified her trigger foods and found an eating plan that works.

"My weight has always been like a yo-yo. I've had a weight problem since I was a child. With diligence, I managed to keep it in check throughout most of my life—until I became pregnant. I've had three pregnancies and gained more weight with each one. In 1970, after my youngest son was born, I was suddenly 30 pounds over-weight. I adopted a low-carbo-hydrate eating plan and it helped me lose all 30 pounds. I stuck with the plan and kept the weight off for almost 20 years. Then in 1989, a number of changes in my life brought my stress levels to their limits. I sent my last child off to college, moved from my Pennsylvania home of 20 years, relocated to Virginia, and

before

**Weight lost:** 30 pounds
**Time kept off:** 2 years
**Weight-loss strategies:** Avoided trigger foods, reduced carbohy-drates, did Pilates or Jazzercise most days of the week

**Weight-maintenance strategies:** Avoids trigger foods and refined carbohydrates, ex-ercises several days a week, maintains good self-esteem

started my own business—all within the span of 3 weeks. For comfort, I turned to my favorite foods like potatoes, anything containing sugar, and any kind of bread. My health paid the price, as did my waistline—once again! That year, I gained 50 pounds.

"Because I was having various health problems, I decided to see a homeopathic physician. He diagnosed me with a sluggish thyroid and suspected that I had several trigger foods that were causing me to gain weight. I immediately went on a diet that avoided my trigger foods. This diet was simple—it rotated a variety of foods in and out of my menus every week. I could not believe the difference it made! My cravings for sugar and other refined carbohydrates disappeared. I learned to listen to my body for hunger signals rather than just resort to food whenever I thought I needed it. Best of all, I started to lose weight again and keep it off.

"I am amazed that eating sugar can cause me to crave food all of the time, even when I am full. I now realize that sugar was behind my mood swings, too. Dairy foods are another trigger food for me. Whenever I eat them, my stomach gets bloated and my head gets congested. I'm so glad I know these things now. I never realized how food can regulate not only my weight, but also my health and mental well-being.

"Now I choose lean protein foods like chicken breasts, lean pork chops and pork tenderloin, orange roughy, and occasionally beef tenderloin. I also limit my carbohydrates to only whole grains, starchy vegetables, and beans. For treats, I snack on fresh fruit. I am also more diligent about my exercise routine. I do Pilates (simple body conditioning) four times a week and attend Jazzercise classes three times a week.

"My new eating and exercise plan has made me more successful in every aspect of my life—particularly the weight-loss aspect! I have more energy and I'm not nearly as depressed (for some reason, sugar depresses me). Everything in my life just looks better. I am more able to stay focused on my weight now that I've found out what works. I also know that reaching my goal weight is as important for my self-esteem as it is for my health and longevity."

Whole Grain Pancakes with Berry Cream Syrup (page 97), Pecan Muffins (page 99), and Chocolate-Raspberry Dip and Fresh Fruit (page 347). Another advantage stevia has over sugar (besides being calorie-free) is that it has a health benefit. Stevia is a probiotic, which means that it provides food for healthy bacteria to multiply in your intestines. This healthy bacteria is important for proper digestion and detoxification.

**Have a taste of Splenda.** You may have seen Splenda, a newly available type of sweetener, in a box next to the sugar on your supermarket's shelves. It's another good option among alternative sweeteners. The primary ingredient in Splenda is sucralose, a sugar substitute processed from real sugar that has been modified so that it isn't absorbed by the body. Sucralose was first discovered in 1976. More than 20 years and 100 studies later, the safety of sucralose has been endorsed by 25 countries. In April 1998, the Food and Drug Adminis-

tration (FDA) approved sucralose for use in everyday foods in the United States. Sucralose is calorie-free, does not affect blood sugar levels, does not promote tooth decay, and maintains its sweetness across a broad range of temperatures.

Splenda, the commercial form of sucralose, is a real breakthrough for low-calorie, low-carbohydrate cooking. It measures cup for cup like sugar; it performs almost like sugar in recipes; and when used in moderate amounts, it doesn't have the cloying aftertaste associated with artificial sweeteners. Splenda is especially useful in baking, but keep in mind that it doesn't caramelize like sugar. If you're reducing your sugar intake, one option is to split the difference and use half sugar and half Splenda. You'll still get the caramelizing and browning properties of sugar, but fewer calories and carbohydrates. See the recipes for Strawberry Cream Cake (page 336), Double Chocolate Pudding

## HIDDEN ROADBLOCK to weight loss

### UNDEREATING

That's right, it's possible that you're not eating enough! Consuming too few calories signals your metabolism to slow down in order to protect your body from what it thinks might be an oncoming famine. Also, if you're not eating enough, chances are good that your body is not getting enough of the nutrients that it needs to efficiently metabolize carbohydrates, proteins, and fats. If you are following one of the specific plans in this book, you will be getting adequate calories— unless you are very active or extremely overweight. If that's you, try eating more protein foods and slightly more fat, rather than more carbohydrates. Keep in mind that no one should consume fewer than 1,200 calories a day, especially without medical supervision. Going too low puts your body into starvation mode, which slows down your metabolism so much that you may not be able to lose any weight.

(page 341), or Cantaloupe Sorbet (page 349). As with any alternative sweetener (or any sweetener for that matter), don't go overboard with Splenda. Moderation and variety are still key.

**Be cautious of artificial sweeteners.** Aspartame and saccharin are two other options you may have considered. Of the two, aspartame is generally considered more safe and palatable. That's the sweetener found in Equal and NutraSweet brands. Though most scientists disagree, some scientists suspect that aspartame may cause brain damage that leads to memory loss, so be cautious. As for saccharin, some research on animals shows that, in very high doses, it may lead to cancer. But many scientists consider it safe for humans at the levels found in food.

**Keep an eye out for sugar replacers in processed foods.** Sucralose, aspartame, and saccharin are all called nonnutritive sweeteners because they don't supply any calories. They're often used in diet sodas and other diet foods. Sugar replacers, on the other hand, are called nutritive sweeteners because they do contain some calories. However, their energy values (calories) are lower than that of sugar because these carbohydrates are slowly and incompletely absorbed. Thus, they have a lower glycemic index than sugar, too. Sugar replacers often crop up in products labeled "sugar-free" or "no sugar added." You can usually spot a sugar replacer because the name ends in "-ol," as in mannitol, xylitol, and sorbitol. Two other sugar replacers are isomalt and hydrogenated starch hydrolysate.

**Use sugar-free products sparingly.** The FDA and several other world health organizations consider sugar replacers to be safe for human consumption. The drawback of sugar replacers is that these less-digestible carbohydrates pull water into the intestine. This can result in diarrhea if you eat too much. Also, bacteria in the colon ferment this kind of carbohydrate, which can cause flatulence or gas. Use caution. One half-stick of sugar-free chewing gum is enough to cause some people discomfort!

**Know what the labels mean.** The Nutrition Labeling and Education Act of 1990 established the following guidelines for labeling sugar content in processed foods. Keep these in mind when making low-carb choices.

**Sugar-free:** Must contain less than 0.5 gram of sugar per serving

**Reduced sugar or less sugar:** Sugar content has been reduced by 25 percent

**No sugar added:** No sugars added during processing, but may have a natural sugar content, as with canned fruit with no sugar added

## CHOOSE THE BEST OILS

Most liquid oils are a more healthy choice than saturated or solid fats such as butter and bacon drippings. Various types of oil are used throughout this book. The big two are olive oil and canola oil. Nut oils such as walnut oil are suggested in a few recipes for their tremendous flavor. But other oils can be substituted in most cases. Here's the

*(continued on page 64)*

# SMART LOW-CARB SUBSTITUTIONS

Keeping carbs in check doesn't mean eliminating your favorite food groups. A simple switch within the same group may be all it takes. You can dodge nearly 40 grams of carbohydrate by snacking on a cup of popcorn instead of a handful of pretzels. Or skip 25 grams by opting for whole wheat bread instead of a bagel. Try these substitutions in the kitchen and when you eat out.

| INSTEAD OF . . . | TRY . . . | CARBS SAVED (G). . . |
|---|---|---|
| **Breads, Pasta, and Flour** | | |
| Bagel, plain (4") | Bread, whole wheat (1 slice) | 25 |
| Bread, white (1 slice) | Bread, light whole wheat (1 slice) | 2.3 |
| Flour, all-purpose or whole wheat (¼ cup) | Flour, soy (¼ cup) | 14 |
| | Flour, oat (¼ cup) | 12 |
| French toast (1 slice) | Omelette, ham and cheese (2 eggs) | 12 |
| Lasagna noodles (2 oz dry) | Eggplant or zucchini slices (1 cup) | 35 |
| Pancakes, from mix (two 6") | Eggs, large (2) | 56 |
| Spaghetti, cooked (1 cup) | Squash, spaghetti, cooked (1 cup) | 30 |
| Tortilla, flour (6") | Tortilla, corn (6") | 6 |
| **Desserts, Sweets, and Dairy Foods** | | |
| Cake, yellow, w/van frosting (1 slice) | Cheesecake (1 slice) | 18 |
| Ice cream (½ cup) | Gelatin, diet (½ cup), w/whipped cream (2 Tbsp) | 14 |
| Milk, chocolate (1 cup) | Milkshake, chocolate, high-protein, low-carb (1 cup) | 26 |
| Maple syrup, pure (2 Tbsp) | Maple syrup, low-calorie (2 Tbsp) | 14 |
| Milk, skim (1 cup) | Milk, soy, unsweetened (1 cup) | 9 |
| Pie, apple (1 slice) | Pie, pumpkin (1 slice) | 10 |
| Sugar, granulated (½ cup) | Splenda (¼ cup) or stevia (⅛ tsp) | 48 |
| Sugar, granulated (¼ cup) | Brown sugar (¼ cup) | 15 |
| | All-fruit spread (¼ cup) | 9 |
| | Fruit juice bar (2.5 oz) | 2 |
| Yogurt, frozen soft (½ cup) | Yogurt, plain, unsweetened (1 cup) | 30 |
| Yogurt, with fruit (1 cup) | | |
| **Fruits** | | |
| Apple | Celery (1 rib) | 18 |
| Banana (6") | Kiwifruit | 10 |

| INSTEAD OF . . . | TRY . . . | CARBS SAVED (G). . . |
|---|---|---|
| Blueberries, fresh (½ cup) | Strawberries, fresh (½ cup) | 5 |
| Cranberry sauce, canned (¼ cup) | Cranberry sauce, made w/Splenda (¼ cup) | 22 |
| Honeydew (¼ med) | Grapefruit (½ medium) | 13 |
| Juice, apple (1 cup) | Cider, apple (1 cup) | 8 |
| Strawberries, frozen in syrup (½ cup) | Strawberries, frozen, no sugar added (½ cup) | 23 |

**Main Dishes, Sauces, and Soups**

| | | |
|---|---|---|
| Beef pot pie, frozen (1 serving) | Meat loaf (1 serving) | 40 |
| Linguine w/white clam sauce (1 serving) | Manicotti w/tomato sauce (1 serving) | 31 |
| Mayonnaise, regular (1 Tbsp) | Mayonnaise, no sugar added (1 Tbsp) | 1 |
| Pasta salad, seafood (1½ cups) | Tuna salad (1½ cups) | 3 |
| Sandwich, chicken, fast food | Hamburger, fast food | 8 |
| Sandwich, roast beef, fast food (1) | Soup, chicken rice, (1 can) | 29 |
| Soup, tomato, canned (1 cup) | Gazpacho soup (1 cup) | 12 |
| Thousand Island dressing (2 Tbsp) | Oil and vinegar (1 Tbsp each) | 4 |
| Vinaigrette, bottled (2 Tbsp) | Oil and vinegar (1 Tbsp each) | 2 |

**Snacks and Beverages**

| | | |
|---|---|---|
| Cashews, dry-roasted (⅓ cup) | Brazil nuts, dry-roasted (⅓ cup) | 9 |
| Cola (12 oz) | Diet cola, seltzer, or club soda (12 oz ) | 38 |
| Fig bars (2) | Gingersnaps (2) | 20 |
| Jelly beans, large (10) | Apricots, dried (10 halves) | 5 |
| Pretzels, hard twists (10) | Popcorn, air-popped (2 cups) | 35 |
| Vanilla wafers (5) | Cookies, oatmeal (2) | 2 |

**Vegetables and Side Dishes**

| | | |
|---|---|---|
| Carrot | Celery (1 rib) | 5 |
| Onion rings, fried (8) | Mozzarella sticks, fried (5) | 9 |
| Onions, chopped (½ cup) | Scallions, chopped (½ cup) | 3 |
| Potato, baked (1 med) | Corn-on-the-cob (1 med) | 34 |
| Potatoes, mashed (1 cup) | Turnips, mashed (1 cup) | 26 |
| Potato pancake (1 med) | Hash brown potatoes (½ cup) | 6 |
| Potato salad (½ cup) | Cauliflower salad (½ cup) | 11 |

skinny on several types of oils. Choose the ones you like best.

**Olive oil.** One of the best oils for healthy cooking, olive oil is high in heart-healthy monounsaturated fats and holds up fairly well to heat. Use it for dressings, sauces, marinades, sautéing, stir-frying—and even baking. There are three main classes of olive oil: Extra-virgin, classic, and extra-light taste. Each contains 120 calories, 14 grams of fat, and 0 grams of carbohydrate per tablespoon. *Extra-virgin* olive oil has a bold flavor and dark green color. Its flavor holds up best in uncooked dishes such as dressings, marinades, and sauces. Or add it at the end of cooking to boost the flavor of pasta or vegetables, for example. *Classic* olive oil is more golden in color and mild in flavor. This is a good all-purpose choice for sautéing and cooking. *Extra-light* olive oil has a less noticeable olive flavor. If you have never tasted olive oil or used it in your cooking, this type is probably the best to start with. Use it for sautéing, stir-frying, or baking. Among all the olive oil varieties, extra-light holds up best to high temperatures. Many people stock a large bottle of classic olive oil and smaller bottles of extra-virgin or extra-light olive oil for special uses. Keep olive oil away from heat and light for the longest storage—up to 2 years. The refrigerator is a good place. Don't worry if the oil becomes cloudy. Its translucence will return when the oil reaches room temperature.

**Canola oil.** This type of oil, made from rapeseed, got its name from the term Cana-

Smart-Carb Insider Tip

## FLAVOR UP

If your kitchen isn't stocked with a slew of herbs and spices, it might be time to invest in some. Seasoning foods in different ways will ward off flavor fatigue and help you save carbohydrate grams. For example, a dash of cinnamon or nutmeg makes whole grain cereals, fruits, and baked goods taste a little sweeter—without adding sugar or carbohydrates. Use flavored vinegars to perk up beans or salads. Mustard, hot-pepper sauce, horseradish, salsa, soy sauce, Worcestershire sauce, citrus fruit, dried mushrooms, and sun-dried tomatoes are a few other low-carb flavor boosters to keep on hand. You might also want to keep a bottle of diet maple syrup in the fridge. Compare brands for the lowest carbohydrate count.

dian oil. Although usually considered a monounsaturated fat, canola oil has about 20 percent less monounsaturated fat than olive oil. Canola oil is nearly flavorless, so it won't interfere with other flavors in a dish. It's a good all-purpose oil for cooking and baking.

**Vegetable oil.** Usually the least expensive type of oil, vegetable oil is an all-purpose blend of oils that may come from vegetables, nuts, and seeds. Most vegetable oils are made from soybeans. As with canola oil, use vegetable oil for cooking, baking, dressings, marinades, and sauces.

**Safflower oil.** This light-tasting oil does not solidify when chilled, so it's great for salad dressings, mayonnaise, and dips. It can also be used for baking. Safflower oil is also an excellent choice for sautéing and pan frying because of its high smoke point (450°F).

**Nut oils.** Pure nut oils have a fragrant, nutty flavor achieved by grinding whole nuts or big pieces of nuts, roasting the ground nuts, and only lightly filtering the oil. These oils make a good choice for both flavor and high monounsaturated fat content. Remember that price equals flavor. Avoid the less-expensive nut oils, which are often a very mild-tasting mixture of mascerated nuts and vegetable oil. Pure walnut, almond, and macadamia nut oils are good types to try if you're new to nut oils. *Walnut oil*, made from English walnuts, is topaz in color with a delicate toasted walnut flavor. The walnut flavor is destroyed by cooking, so use walnut oil for dressings, dips, or adding to hot dishes just before serving. See the recipe for Asparagus with Orange-Walnut Vinaigrette (page 307). *Almond oil* is fairly mild-tasting and holds up to heat better than walnut oil. It's a good choice for dressings, light sautéing, or baking. Try almond oil in muffins or on green beans with almonds. *Macadamia nut oil* is even higher in monounsaturated fats than olive oil (79 percent versus 71 percent). If you like the taste of macadamia nuts, you'll love macadamia nut oil. It can withstand the heat of sautéing and stir-frying, so it can be used in both hot and cold dishes. As with all nut oils, a little goes a long way (another reason why they're slightly higher in price). Nut oils are more prone to rancidity than vegetable oils, so buy only small quantities and keep them in a cool, dark place such as the refrigerator, where they will last for up to a year.

## Eat Beans — They're Easy and Filling

Beans are one kind of starch you can't complain about getting bored with. There are more than 100 different varieties. Beans provide all the protein, carbohydrate, fats, vitamins, and minerals needed for plants to grow and mature. That's why they're so nutrient rich and healthy for us to eat. It's true that beans are not superlow in carbohydrates, but they are one of the best sources of fiber, which gives them a low glycemic index. Numerous studies have demonstrated the cardiovascular benefits of eating beans.

**Use canned beans for convenience.** Canned beans are already soaked and cooked, so they are ready to use. Keep several varieties in your pantry. Add canned beans to salads and pasta dishes, or use them to make dips. For instance, see the recipe for White Beans with Cheese and Basil (page 114). To reduce the sodium content of canned beans, drain and rinse them before using. Rinsing until all the bubbles disappear removes up to 40 percent of the sodium as well as some of the gas-producing oligosaccharides. One drained can (15½ ounces) of beans yields about 1⅔ cups.

**Use dried beans for more flavor.** Some recipes, such as soup, taste remarkably better made with dried beans. That's because as the beans cook, they release their

# FOOD LABELS FOR THE CARB-SAVVY

The "Nutrition Facts" label made great strides in clarifying nutrition information on food products. However, the details of carbohydrate content can still be confusing. Here are seven tips that clear things up.

**1. Check the serving size first.** This number is right at the top because all the figures below it are based on that serving size. If you are going to eat a larger serving, increase all of the nutritional figures, including the number of carbohydrates.

**2. Read the "As Prepared" figures.** Packaged products sometimes call for the addition of eggs or milk to finish preparation. Read the as-prepared figures to see if the carbohydrates go up.

**3. Stay to the left.** Look at the total calories, grams, and milligrams that appear on the left side of the label. The "% Daily Value" on the right is based on 2,000 calories a day, which may not be what you're eating.

**4. Focus on the "Total Carbohydrate" figures.** These are the most important figures to look at when you're watching carb intake. The total-carbohydrate figure represents the sum of sugars plus starch plus soluble fiber plus insoluble fiber. Specific figures for sugars and fiber may be listed underneath. If they are, you might notice that the numbers don't add up to the "Total Carbohydrate." This happens because sugars and fibers must be exactly measured in the laboratory and calculated separately from the total-carbohydrate figure. But total carbohydrate is calculated with the following formula:

**Total carbohydrate = total weight of food − [weight of protein + total fat + moisture + ash].**

Choose foods that will balance out your overall carbohydrate intake for the day or week.

**5. Strive for fiber.** Eat foods with the most fiber when you can. Fiber helps to make you feel full so that you don't overeat. Fiber also helps to slow the absorption of sugar in carbohydrate-containing foods. Try to get 25 to 35 grams of fiber a day.

**6. Convert grams of sugar to teaspoons.** Teaspoons of sugar are easier to visualize than grams. To convert grams to teaspoons, simply divide the number of grams by 4. For instance, if the label lists 8 grams of sugar, dividing by 4 tells you that the product contains 2 teaspoons of sugar per serving. Keep in mind that the total recommended amount of sugar intake per day is less than 10 teaspoons. Choose foods with the least sugar when you can.

**7. Go high-pro.** Look for foods that are high in protein, especially breads and other starchy foods. Depending upon your calorie intake and weight-loss goals, you should get approximately 75 to 150 grams of protein a day.

---

delicious flavors into the soup (some of the flavor of canned beans goes down the drain with the canning liquid). Many of the soup recipes in the book use dried beans instead of canned. Don't be scared off by using dried beans. They only need to be soaked before cooking. Here's what you need to know.

**Soak dried beans the quick way.** First, spread the dried beans on a clean surface and pick out any pebbles, debris, or mis-shapen beans. Put the sorted beans in a colander and rinse them, then transfer to a large pot (big enough to hold at least twice the volume of the beans). Cover with cold water and soak overnight, then drain and rinse. Or to soak dried beans the quick way, add 10 cups of hot water for each 2 cups (1 pound) of beans. Bring the pot to a boil over medium-high heat, then boil for 2 to 3 minutes. Cover and let soak for 1 to 4 hours. Drain off the soaking water and rinse the beans. At this point, the beans are ready for cooking as directed in most recipes. Or if you want to cook 1 pound of soaked beans for another purpose, put them in a 3- to 4-quart pot and add 6 cups hot water, 2 tablespoons oil, and 2 teaspoons salt. Simmer over medium heat for 1 to 2 hours, or until tender but not mushy. Avoid overcooking beans that will be used in salads or casseroles; they should remain somewhat firm. One pound (2 cups) of dry beans makes 4 to 6 cups cooked beans. A few more tips: If you have hard water, shorten cooking time by adding baking soda to the cooking water; use $\frac{1}{8}$ to $\frac{1}{4}$ teaspoon per pound of beans. Also, hold off on adding acidic ingredients such as tomatoes or vinegar until the end of cooking time because acidic ingredients will slow down the cooking of beans. Keep dry beans in a cool, dry place in airtight glass or metal containers. If you have left-over cooked or canned beans, drain them and freeze them for up to 6 months. Thaw before using.

## GIVE SOY A TRY

Soybeans are one of the most nutrient-dense beans available. Numerous studies show that soy protein helps to lower blood cholesterol levels and may help reduce the risk of osteoporosis and some forms of cancer. The easiest way to get these benefits is to include some soy milk, tofu, and soy flour in your kitchen.

**Sample soy milk.** Soy milk is made from soybeans that have been soaked and squeezed to release their liquid. One big advantage of soy milk is that it's lower in carbohydrates than cow's milk because it does not contain lactose. Its protein content is about the same as that of cow's milk. And most brands are fortified with calcium, vitamin D, and vitamin $B_{12}$ so that the milk is nutritionally similar to cow's milk. Soy milk can stand in for cow's milk in cereal, shakes or smoothies, sauces, baking, and for almost any recipe. The best-tasting varieties are often sold in the refrigerated dairy case in the grocery store. Try a few brands to see which you like best. Read labels carefully. Some brands of soy milk are sweetened with malt, rice syrup, or other sweeteners. The carbohydrate content can range from 8 to 36 grams. Buy unsweetened soy milk for the fewest carbs. If you buy a brand sold in a shelf-stable container, it can be stored for several months in a cool, dry place. Once opened, all soy milk will keep in the fridge for 5 to 7 days. You can buy powdered soy milk, too. Store it in the refrigerator in a sealed container for up to 6 months. Once rehydrated with water, it will also last for up to 7 days in the refrigerator.

**Try tofu.** No doubt you've heard about the possibilities for tofu in the kitchen. If you eat meat, there's no reason to replace meat with tofu. But you might want to use tofu in other ways for the health benefits associated with soy protein. Firm tofu can be cut into cubes, browned, and tossed into a stir-fry. Or it can be cut into thick slabs, marinated, and grilled, baked, or broiled. You can also buy premarinated, prebaked tofu that's ready to be eaten right out of the package or tossed into salads or stir-fries. Soft tofu and silken tofu have a more cus-tardlike texture than firm tofu. Soft tofu can be pureed as the basis for dips, sauces, and puddings. Either way, it's worth checking out at least once.

**Stock a small bag of soy flour.** Lower in carbohydrates than wheat flour, soy flour is a smart addition to your shopping list. The regular roasted variety (not defatted) is the best-tasting one with the fewest carbohydrates. Soy flour is excellent for dredging and sautéing foods such as fish fillets or chicken because it browns beautifully and quickly. That's an easy switch from wheat flour. In baking, things get a little trickier. It's best to replace no more than one-quarter of the wheat flour (or other flour) called for in a baking recipe with soy flour. Baked goods made with soy flour tend to brown more quickly and have a more

grainy texture. In certain cases, the effect is desirable. For instance, a little bit of soy flour makes wonderfully crisp, browned waffles. You can add soy flour to muffins and pancakes, too. If the food is browning too quickly, reduce the oven temperature or shorten the baking time. Keep in mind that soy flour doesn't work as well with delicate cakes. Soy flour has a higher fat content than most refined flours, so store it tightly wrapped in the fridge or freezer to prevent rancidity. It also packs down during storage. Before measuring, stir or sift it.

**Use soy grits instead of corn grits.** Soy grits are easy to work with and make a good substitute for corn (hominy) grits. Or use soy grits as a bread substitute for stuffing when serving poultry. Look for soy grits in the baking aisle of the health food store or supermarket. See the recipe for Roast Chicken with Vegetable-Grits Stuffing (page 186).

## Go Whole Grain

Here they are again: whole grains. We can't recommend them enough. They offer more nutritional benefits than refined grains, and they can help you lose weight. Refined grains, on the other hand, may actually sabotage your weight-loss plans. Take a look at a few of the nutrients lost when whole wheat flour is refined into all-purpose white flour:

| Bran | 100% |
| Manganese | 86% |
| Vitamin E | 86% |

| Magnesium | 85% |
|-----------|-----|
| Vitamin B$_6$ | 72% |
| Copper | 68% |
| Chromium | 40% |

Similar nutrients are lost when other grains such as rice are refined. For healthy weight loss, fiber is the most crucial nutrient retained in whole grains. Fiber helps you to feel full so you're not tempted to overeat, and it can reduce your risk of heart disease. Here are some tips on using fiber- and vitamin-rich whole grains.

**Switch to whole wheat pasta.** Swap white pasta for whole wheat pasta one for one and you'll get more fiber, a lower glycemic index, and—believe it or not—more flavor! Whole wheat pasta has a more complex, nutty taste than refined white pasta. Use whole wheat pasta in any of your favorite recipes. Most supermarkets carry both strand and shaped whole wheat pastas such as spaghetti, linguine, and rotelle. Look for them right next to the refined white pastas. Whole wheat couscous is another type of higher-fiber tiny pasta that can be used in place of regular couscous. It's excellent for making grain salads and pilafs. See the recipe for Couscous Salad with Lime-Cumin Dressing (page 324).

**Don't settle for boring white rice.** Here's another simple trade-in. Use brown rice instead of white. Brown rice is higher in fiber and vitamins than white rice, and it has a more chewy texture and nutty flavor. Both short- and long-grain varieties work well in casseroles and as simple side dishes. For ex-

ample, see the recipe for Brown Rice Pilaf with Hazelnuts (page 328). Many grocery stores also carry whole-grain rice mixes that include various types of wild rice and brown rice. The taste of these rice mixes beats plain white rice hands down. Of course, white rice has its place—alongside a stir-fry, for instance. If you must choose white rice, go for parboiled rice instead of regular white rice. It has a lower glycemic index.

**Reach for whole grain bread.** Good choices here include 100 percent whole wheat bread and 100 percent rye bread. Read the label to make sure that at least the first flour used is a whole grain flour, such as whole rye, whole wheat, or whole oat flour. Light whole wheat bread is the best choice for reducing carbohydrates; it is cut thin and is slightly smaller than a traditional loaf. Slice for slice, light whole wheat bread has 5 fewer grams of carbohydrate than white bread.

**Coat foods with whole grain bread crumbs.** For breading fish or chicken, use whole wheat bread crumbs instead of regular bread crumbs. To make ½ cup of fresh whole wheat bread crumbs, place two slices of whole wheat bread in a food processor and process until fine crumbs form. Use immediately or freeze to use another time. For a taste of how good whole wheat bread crumbs can be, see the recipe for Breaded Baked Cod with Tartar Sauce (page 234).

**Use whole grain flours when you can.** If you bake, try mixing in some whole grain flour along with the all-purpose flour. You can even use whole grain flours for thickening sauces and dredging meats. (See page 68 for tips on using soy flour.) Here's what you need to know about using the most popular whole grain flours.

- **Whole wheat flour.** If you bake bread, whole wheat flour makes a good stand-in for bread flour. Look for 100% stone-ground whole wheat flour for the best texture and flavor. For most other uses in the kitchen, whole wheat pastry flour is the better choice. This finely milled flour is made from soft wheat. In most quick-bread recipes, you can replace all of the all-purpose flour with whole wheat pastry flour. Its texture is similar to all-purpose flour and it works well as a thickener; for dredging meats, poultry, and fish; and in baking. For delicate baked goods like cakes, use a combination of whole wheat pastry flour and oat flour to create a lighter texture. For instance, to replace 1 cup all-purpose flour, use ½ cup whole wheat pastry flour plus ½ cup oat flour. See the recipe for Strawberry Cream Cake (page 336) for a good example of how well these flours work together. You can also achieve a lighter texture from whole wheat pastry flour by sifting it a few times before using. Because whole wheat pastry flour soaks up more liquid than all-purpose flour, you might need to add a few tablespoons of liquid to your recipe or use a few tablespoons less whole wheat flour than the recipe

calls for. Note that some supermarkets carry whole grain pastry flour rather than whole wheat pastry flour. Whole grain pastry flour is a mix of whole grain flours that generally performs the same way as whole wheat pastry flour.

- **Oat flour.** Made from whole oats, oat flour has about half the carbohydrate content and a lower glycemic index than all-purpose flour. It's a great substitute for wheat and has a slightly sweet taste. It's important to sift oat flour before using it because it clumps easily. As with whole grain pastry flour, when replacing all-purpose flour in a recipe, use a few tablespoons less oat flour than is called for. If you can't find oat flour in your grocery store, you can make it at home by running whole rolled oats through your food processor until finely ground.

- **Kamut® flour.** Pronounced ka-MOOT, this flour is an ancient relative of modern common wheat. It has a higher amino acid and mineral content than common wheat. The gluten content in kamut makes it easy to substitute for white flour in your recipes. The taste is richer and nuttier—with more protein and fiber—than that of all-purpose flour.

- **Buckwheat flour.** Surprisingly, buckwheat is not related to wheat. It is a relative of rhubarb. Technically, buckwheat is not even a grain. It is a type of grass. Buckwheat flour is gluten-free and works well in pancakes, breads, dumplings, and pastas such as soba noodles (buckwheat noodles).

■ **Amaranth flour.** This flour makes an excellent addition to whole wheat and soy flours for baking. It tenderizes the final product somewhat and adds a pleasant nutty flavor. For recipes containing more than one type of flour, substitute 1 cup of amaranth flour for 1 cup of all-purpose flour.

■ **Quinoa flour.** Considered a complete protein, quinoa flour contains all of the essential amino acids. It's also lower in carbohydrates than most of the other flours. However, quinoa lacks gluten, the substance that gives flours elasticity. Rather than use it alone, only use it for up to 50 percent of the flour in a recipe to allow for adequate gluten. When mixed with buckwheat flour, cornmeal, and some all-purpose flour, quinoa flour makes excellent pancakes.

**Store whole grain flours in the fridge.** To best preserve the flavors of whole grain flours, store them tightly wrapped in the refrigerator. For longer storage, keep them in the freezer. Be sure to bring the flour to room temperature before using (unless it's for a pie or biscuit dough that calls for chilled ingredients).

**Sift before using.** Most baked goods made with whole grain flours will be a little heavier than those made with white flour. But you can still get a fairly light product if you sift the flour two or three times to in-corporate some air. If you don't have a sifter, whisk the flour after you put it in a bowl.

**Work quickly but gently.** Here's another tip to ensure light-tasting whole grain baked goods. Preheat the oven and prepare the pans first. This will reduce the amount of time that the whole grain flour has to sit in the bowl and absorb moisture. Avoid letting batters sit. Also, avoid overmixing the batter for quick breads such as pancakes and muffins. The more you mix, the heavier the baked good is likely to be.

**Add extra liquid.** Whole grain flours *love* liquid. The extra fiber in them soaks it up readily. For baking, this means that you'll probably need to add a little extra oil or liquid to the recipe to prevent dryness.

## GET A LITTLE NUTTY

The ancient Romans often served nuts with or after dessert. Hence, we have the phrase "from soup to nuts." Take a tip from the ancients and reap a wealth of health benefits by including nuts in your daily diet. They contain protein, iron, and other important vitamins and minerals. (See "What's a Serving of Nuts?" on page 27 to see how much.) Here are some surprising nut facts:

■ One ounce of almonds (20 to 25 almonds) contains as much calcium as ¼ cup milk. The same amount also supplies 35 percent of the Daily Value of vitamin E, plus trace amounts of mag-

*mastering carbs in and out of the kitchen*

nesium, zinc, phosphorus, fiber, and folic acid.

- Pecans contain 65 to 70 percent oil. Most of this oil is the same kind of heart-healthy monounsaturated fat found in olive oil.
- Walnuts are the oldest tree food, dating back to 7000 B.C. They were traded on English ships throughout the Mediterranean. This is how they came to be called English walnuts. California now produces 99 percent of the commercial U.S. supply and two-thirds of the world supply of these walnuts. It takes 6 to 8 years for trees to yield a crop. But then the tree bears nuts for nearly a century.
- Pine nuts have the highest protein content of any nut. Ounce for ounce, pine nuts contain approximately the same amount of protein as beef.
- Cashews are in the same botanical family as poison ivy, poison oak, poison sumac, and mangoes. All of these plants contain volatile substances that can irritate the skin, and because the shell of cashews contains an irritant, they are never sold in the shell. Cashews have a higher carbohydrate content than most other nuts.

**Choose the freshest nuts for the most flavor.** Autumn and winter are generally considered nut season. But nuts are available all year round. If you buy fresh nuts in bulk, shop at a store with fast turnover. Shelled nuts can become rancid fairly quickly because of their high fat content. For the freshest nuts, buy them in the shell. Avoid any that feel light for their size or have holes or splits in the shell. These are most likely past their prime.

**Keep them in a cool, dark place.** Nuts (and seeds) will generally last about a month at room temperature. They will last longer and taste fresher when stored in a cool, dry place away from light (or in the refrigerator). If you have a large stockpile of nuts, keep them in the freezer in airtight containers, where they will last for up to a year.

**Bring out the flavor.** Toasting nuts enhances their flavor. To toast nuts, place them in a dry skillet over medium heat and stir frequently until lightly colored and fragrant. This should only take 2 to 3 minutes. If your oven is already on, place the nuts on a baking sheet and toast at 350°F for 3 to 5 minutes.

**Add nuts to almost any dish.** Nuts are incredibly versatile. They can be eaten alone as a snack or added to almost any dish—both savory and sweet. Sprinkle nuts on whole grain cereal or yogurt, into bread or cookie batters, into casseroles, on pasta, or over desserts. Pastas and casseroles are typically made with high-GI ingredients like potatoes or bread crumbs. To lower the glycemic index, add nuts. Pine nuts are terrific with pasta or couscous. Pecans, walnuts, and almonds work well with casseroles, vegetables, and rice dishes. Nuts even work with meats. See the recipe for Meat Loaf with Walnuts (page 212).

**Stock up on nut butters.** If you like peanut butter, try the unsweetened variety, also called natural peanut butter. Unsweetened peanut butter is made without hydrogenated fats, sugar, or other flavoring agents. It has a more peanutty taste and a lower glycemic index than most commercial varieties, so it won't raise your blood sugar as rapidly.

Give other nut butters a try, too. Cashew butter is exceptionally rich-tasting and delicious on toast with fruit spread. Creamy macadamia nut butter makes a great sandwich spread. And almond butter is fantastic in sauces. You can use almost any nut butter to make a dip or sauce. See the recipe for Crudités with Spicy Peanut Dipping Sauce (page 118). Tahini (sesame seed butter) is another good choice for making dips and sauces. These nut butters are sold in most health food stores and some large supermarkets.

## FLAVOR UP!

The cardinal rule of any successful eating plan is this: Don't settle for bland-tasting food! Sometimes all a dish needs is a little something. Here are a few last-minute additions to help perk up the flavor of your food.

**Toss in some herbs.** The volatile oils in herbs are teeming with aromas. When using dried herbs, add them early on in the cooking so they have time to release flavor. Crush them before using to release even more flavor. More delicate fresh herbs such as basil and parsley are best added toward the end of cooking.

**Sprinkle on sweet spices.** To enhance sweetness without adding calories or carbohydrates, use sweet spices—especially in baking. A sprinkle of cinnamon, nutmeg, cloves, allspice, or pumpkin pie spice might be all you need to make your cookies, pancakes, or quick bread sing with flavor. See, for example, the recipe for Gingerbread Cake with Peach Whipped Cream (page 334).

**Add a bit of acid.** Acidic foods can help balance out the taste of a dish or add a last-minute shot of flavor. Citrus juices add fresh flavor to everything from chicken and fish to pasta and vegetables. Or look to lemon zest, lime zest, or orange zest to bring out more flavor in baked goods like cookies and muffins. Vinegars add bright flavors too. Splash flavored vinegars such as raspberry onto salads, vegetable side dishes, and beans.

**Look to a salty flavor.** Ditch the salt shaker. Save on sodium by using other salty condiments like reduced-sodium soy sauce, mustard, and Worcestershire sauce.

**Unlock the flavor of dried food.** Dried foods are concentrated sources of wow-that-tastes-good flavor. A handful of chopped sun-dried tomatoes can really deepen the taste of pizza, pasta, and salads. Or add rehydrated dried mushrooms to rice dishes, soups, or casseroles. Dried porcini mushrooms are especially good. If you're making muffins, breads, or a dessert sauce, try dried fruit.

## INSTANT PROTEIN

If you like to get your protein in a powder or a bar, here are some things to keep in mind about both.

**Protein bars.** The carbohydrate content of a protein bar can be as low as 1.5 grams per bar or as high as 44 grams. The caloric range is 190 to 340 calories per bar. Read labels carefully to keep track of what you're eating. Not all protein bars are fortified with vitamins and minerals. Some bars are really just candy bars in disguise, while others may be a suitable meal replacement on occasion.

**Protein powders and shakes.** These include a variety of products marketed mostly to body-builders. The protein sources are usually egg (albumin), soy, or milk (whey) and less frequently, rice or vegetable protein. As with the bars, carbohydrate contents vary widely. Pure protein powder contains from only a trace to about 3 grams of carbohydrate per serving. Flavored varieties are often sweetened with fructose and may contain up to 22 grams of carbohydrate per serving. The shakes make a good snack or occasional meal replacement. The powders can be sprinkled into recipes such as smoothies, muffins, or casseroles. See the recipe for Strawberry Protein Shake on page 124. Both powders and shakes are easiest to find in a health food store, but some large supermarkets carry them, too. At less than $1 per serving, they are very economical compared to meat. Generally, the ready-to-drink versions cost a little more than the powders.

When heated with almost any type of liquid, the rich, sweet flavor of dried apricots, dates, figs, and raisins blossoms beautifully.

**Kick it up!** Nothing perks up a dish like hot sauce. Salsa, hot-pepper sauce, or even crushed red pepper flakes may be just the thing to boost the flavor of a dish.

## BRIGHTEN UP BREAKFAST

Let's get specific and talk about smart choices you can make at each meal throughout the day. Many of the people we talked with said that they skip breakfast or eat the same thing every morning. Neither approach is the best way to start the day.

The key to a healthy diet is variety. And breakfast time may be the best time to eat carbohydrates. One study shows that our bodies are more receptive to the insulin rush of carb-rich foods in the morning. Keep breakfast time fresh with some of these ideas.

**Switch to whole grain starches.** If you're married to your morning cereal, try a whole grain or high-fiber version such as All-Bran, oat bran or oatmeal, whole rolled wheat or rye, kasha (buckwheat), or unsweetened puffed grains such as brown rice, corn, or whole wheat. Top with a bit of cow's milk or soy milk and some fruit such as blueberries or strawberries. Or try a few whole grain crackers, a whole wheat matzo, a whole wheat tortilla, or some whole wheat toast spread with cream cheese, almond butter, or macadamia nut butter.

**Get creative with eggs.** This excellent source of protein can be scrambled, hard-cooked, poached, fried, or made into an omelette, frittata, or even an egg salad for breakfast. Add leftover vegetables, meats, and some reduced-fat cheese to eggs to make a quick omelette or frittata. Leftover quiche also makes an excellent breakfast dish in a pinch.

**Find new uses for cottage cheese.** Cottage cheese can be mixed with a teaspoon of all-fruit spread, cut-up whole fruit, and a sprinkle of cinnamon for breakfast. Or try it with some chopped vegetables or a chopped hard-cooked egg.

**Think different.** Pressed for time? Remember that breakfast doesn't have to be as you've always known it. Be daring. Who says you can't reheat leftovers from supper or have a bowl of soup? In Japan, it is customary to start the day with a bowl of warming soup. In Mexico and Britain, beans are often served with breakfast. Beans are a terrific source of protein and make an excellent accompaniment to eggs. Or try some seasoned lentils or kidney, pinto, navy, or northern beans.

## Enjoy a Good Lunch

For most Americans, lunch is a grab-and-go meal. Fortunately, plenty of satisfying low-carb lunches are out there. You just need to know where to look.

**Make a salad out of almost anything.** With so many varieties of greens and prepared salads readily available in today's supermarkets and fast food restaurants, there's no reason to get bored with salad. Try all different kinds. Mix cut-up, raw vegetables with cooked ones. For instance, the contrast of raw, leafy vegetables with hot, cooked cauliflower or sugar snap peas tastes fantastic. For protein, add chunks or slices of meat, poultry, fish, hard-cooked eggs, shellfish, or some chickpeas or other beans to a salad. Get creative with toppings like Parmesan cheese or other shredded cheeses, real bacon bits, olives, sunflower seeds, or croutons.

**Make a wrap with lettuce.** Soft lettuce leaves such as Boston make excellent sandwich wrappers. Top a large lettuce leaf with tuna, egg, chicken, turkey, shrimp, or crabmeat salad and roll it into a neat package. Fasten with toothpicks to take with you.

**Switch to spinach.** Try using spinach instead of lettuce now and then. Spinach is packed with vitamin A, folate, and magnesium. And it contains some vitamin C, calcium, potassium, fiber, and important B vitamins. Whenever you make a sandwich, try using spinach instead of lettuce. Having salad? Make it a spinach salad. Baby spinach comes prewashed in bags and ready to eat.

**Have a real sandwich.** If you like sandwiches at lunchtime, just remember to use whole grain bread, light whole wheat

## EATING OUT LOW-CARB

Reducing your carbohydrate intake doesn't mean settling for boring restaurant meals. In fact, most restaurant main dishes focus on protein rather than carbohydrates, so it shouldn't be too hard to choose a great-tasting, low-carb meal. Just keep your eyes open for menu terms that may indicate extra carbohydrates and ask whether foods are prepared with flour, bread crumbs, or sugar. For example, meats, poultry, or fish may be dredged in flour, or a dish may include a gravy or sauce not specified on the menu. Here are a few menu terms that may indicate extra carbohydrate content:

- à la mode
- barbecued
- breaded
- creamed
- crispy
- honey-baked
- loaf
- parmigiana
- pot pie
- stuffed
- crust
- fruited
- glazed
- gravy
- stuffing
- sweet and sour
- tetrazzini

When ordering, don't be bashful. Ask questions. Many restaurants are willing to make something special or to substitute a serving of vegetables or small salad for a potato, rice, pasta, or other starchy dish. If you have bread with the meal, remember that an average-size dinner roll is the equivalent of two servings of starch. It's unlikely that you'll be able to get whole grain bread or pastas or brown rice in some restaurants. But if you eat out only occasionally, it won't hinder your weight loss or adversely affect your health to enjoy the refined versions of these foods now and then.

bread, whole wheat pitas, or whole wheat tortillas for wraps. You could also make an open-face sandwich with just one slice of bread to reduce your carb intake. Top with a lettuce leaf instead of another slice of bread. See the sandwich recipes beginning on page 127.

**Have eggs for lunch.** If you haven't had eggs for breakfast, an omelette can be very satisfying at lunchtime. Include some finely chopped vegetables and cheese, meat, poultry, or fish.

**Make extra servings.** One of the eas-iest ways to plan for lunch is to make extra servings of dinner the night before. Pack an extra serving in a microwaveable container and keep it refrigerated until lunchtime. You can also add leftover chicken, turkey, beef, pork, or fish to a store-bought salad. Whenever you have time in the kitchen, make one of your favorite casseroles or soups, then freeze individual portions in microwaveable containers. With these frozen assets, you'll never be at a loss for smart lunchtime solutions.

## SIMPLE DINNER IDEAS

Dinner is by far the easiest low-carb meal to plan because most dinner menus have some type of protein food at the center, a serving or two of vegetables, and relatively few carbohydrates. This book includes more than 100 main-dish recipes that serve as excellent examples. Here are a few things to keep in mind when planning dinner.

**Get balance.** Try to include at least one protein food, one to two vegetables (cooked or raw), and a starch if you have not already eaten much from these food groups earlier in the day.

**Vary your protein source.** Eating the same food over and over may hinder or even halt your weight loss. To avoid flavor fatigue and trigger foods (which could wreak havoc on your weight-loss plans), rotate different sources of protein in and out of your diet every few days. If you can, make enough food to have the leftovers the next day for lunch. Below are 4 days of menus that help explain this principle of variety.

- **Day One** (lunch and supper): beef, lamb, cod, haddock, or pollack
- **Day Two** (lunch and supper): chicken, Cornish hen, tuna, or mackerel
- **Day Three** (lunch and supper): pork, shrimp, crab, lobster, flounder, halibut, sole, or turbot
- **Day Four** (lunch and supper): turkey, salmon, perch, croaker, whitefish, or bass

## MAKE SNACKS A HEALTHY HABIT

Here's some great news for weight watchers: Snacks are good for you! In fact, you should eat or drink something every 2 to 4 hours to avoid setting yourself up for a starvation-binge scenario. If you're used to having breakfast, lunch, and dinner every day, fill in the gaps with smart snack choices. Here are a few simple ideas for keeping carbs low. See the recipes beginning on page 105, too.

**Snack on nuts.** Nutritious, filling, and a source of protein and monounsaturated fats, nuts make a perfectly healthy snack. It takes a few minutes after eating nuts to feel satisfied, so eat them slowly. Allow yourself at least 10 minutes before reaching for something else.

**Stuff some celery.** Spread with a little peanut butter or seasoned cream cheese, celery sticks make an easy, satisfying, and quite portable snack.

**Try a little fruit.** Fruit is a natural at snacktime. Try to combine it with nuts to lessen its effect on your blood sugar. For instance, have a banana or apple with some peanut butter. Or munch on GORP (good ol' raisins and peanuts).

**Go with crackers.** Whole grain crackers with nut butter or reduced-fat cheese make a satisfying, low-carbohydrate nibble that you can enjoy anytime.

## ABOUT THE RECIPES IN THIS BOOK

All of the basic principles of smart low-carb cooking have been discussed above. To see these principles in action, turn to the recipe section and try a recipe that strikes your fancy. How about Pecan Muffins (page 99)? Pesto Chicken Sandwich with Roasted Peppers (page 156)? Or Chocolate-Almond Meringue Cookies (page 331)? All 200 recipes come together quickly and use easy-to-find ingredients. Here are a few general notes about the recipes to keep in mind.

**Some recipes are higher in carbohydrates.** Most of the 200 recipes in this book are low to moderate in carbohydrates. You may notice that some recipes are higher in carbs than you might expect (30 grams or more per serving). Don't worry. In most cases, these recipes have a low glycemic index. For instance, oats are fairly high in carbs, but their relatively low glycemic index makes them a healthy food. Other higher-carb recipes are intended as splurge foods to be eaten occasionally as an indulgence. These high-carb treats are important to sticking with a reduced-carb plan in the long run. If you're eating about 180 grams of carbohydrate a day (the amount recommended for most folks), one dish with 30 grams of carbohydrate can be easily fit into a day's worth of meals. Either way, don't get too hung up on just counting carbohydrates. Balancing both low-carbohydrate foods and low-glycemic index foods is the real cornerstone of smart low-carb eating.

**Some recipes are higher in fat.** Don't be alarmed if you see that some of these recipes are higher in fat than what you might expect (20 grams or more). These recipes are still good for you. We've just been so conditioned to believe that all fat is bad. But in fact, several types of fat are essential for your body's long-term health. These mono- and polyunsaturated fats are the types used most often in the higher-fat recipes in this book. It's okay to eat a bit more of these now and then. Notice that saturated fat is kept to a minimum. See page 25 for more on healthy versus less-healthy fats.

**Consider using the Diet Exchanges.** Every recipe in this book comes with a complete nutrition analysis that was calculated with Food Processor version 7.6, ESHA Research Professional Nutritional Analysis Software and Databases. Optional ingredients have not been included in the analysis. When a recipe offers an alternative ingredient, only the first ingredient has been used for analysis. Each nutrition analysis includes calories, protein, carbohydrates, fat, saturated fat, cholesterol, sodium, and fiber. As with any food you eat, use these nutrition facts to make smart choices and eat a balanced diet overall. To get balance by looking broadly at food groups, use the Diet Exchanges, too. Diet Exchanges make it easier to keep track of how much you are eating from each food group. The basic food groups include milk (dairy products), vegetable, fruit, bread (starches), meat (protein foods), and fat. In the Diet Exchanges, the number in front of each food group shows how many servings from that group are provided by the recipe. You might notice that certain recipes contain no meat, yet have a number in front of the meat group. That's because all protein foods, including nuts and eggs, are counted as meat (protein). If you're following one of the suggested plans in this book, the Diet Exchanges will help you to eat the right amount from each food group and reach your weight-loss goals.

**Enjoy your food.** No matter how you decide to implement the principles of smart low-carb eating, it's important to enjoy your food. When you try one of these recipes, or when you eat any food, take the time to really savor it. Many people say that when they slow down and enjoy their food, they are rewarded with an eating satisfaction that leaves them feeling less hungry later on.

# eggs & breakfast foods

## ALL-PURPOSE FRUIT SYRUP
*66 calories, 14 g carbs*

1½   cups apple cider

2    cups blueberries, raspberries, or chopped fresh or frozen strawberries

Place the cider and the berries in a deep saucepan set over medium heat. Simmer uncovered until thickened, 55 to 60 minutes, stirring occasionally and skimming off any froth that appears on the surface.

Strain the syrup into a bowl, pressing on the solids to push through some of the pulp. Discard the seeds and the pulp that doesn't pass through easily. Use right away or cover and refrigerate for up to 3 weeks. Or freeze for up to 2 months.

**Makes ½ cup**

---

**Per 2 tablespoons:** 66 calories, 1 g protein, 14 g carbohydrates, 0 g fat, 0 g saturated fat, 0 mg cholesterol, 10 mg sodium, 2 g fiber

**Diet Exchanges:** 0 milk, 0 vegetable, 1 fruit, 0 bread, 0 meat, 0 fat

## BREAKFAST BERRY "SUNDAES"
*200 calories, 24 g carbs*

2    cups plain yogurt

½    teaspoon vanilla extract

2    teaspoons toasted wheat germ (optional)

½    teaspoon ground cinnamon

3    tablespoons dried cranberries or cherries

3    tablespoons granola or muesli

2    cups blueberries (1 pint)

3    tablespoons toasted pecans, chopped

Divide the yogurt among 4 bowls, reserving ¼ cup. Drizzle the vanilla over the yogurt in each bowl and sprinkle with the wheat germ (if using) and cinnamon. Scatter the cranberries or cherries and granola or muesli over each. Spoon the blueberries over the granola, and top each serving with 1 tablespoon of the remaining yogurt. Sprinkle with the pecans.

**Makes 4 servings**

---

**Per serving:** 200 calories, 6 g protein, 24 g carbohydrates, 10 g fat, 3 g saturated fat, 16 mg cholesterol, 63 mg sodium, 3 g fiber

**Diet Exchanges:** ½ milk, 0 vegetable, 1 fruit, ½ bread, 0 meat, 1½ fat

# BAKED APPLES
*176 calories, 27 g carbs*

| | |
|---|---|
| **4** | **Rome apples** |
| **5** | **large pitted prunes or dried apricots, chopped** |
| **2** | **tablespoons pine nuts** |
| **2** | **teaspoons apricot or other fruit spread (optional)** |
| **½** | **teaspoon pumpkin pie spice** |
| **4** | **teaspoons butter, cut into 4 equal pieces** |
| **¾** | **cup apple cider or water** |
| **¼** | **cup plain yogurt** |

Preheat the oven to 375°F.

Core the apples to within ½" of their bottoms. Using a paring knife, remove a ½"-wide strip around the top edges. If necessary, trim a thin slice from each bottom so the apples sit flat.

In a small bowl, combine the prunes or apricots, nuts, fruit spread (if using), and pumpkin pie spice. Spoon into the apple cavities and place the apples in a shallow baking dish. Slip a piece of butter into each cavity and pour the cider or water over the apples (the liquid should be ¼" to ½" deep in the pan).

Bake, uncovered, basting with the pan juices occasionally (add a little hot water if necessary), until the apples are tender when pierced with a fork, 30 to 45 minutes. Place on plates and spoon the pan juices over them. Serve hot, warm, or at room temperature topped with a dollop of the yogurt.

**Makes 4 servings**

---

**Per serving:** 176 calories, 2 g protein, 27 g carbohydrates, 7 g fat, 3 g saturated fat, 12 mg cholesterol, 54 mg sodium, 5 g fiber

**Diet Exchanges:** ½ milk, 0 vegetable, 1½ fruit, 0 bread, 0 meat, 1 fat

## Time-Savers

For a quick breakfast, make the apples up to 3 days ahead and keep them in a covered container in the refrigerator. Reheat at 350°F in a covered baking dish with 2 to 3 tablespoons water until heated through, 10 to 15 minutes. These apples also travel well for brown-bag lunches; eat them at room temperature or reheat in the microwave oven.

# BANANAS, DATES, AND WALNUTS IN YOGURT SAUCE
*226 calories, 43 g carbs*

| | |
|---|---|
| 1 | **cup plain low-fat yogurt** |
| 2 | **tablespoons orange juice or apple cider** |
| 4 | **medium pitted dates (2 ounces), chopped** |
| 4 | **bananas (1 pound), sliced** |
| 3 | **tablespoons toasted walnuts, chopped** |
| 2 | **teaspoons toasted wheat germ or ground flaxseed** |

Place the yogurt in a glass measure and stir in the orange juice or cider to make a pourable, but still thick, dressing.

In a large bowl, lightly toss the dates, bananas, and walnuts. Gently stir in the yogurt mixture. Spoon the fruit mixture into bowls, sprinkle with the wheat germ or flaxseed, and serve.

**Makes 4 servings**

---

**Per serving:** 226 calories, 7 g protein, 43 g carbohydrates, 5 g fat, 1 g saturated fat, 4 mg cholesterol, 45 mg sodium, 5 g fiber

**Diet Exchanges:** ½ milk, 0 vegetable, 2½ fruit, 0 bread, ½ meat, ½ fat

## Time-Saver

Make the yogurt dressing 2 to 3 days ahead and store it in a covered container in the refrigerator for busy weekday mornings. Briefly stir before serving.

## HIDDEN ROADBLOCK to weight loss

### HIDDEN CARBOHYDRATES

Without knowing it, you may be consuming extra carbohydrates. Some are tricky to identify. The next time you open a food package, read the ingredients carefully. Always look for words that end in "-ose" or "-ol," which indicate sugars. Look for syrup, fruit juice, food starch, dextrin, and maltodextrin—more sources of carbohydrates. Notice where these ingredients fall in the list because they're required to be listed from most quantity to least quantity. For instance, if maltodextrin is listed first in the list, maltodextrin is the main ingredient in that food. Keep in mind that sugar-free mints and gum contain carbohydrates, too. A few pieces every day could really slow down your weight-loss efforts. Likewise, if you eat fast food frequently, ask for a nutritional analysis brochure or check the restaurant's Web site to make the healthiest choices. Or turn to page 62 for a list of low-carb substitutions for common high-carb foods.

# FRIED EGGS WITH VINEGAR
*206 calories, 1 g carbs*

| | |
|---|---|
| 2 | **tablespoons butter** |
| 8 | **large eggs** |
| 1 | **teaspoon salt** |
| ¼ | **teaspoon ground black pepper** |
| ⅛ | **teaspoon dried marjoram or basil** |
| 4 | **teaspoons red wine vinegar** |
| 1 | **teaspoon chopped parsley (optional)** |

Melt 1 tablespoon of the butter in a large nonstick skillet over medium-low heat. Add the eggs and sprinkle with the salt, pepper, and marjoram or basil (work in batches if necessary). Cover and cook until the whites are set and the yolks are almost set, 3 to 5 minutes. (For steam-basted eggs, add 1 teaspoon water to the pan and cover with a lid.)

Remove to plates. Place the skillet over low heat and add the remaining 1 tablespoon butter. Cook until the butter turns light brown, 1 to 2 minutes. Add the vinegar. Pour the vinegar mixture over the eggs. Sprinkle with the parsley (if using). Serve hot.

**Makes 4 servings**

---

**Per serving:** 206 calories, 13 g protein, 1 g carbohydrates, 16 g fat, 7 g saturated fat, 440 mg cholesterol, 764 mg sodium, 0 g fiber

**Diet Exchanges:** 0 milk, 0 vegetable, 0 fruit, 0 bread, 2 meat, 2½ fat

## Time-Savers

Cook the eggs 1 to 2 days ahead and keep them in the refrigerator in a covered container for a speedy breakfast or brown-bag lunch. Reheat in a 350°F oven for 8 to 10 minutes. Or serve at room temperature in a sandwich with sprouts and sliced cheese.

Baked Eggs with Cheese and Zucchini and Sesame Buttermilk Biscuits (p. 101)

# Baked Eggs with Cheese and Zucchini
*256 calories, 6 g carbs*

| | |
|---|---|
| 2 | **teaspoons butter** |
| 2 | **teaspoons olive oil** |
| ½ | **small onion, chopped** |
| 2 | **zucchini or yellow squash (12 ounces), thinly sliced** |
| ½ | **teaspoon dried basil** |
| ½ | **teaspoon salt** |
| ¼ | **teaspoon ground black pepper** |
| ⅓ | **cup (1 ounce) shredded sharp provolone or Swiss cheese** |
| 8 | **large eggs** |
| 1 | **tablespoon heavy cream or chicken broth** |

Preheat the oven to 350°F.

Heat the butter and oil in a large non-stick skillet over medium heat until the butter has melted. Add the onion, zucchini or squash, basil, ¼ teaspoon of the salt, and ⅛ teaspoon of the pepper. Cook, stirring occasionally, until crisp-tender, 5 to 8 minutes.

Spread the zucchini mixture over the bottom of 4 individual, shallow baking dishes (or use 1 large baking dish). Sprinkle with 2½ tablespoons of the cheese and add the eggs (without breaking the yolks or stirring). Sprinkle with the remaining ¼ teaspoon salt, the remaining ⅛ teaspoon pepper, and the remaining 2½ tablespoons cheese. Drizzle with the cream or broth. Cover with foil and bake until the whites are set and the yolks begin to thicken, about 15 minutes for individual dishes or 20 minutes for 1 large dish.

**Makes 4 servings**

---

**Per serving:** 256 calories, 17 g protein, 6 g carbohydrates, 18 g fat, 7 g saturated fat, 439 mg cholesterol, 496 mg sodium, 1 g fiber

**Diet Exchanges:** 0 milk, 1 vegetable, 0 fruit, 0 bread, 2 meat, 2½ fat

## Time-Savers

Make extra servings of this dish and refrigerate them in a covered container for up to 2 days. Reheat, covered, at 350°F for 10 to 15 minutes. For an on-the-go breakfast sandwich, tuck the eggs into a roll or between slices of bread.

# Puffy Frittata with Ham and Green Pepper
*290 calories, 8 g carbs*

| | |
|---|---|
| 2 | tablespoons butter |
| 1 | small onion, chopped |
| 1 | green bell pepper, chopped |
| ½ | teaspoon salt |
| ½ | teaspoon ground black pepper |
| 8 | slices (6 ounces) ham, chopped |
| 8 | large eggs, at room temperature |
| ¼ | cup water |
| ½ | cup shredded Cheddar cheese (optional) |

Preheat the oven to 250°F.

Melt 1 tablespoon of the butter in a large (12") nonstick skillet over low heat. Add the onion, bell pepper, ¼ teaspoon of the salt, and ¼ teaspoon of the pepper. Cook, stirring occasionally, until tender-crisp, 3 to 4 minutes. Stir in the ham and cook for 1 minute, stirring occasionally. Transfer to a plate.

Separate the eggs, placing the yolks in a medium-size bowl and the whites in a large bowl. Lightly beat the yolks with the water, the remaining ¼ teaspoon salt, and the remaining ¼ teaspoon pepper. Beat the egg whites until they form stiff, but not dry, peaks. Fold the yolks into the whites.

Melt the remaining 1 tablespoon butter in the skillet over low heat. Pour in the eggs and spread them evenly with a rubber spatula. Scatter the ham mixture and cheese (if using) over the top, cover, and cook until the eggs are set, 25 to 30 minutes. Slide the frittata onto a plate and serve immediately (puffiness will subside in 5 to 7 minutes).

**Makes 4 servings**

---

**Per serving:** 290 calories, 22 g protein, 8 g carbohydrates, 19 g fat, 5 g saturated fat, 448 mg cholesterol, 467 mg sodium, 2 g fiber

**Diet Exchanges:** 0 milk, 1½ vegetable, 0 fruit, 0 bread, 3 meat, 2 fat

## Time-Savers

Extra servings make wonderful sandwiches at room temperature or hot. Refrigerate the frittata for up to 2 days. To reheat: Place the frittata on a baking sheet coated with cooking spray, cover, and bake at 350°F for about 10 minutes.

Puffy Frittata with Ham and Green Pepper

# SUMMER SQUASH AND MUSHROOM FRITTATA

*242 calories, 9 g carbs*

| | |
|---|---|
| 2 | **tablespoons butter** |
| 1 | **small onion, chopped** |
| 1 | **yellow squash or zucchini (6 ounces), thinly sliced** |
| 4 | **large mushrooms (4–5 ounces), chopped** |
| ½ | **large red bell pepper, chopped** |
| ½ | **teaspoon salt** |
| ¼ | **teaspoon dried thyme** |
| ¼ | **teaspoon ground black pepper** |
| 8 | **large eggs, at room temperature** |
| 1½ | **tablespoons grated Parmesan cheese (optional)** |

Place the broiler rack in the lowest position (6" to 7" from the heat source) and preheat the broiler.

Melt 1 tablespoon of the butter in a large (10" to 12") nonstick skillet with a heatproof handle over medium heat. Add the onion, squash or zucchini, mushrooms, bell pepper, ¼ teaspoon of the salt, the thyme, and ⅛ teaspoon of the pepper. Cook, stirring occasionally, until the vegetables are tender and no juices remain in the pan, 8 to 10 minutes.

In a large bowl, combine the eggs, the remaining ¼ teaspoon salt, the remaining ⅛ teaspoon pepper, and the grated cheese (if using).

Melt the remaining 1 tablespoon butter in the skillet over very low heat. Pour in the egg mixture. Cook, uncovered and without stirring, until only the top remains runny, 15 to 20 minutes. Place the skillet under the broiler and cook until the eggs are just set, about 2 minutes. Slide the frittata onto a large serving plate and serve hot, warm, or at room temperature.

**Makes 4 servings**

---

**Per serving:** 242 calories, 15 g protein, 9 g carbohydrates, 17 g fat, 7 g saturated fat, 440 mg cholesterol, 478 mg sodium, 2 g fiber

**Diet Exchanges:** 0 milk, 1½ vegetable, 0 fruit, 0 bread, 1½ meat, 2½ fat

## Time-Saver

Completely prepare the frittata up to 3 days ahead, cover, and refrigerate. Reheat, covered, at 350°F until warm, about 10 minutes.

# ASPARAGUS AND GOAT CHEESE OMELETTES
*292 calories, 7 g carbs*

| | |
|---|---|
| 16 | asparagus spears (10 ounces), trimmed and cut into ½" lengths |
| 8 | large eggs |
| ¾ | cup 1% milk |
| ¼ | cup chopped fresh basil |
| ½ | teaspoon salt |
| ½ | teaspoon ground black pepper |
| 4 | teaspoons butter |
| I | garlic clove, minced |
| ½ | cup (3 ounces) crumbled goat cheese |

Preheat the oven to 250°F. Coat a large baking sheet with cooking spray.

Cook the asparagus in boiling water over high heat until tender-crisp, 2 to 5 minutes. Drain in a colander and pat dry on paper towels.

To make one omelette at a time: Break 2 of the eggs into a small bowl. Add 3 tablespoons milk and lightly beat with a fork. Stir in 1 tablespoon of the basil, ⅛ teaspoon of the salt, and ⅛ teaspoon of the pepper. Melt 1 teaspoon of the butter in an 8" nonstick skillet over medium heat.

Add one-fourth of the garlic and cook until soft, 2 minutes. Stir in one-fourth of the asparagus, then pour in the egg mixture. Cook until the eggs are almost set, 4 minutes, lifting the edge occasionally to let the raw eggs flow under. Spoon 2 tablespoons of the goat cheese along the center. Fold the omelette in half, remove to the prepared baking sheet, and place in the oven to keep warm.

Prepare 3 more omelettes in the same fashion.

**Makes 4**

**Per serving:** 292 calories, 20 g protein, 7 g carbohydrates, 20 g fat, 10 g saturated fat, 450 mg cholesterol, 570 mg sodium, I g fiber

**Diet Exchanges:** 0 milk, I vegetable, 0 fruit, 0 bread, 2½ meat, 2½ fat

▶**Flavor Tip**

*Omelettes taste much better when made individually. If you make one large omelette, the eggs are bound to become overcooked and rubbery.*

# CREAMY SCRAMBLED EGGS WITH SAUSAGE AND SCALLIONS

*257 calories, 2 g carbs*

| | |
|---|---|
| 5–6 | ounces breakfast turkey sausage patties or links, cut into bite-size pieces |
| 8 | large eggs |
| 3 | scallions, thinly sliced |
| ¼ | teaspoon salt |
| ¼ | teaspoon ground black pepper |
| 6 | drops hot-pepper sauce |
| 2 | teaspoons butter |

Warm a large nonstick skillet over medium heat. Add the sausage and cook until heated through, 8 to 10 minutes.

Meanwhile, break the eggs into a bowl and beat lightly with a fork. Stir in the scallions, salt, pepper, and hot-pepper sauce.

Melt the butter in the skillet with the sausage over medium-low heat. Pour in the eggs. Cook, stirring almost continually, until the eggs are set but still soft and creamy, 6 to 8 minutes. Serve hot.

**Makes 4 servings**

---

**Per serving:** 257 calories, 20 g protein, 2 g carbohydrates, 18 g fat, 7 g saturated fat, 458 mg cholesterol, 540 mg sodium, 0 g fiber

**Diet Exchanges:** 0 milk, ½ vegetable, 0 fruit, 0 bread, 3 meat, 2 fat

## Time-Saver

Store the eggs in a covered container in the refrigerator for up to 2 days. Serve warm or at room temperature. Reheat the eggs in foil at 350°F for 5 minutes.

# POACHED EGGS ON TOMATO-EGGPLANT BEDS

*258 calories, 12 g carbs*

| | |
|---|---|
| 1½ | tablespoons distilled white vinegar |
| 1 | small eggplant (3" diameter), peeled and cut into 8 rounds (each ¼" thick) |
| 1 | tablespoon olive oil |
| ½ | teaspoon salt |
| ½ | teaspoon ground black pepper |
| 2 | tomatoes, cut into 8 slices (each ¼" thick) |
| ¼ | teaspoon garlic powder (optional) |
| 4 | slices (3 ounces) ham, halved |
| 8 | large eggs |
| 3 | tablespoons chopped fresh basil (optional) |

Preheat the oven or toaster oven to 425°F. Fill a large, deep skillet or braising pan with hot water to within 1" from the top. Add enough of the vinegar to the water so it tastes faintly of vinegar. Bring to a simmer over medium heat.

Meanwhile, brush both sides of the eggplant slices with the oil and season with ¼ teaspoon of the salt and ¼ teaspoon of the pepper. Place on a baking sheet in a single layer. Bake just until tender, 5 to 8 minutes. Remove to a platter or plates. Place 1 slice of tomato on top of each, and season with ⅛ teaspoon of the salt, ⅛ teaspoon of the pepper, and the garlic powder (if using). Top each with 1 slice of ham.

Break the eggs one at a time into a bowl, then slip them one at a time into the simmering water. Cook, uncovered, until the whites are set and the yolks are almost set, 3 to 5 minutes. Remove with a slotted spoon, drain well, and place on top of the ham. Sprinkle all with the remaining ⅛ teaspoon salt, the remaining ⅛ teaspoon pepper, and the basil (if using). Serve hot.

**Makes 4 servings**

---

**Per serving:** 258 calories, 18 g protein, 12 g carbohydrates, 15 g fat, 4 g saturated fat, 436 mg cholesterol, 429 mg sodium, 3 g fiber

**Diet Exchanges:** 0 milk, 2½ vegetable, 0 fruit, 0 bread, 2 meat, 2 fat

# Whole Grain Crepes with Banana and Kiwifruit
*215 calories, 34 g carbs*

### CREPES

| | |
|---|---|
| 1 | **cup whole grain pastry flour** |
| ¼ | **teaspoon salt** |
| 1 | **egg** |
| 1 | **cup + 3 tablespoons unsweetened soy milk or whole milk** |
| 1½ | **teaspoons vanilla extract** |
| 2 | **teaspoons butter** |
| 1–2 | **tablespoons water** |

### FILLING

| | |
|---|---|
| ½ | **cup plain yogurt** |
| 1 | **banana, cut into 24 diagonal slices** |
| 2 | **kiwifruit, peeled, cut in half lengthwise, and sliced** |
| 2 | **teaspoons lime juice (optional)** |
| ½ | **teaspoon ground cinnamon** |

**To make the crepes:** In a large bowl, combine the flour and salt.

In a small bowl, beat the egg, then stir in the milk and vanilla. Pour into the flour and mix well.

Melt ½ teaspoon of the butter in an 8" nonstick skillet over medium heat. Pour 3 tablespoons of batter into the skillet and tilt the skillet to coat the bottom in a thin layer (if the batter seems too thick add 1 to 2 tablespoons water). Cook the first side until nicely browned, about 2 minutes. Using a spatula, turn the crepe and cook the second side for 1 to 2 minutes (the second side will look spotty). Slide the crepe onto a plate and cover with foil to keep warm. Continue making crepes in the same fashion, rebuttering the pan after every second crepe, until all the butter and batter are used.

**To make the filling and assemble:** Place a crepe on a serving plate, attractive side down, and spread with 1 tablespoon of yogurt. Arrange the 2 banana slices and a quarter of a kiwifruit in strips one-third of the way from one edge. Sprinkle with ¼ teaspoon of the lime juice and a pinch of the cinnamon, and roll up. Continue assembling the remaining crepes.

**Makes 4 servings (Eight 6" to 7" crepes)**

---

**Per serving:** 215 calories, 8 g protein, 34 g carbohydrates, 6 g fat, 3 g saturated fat, 62 mg cholesterol, 198 mg sodium, 6 g fiber

**Diet Exchanges:** ½ milk, 0 vegetable, 1 fruit, 1 bread, 0 meat, 1 fat

## Time-Saver

To make these ahead, cook the crepes, stack and cover with foil, and refrigerate or freeze. Thaw if frozen, then reheat the foil-wrapped stack on a baking sheet at 350°F until the crepes are warm and pliable, 5 to 8 minutes, or in a skillet on the stovetop. Assemble as directed.

*Whole Grain Crepes with Banana and Kiwifruit*

*Whole Grain Pancakes with Berry Cream Syrup*

# WHOLE GRAIN PANCAKES WITH BERRY CREAM SYRUP

*285 calories, 31 g carbs*

### PANCAKES

| | |
|---|---|
| ¾ | **cup whole grain pastry flour** |
| ¼ | **cup buckwheat flour** |
| 1½ | **teaspoons baking powder** |
| ½ | **teaspoon baking soda** |
| ⅛ | **teaspoon salt** |
| 1 | **cup buttermilk** |
| 1 | **large egg, at room temperature, separated** |
| 3 | **tablespoons + 2 teaspoons melted butter** |
| 8 | **drops liquid stevia** |

### SYRUP

| | |
|---|---|
| ¼ | **cup red or black raspberry fruit spread** |
| 2 | **tablespoons heavy cream** |
| 3–4 | **teaspoons orange juice or apple cider (optional)** |

**To make the pancakes:** In a large bowl, combine the pastry flour, buckwheat flour, baking powder, baking soda, and salt.

In a glass measure, mix the buttermilk, egg yolk, 3 tablespoons butter, and the stevia. Stir into the flour mixture until well-combined. In a small bowl, whip the egg white until it forms stiff, but not dry, peaks. Fold into the batter. (The batter will be light but not fluid.)

Heat a nonstick griddle over medium-low heat and add half of the remaining melted butter. For each pancake, spoon ¼ cup batter onto the griddle, making 4 cakes at a time, each about 4" in diameter. Cook the first side until the edges begin to look dry, about 3 minutes. Flip the cakes and cook the second side for 2 to 3 minutes. Continue making cakes in the same manner until all the butter and batter are used. Serve hot with the syrup.

**To make the syrup:** In a small bowl, combine the fruit spread, cream, and enough juice or cider (if using) to make a syrup. (Without the juice or cider, the topping will have the consistency of a spread.)

**Makes 4 servings (eight 4" pancakes)**

---

**Per serving:** 285 calories, 7 g protein, 31 g carbohydrates, 15 g fat, 10 g saturated fat, 93 mg cholesterol, 564 mg sodium, 2 g fiber

**Diet Exchanges:** ½ milk, 0 vegetable, 0 fruit, 1½ bread, 0 meat, 2½ fat

## ▶ Flavor Tip

*For an elegant blueberry variation on this dish, see the cover photo. To prepare, fold ⅓ cup blueberries into the finished batter and prepare as above. Serve with low-calorie syrup, fresh berries, and a dollop of whipped cream.*

# Kamut Crepes with Cottage Cheese and Fruit
*206 calories, 26 g carbs*

### CREPES

| | |
|---|---|
| ⅓ | **cup Kamut flour** |
| 2 | **tablespoons white whole wheat flour or whole grain pastry flour** |
| 1 | **tablespoon unflavored protein powder** |
| ⅛ | **teaspoon salt** |
| ⅓ | **cup apple cider** |
| ½ | **cup + 1–2 tablespoons water** |
| 1 | **large egg, lightly beaten** |
| 4 | **teaspoons butter, melted** |

### FILLING

| | |
|---|---|
| 1 | **cup small-curd 2% cottage cheese or ricotta cheese, at room temperature** |
| 2 | **pears (10 ounces), at room temperature, peeled and thinly sliced** |
| ¼ | **cup low-calorie maple syrup** |

**To make the crepes:** In a large bowl, stir together the Kamut flour and whole wheat flour or pastry flour, protein powder, and salt.

In a small bowl, whisk together the apple cider, water, egg, and 2 teaspoons of the butter. Whisk into the flour mixture to make a smooth batter.

Spread ½ teaspoon of the remaining butter in an 8" nonstick skillet over medium heat. Pour 3 tablespoons of batter into the skillet and tilt the skillet to coat the bottom in a thin layer (if the batter seems too thick, add 1 to 2 tablespoons of water). Cook the first side until lightly browned, about 1 minute. Using a spatula, turn and cook the second side for 30 to 60 seconds (the second side will look spotty). Slide the crepe onto a plate and cover with foil to keep warm. Continue making crepes in the same fashion, rebuttering the pan after every second crepe, until all the butter and batter are used.

**To make the filling and assemble:** Place a crepe on a plate, attractive side down. Arrange the cottage cheese or ricotta cheese and pear in a line ⅓ of the way from one edge, and roll up. Fill the remaining crepes in the same manner. Serve drizzled with syrup.

**Makes 4 servings (Eight 6" to 7" crepes)**

**Per serving:** 206 calories, 11 g protein, 26 g carbohydrates, 7 g fat, 4 g saturated fat, 68 mg cholesterol, 402 mg sodium, 3 g fiber

**Diet Exchanges:** 0 milk, 0 vegetable, ½ fruit, 1 bread, 1 meat, 1 fat

## ▶Flavor Tip
*Crepes cooked in butter brown beautifully. If you substitute cooking spray, increase the heat to medium-high, and the crepes will brown moderately well.*

# Pecan Muffins

*218 calories, 20 g carbs*

| | |
|---|---|
| 1½ | **cups whole grain pastry flour** |
| ¼ | **cup soy flour** |
| 2½ | **teaspoons baking powder** |
| ½ | **teaspoon salt** |
| ½ | **teaspoon ground nutmeg** |
| ½ | **cup toasted pecans, chopped** |
| ½ | **cup vegetable oil** |
| ½ | **cup apricot or peach fruit spread** |
| 2 | **large eggs, lightly beaten** |
| 1½ | **teaspoons vanilla extract** |
| ⅛ | **teaspoon liquid stevia** |

Place a rack in the middle position in the oven and preheat the oven to 375°F. Coat a 12-cup muffin pan with cooking spray or line with paper cups.

In a large bowl, whisk together the pastry flour, soy flour, baking powder, salt, nutmeg, and pecans.

In a small bowl, combine the oil, fruit spread, eggs, vanilla, and stevia. Add to the flour mixture and stir just until the dry ingredients are moistened.

Spoon into the prepared muffin cups until ¾ full. Bake until a toothpick inserted in the center of a muffin comes out clean, 12 to 14 minutes. Serve warm.

**Makes 12 muffins**

**Per serving:** 218 calories, 4 g protein, 20 g carbohydrates, 12 g fat, 1 g saturated fat, 35 mg cholesterol, 193 mg sodium, 3 g fiber

**Diet Exchanges:** 0 milk, 0 vegetable, 0 fruit, 1 bread, ½ meat, 2½ fat

## Time-Savers

Make a double batch and cut preparation time in half. To store: Let the muffins cool, then wrap them individually and place in a self-sealing bag. Keep for up to 2 days in the refrigerator or 2 months in the freezer. Thaw the muffins at room temperature and reheat on a baking sheet at 350°F for 5 to 10 minutes.

# RAISIN SPICE QUICK BREAD

*168 calories, 29 g carbs*

1   cup whole grain pastry flour

1   cup oat flour

2   teaspoons baking powder

1½  teaspoons allspice

½   teaspoon cinnamon

½   teaspoon salt

1   large egg, at room temperature

1   cup 2% milk

¼   cup brown sugar

2   tablespoons butter, melted

1   teaspoon vanilla extract

⅛   teaspoon liquid stevia (optional)

½   cup raisins

Preheat the oven to 350°F. Oil an 8" × 4" loaf pan.

In a large bowl, combine the pastry flour, oat flour, baking powder, allspice, cinnamon, and salt.

In a medium bowl, lightly beat the egg with the milk, sugar, butter, vanilla, and stevia (if using). Pour into the flour mixture and stir until just combined. Fold in the raisins.

Pour the batter into the prepared pan and smooth the top.

Bake until a toothpick inserted into the middle comes out clean, 45 to 50 minutes. Cool in the pan on a rack for 10 minutes. Turn out onto rack to cool. Serve warm or at room temperature in thick slices.

**Makes 1 loaf (10 slices)**

**Per slice:** 168 calories, 5 g protein, 29 g carbohydrates, 4 g fat, 2 g saturated fat, 29 mg cholesterol, 235 mg sodium, 3 g fiber

**Diet Exchanges:** 0 milk, 0 vegetable, ½ fruit, 1½ bread, 0 meat, ½ fat

## Time-Savers

This bread stores well and is excellent for lunch. Let the loaf cool, then wrap it in plastic wrap and place it in a self-sealing bag. Keep at room temperature for up to 3 days. Reheat at 350°F. For a special treat, spread bread slices with apricot fruit spread and rewarm them topped with a pat of butter. If you prefer muffins instead of a whole loaf, pour the batter into a 12-cup muffin pan coated with cooking spray and bake for 20 minutes.

# SESAME BUTTERMILK BISCUITS *(photo on page 86)*

*190 calories, 20 g carbs*

| | |
|---|---|
| 1¼ | cups + 2 tablespoons whole wheat pastry flour |
| ½ | cup soy flour |
| 2½ | teaspoons baking powder |
| ½ | teaspoon baking soda |
| ½ | teaspoon salt |
| 1 | tablespoon toasted sesame seeds |
| 6 | tablespoons cold butter, cut in pieces |
| ¾ | cup cold buttermilk |
| ⅛ | teaspoon liquid stevia (optional) |

Place a rack in the middle position in the oven and preheat the oven to 425°F.

In a large bowl, combine 1¼ cups of the pastry flour, the soy flour, baking powder, baking soda, salt, and sesame seeds. Using a pastry cutter or fork, cut the butter into the flour mixture until the mixture looks like coarse meal.

In a small bowl, combine the buttermilk and stevia (if using). Using a fork, stir into the flour mixture just until the dry ingredients are moistened and form a rough mound. Dust a working surface with the remaining 2 tablespoons whole wheat pastry flour and turn out the dough. Press together (the dough will be moist) and knead gently, about 5 or 6 times.

Using a floured rolling pin, roll out the dough to form a ¾"-thick circle. Using a 2½"-diameter cookie cutter, cut out circles and place 1" apart on an ungreased baking sheet. Pinch together the scraps, reroll, and cut out additional biscuits.

Bake until the bottoms are golden and tops lightly colored, 11 to 13 minutes. Serve hot, warm, or at room temperature.

**Makes 8 biscuits (2½" diameter)**

---

**Per serving:** 190 calories, 5 g protein, 20 g carbohydrates, 10 g fat, 6 g saturated fat, 24 mg cholesterol, 437 mg sodium, 4 g fiber

**Diet Exchanges:** ½ milk, 0 vegetable, 0 fruit, 1 bread, 0 meat, 1½ fat

## Time-Savers

Toast the sesame seeds in a small baking dish in the oven while it preheats. To save preparation time, make a double batch of these biscuits and freeze for later. Let the biscuits cool, wrap them individually in plastic wrap, and place in a self-sealing bag. Keep at room temperature for up to 2 days or in the freezer for up to 2 months. Reheat on a baking sheet at 350°F for 5 to 10 minutes.

*eggs and breakfast foods*

# Oatmeal with Ricotta, Fruit, and Nuts

*184 calories, 30 g carbs*

- **2**    **cups apple cider**
- **2**    **cups water**
- **2**    **cups rolled oats**
- **⅛**    **teaspoon salt**
- **½**    **teaspoon ground cinnamon**
- **¼**    **cup (2 ounces) ricotta cheese**
- **1**    **large peach or plum (4 ounces), chopped**
- **2**    **tablespoons sunflower seeds or toasted almonds, chopped**

Combine the cider, water, oats, and salt in a medium saucepan. Bring to a boil over medium heat. Reduce the heat to low. Cook, uncovered, until thick and creamy, stirring occasionally, 3 to 5 minutes.

Spoon into bowls and sprinkle with the cinnamon. Top with the ricotta, peach or plum, and nuts or seeds. Serve hot.

**Makes 6 servings**

---

**Per serving:** 184 calories, 6 g protein, 30 g carbohydrates, 4 g fat, 1 g saturated fat, 5 mg cholesterol, 81 mg sodium, 4 g fiber

**Diet Exchanges:** 0 milk, 0 vegetable, 1 fruit, 1 bread, ½ meat, ½ fat

## ▶Flavor Tips

*For more chewy oatmeal, bring the cider, water, and salt to a boil, then stir in the oats. For sweeter oatmeal, drizzle each serving with 1 to 2 teaspoons low-calorie maple syrup.*

# CREAMY QUINOA

*332 calories, 46 g carbs*

2½  **cups milk**

⅛  **teaspoon salt**

1  **cup quinoa, thoroughly rinsed until the water runs clear**

¼  **cup chopped dried figs or dates**

2  **tablespoons butter (optional)**

⅛  **teaspoon ground cardamom**

8  **drops liquid stevia**

¼  **cup toasted walnuts, chopped**

Combine the milk and salt in a saucepan and bring to a boil. Stir in the quinoa and reduce the heat to low. Cover and cook until all the liquid has evaporated and the grains are tender-crunchy, about 15 minutes. Stir in the figs or dates, butter (if using), cardamom, and stevia.

Remove from the heat. Sprinkle each serving with the walnuts. Serve hot.

**Makes 4 servings**

**Per serving:** 332 calories, 13 g protein, 46 g carbohydrates, 12 g fat, 4 g saturated fat, 21 mg cholesterol, 178 mg sodium, 4 g fiber

**Diet Exchanges:** 1 milk, 0 vegetable, ½ fruit, 2 bread, 0 meat, 1½ fat

## Smart-Carb Insider Tip

### WHY NOT EGGS?

Always have eggs in the refrigerator. They are a great source of protein and B vitamins, low in saturated fat, and have less than 1 gram of carbohydrate each. Hard boil a half-dozen at a time for quick breakfasts or snacks on the run. Or shell two or three of them, place in a zip-top bag with some mayonnaise, mustard, onion powder, and pepper, then seal and "smush" to desired consistency. Cut off a corner of the bag and squeeze out the egg salad onto a lettuce leaf and roll up into a sandwich; or squeeze the mixture into a cucumber, zucchini, or celery boat for an instant lunch. Other ideas: Reheat some leftover veggies, beat some eggs, pour them over the veggies, and pop into the microwave or heat in a skillet for a satisfying vegetable-egg scramble.

# CHERRY CREAM OF RYE CEREAL

*208 calories, 45 g carbs*

| | |
|---|---|
| 1¼ | cups water |
| 1¼ | cups apple cider |
| ¼ | teaspoon salt |
| 1 | cup cream of rye cereal |
| 1¼ | tablespoons cherry fruit spread |
| ⅛ | teaspoon ground nutmeg |
| ⅛ | teaspoon ground cardamom |
| 1½ | tablespoons chopped hazelnuts (optional) |

Combine the water, cider, and salt in a saucepan and bring to a boil over medium heat. Stir in the cereal and reduce the heat to low. Cook, uncovered, until thick, stirring occasionally, 3 to 5 minutes. Remove from the heat and stir in the fruit spread.

Spoon into bowls and sprinkle with the nutmeg, cardamom, and hazelnuts (if using). Serve hot.

**Makes 4 servings (3 cups)**

---

**Per serving:** 208 calories, 4 g protein, 45 g carbohydrates, 1 g fat, 0 g saturated fat, 0 mg cholesterol, 168 mg sodium, 6 g fiber

**Diet Exchanges:** 0 milk, 0 vegetable, 1 fruit, 2 bread, 0 meat, 0 fat

# snacks, appetizers & beverages

# CHEESE, APPLE, AND NUT BUTTER ROLL-UPS

*143 calories, 5 g carbs*

4     thin slices (¼ pound) Swiss or
      Muenster cheese, at room
      temperature

½     large apple (3 ounces),
      thinly sliced

1     tablespoon macadamia nut
      butter or 2 teaspoons
      unsweetened peanut butter

**Per serving:** 143 calories, 9 g protein, 5 g carbohydrates, 11 g fat, 6 g saturated fat, 30 mg cholesterol, 51 mg sodium, 1 g fiber

**Diet Exchanges:** 0 milk, 0 vegetable, ½ fruit, 0 bread, 1 meat, 1 fat

Place the cheese on a cutting board. Arrange the apple slices in a horizontal row 1" from a narrow end of each cheese slice, drizzle or spread with the nut butter, and roll up. Secure with toothpicks.

**Makes 4 servings**

## Time-Saver

Make this easy snack whenever you have a few minutes. It keeps in the refrigerator or at room temperature for 2 to 3 hours. If making ahead, be sure to completely cover the apple slices with nut butter to keep them from browning.

## HIDDEN ROADBLOCK to weight loss

### NOT ENOUGH FAT

Believe it or not, a lack of fat in your daily diet may slow down your weight-loss efforts. Fats make up the basic structure of our cell membranes and are needed for several vital functions. Plus, fats satisfy our hunger. If you don't eat enough fats, you may end up overeating other foods to make up for what's missing. If you think that eating fat is not conducive to weight loss, consider this: In 1998, several teams of researchers studied the impact of all macronutrients on the development of obesity. Keeping calorie intake constant, they found that there is no data to substantiate the theory that fat promotes the development of obesity more than any other macronutrient. Of course, this doesn't mean it's okay to gorge yourself on butter, steaks, and bacon. Just be sure to choose a variety of healthy fats every day, like those found in nuts, seeds, olives, avocados, salmon, and vegetable oils. By the same token, try to minimize the saturated fats and trans fats found in butter, margarine, lard, and processed snack foods such as crackers.

# SOFT YOGURT CHEESE WITH OLIVES
*143 calories, 11 g carbs*

| 1 | cup **Soft Yogurt Cheese (below)** |
| 2 | tablespoons olive oil |
| ½–¾ | teaspoon flaxseed oil (optional) |
| 10 | pitted black kalamata or green Spanish olives (1½ ounces), chopped |
| ¼ | teaspoon salt |
| ⅛ | teaspoon ground black pepper |
| 15 | celery ribs, cut into 3"–4" pieces |

Place the yogurt cheese in a large bowl and gradually stir in the olive oil. Stir in the flax-seed oil (if using), olives, salt, and pepper.

Serve right away or chill for 1 hour or up to 5 days. Use as a dip or spread with the celery.

**Makes 4 servings**

**Per serving:** 143 calories, 4 g protein, 11 g carbo-hydrates, 10 g fat, 2 g saturated fat, 4 mg cholesterol, 411 mg sodium, 3 g fiber

**Diet Exchanges:** ½ milk, 1 vegetable, 0 fruit, 0 bread, 0 meat, 1½ fat

# SOFT YOGURT CHEESE
*53 calories, 6 g carbs*

**2¾ cups plain low-fat yogurt**

Rinse a 14" to 16" length of cheesecloth in cold water and wring out. Fold in half and line a large strainer, leaving overhanging sides. Spoon the yogurt into the strainer, place over a larger bowl, cover with plastic wrap, and refrigerate for 10 to 12 hours or overnight. Discard the liquid in the bowl.

Lift the cheesecloth by the sides and turn the cheese into a clean bowl. Use right away or refrigerate for up to 5 days.

**Makes 1 cup**

**Per 2 tablespoons:** 53 calories, 4 g protein, 6 g carbohydrates, 1 g fat, 1 g saturated fat, 5 mg cho-lesterol, 59 mg sodium, 0 g fiber

**Diet Exchanges:** ½ milk, 0 vegetable, 0 fruit, 0 bread, 0 meat, 0 fat

▶Flavor Tips

*To make a salad dressing, mix the yogurt cheese with 1 tablespoon prepared mustard, 1 teaspoon lemon juice or vinegar, 2 tablespoons oil, and 2 to 4 tablespoons unsweetened soy milk to make it pourable.*

# Zucchini Chips
*54 calories, 5 g carbs*

**2**   large zucchini (24–28 ounces)

**1**   tablespoon olive oil

**¼**   teaspoon salt

**¼**   teaspoon garlic powder (optional)

Preheat the oven to 400°F. Coat 2 baking sheets with cooking spray.

Thinly slice the zucchini on the diagonal, about ⅛" thick. Place the slices in a large bowl and toss well with the oil, salt, and garlic powder (if using). Arrange in a single layer on the baking sheets.

Bake, turning often, for 25 minutes. Reduce the oven temperature to 300°F and bake until splotchy brown and crisp, 10 to 15 minutes. Remove to paper towels and let cool. These will keep at room temperature, uncovered, for several hours.

**Makes 4 servings**

**Per serving:** 54 calories, 2 g protein, 5 g carbohydrates, 3 g fat, 0 g saturated fat, 0 mg cholesterol, 150 mg sodium, 2 g fiber

**Diet Exchanges:** 0 milk, 1 vegetable, 0 fruit, 0 bread, 0 meat, 1 fat

## Smart-Carb Insider Tip
### STOCK SNACKS

Keep a few low-carbohydrate snacks in your kitchen, desk, car, or carry-bag. Nuts and cheeses are really satisfying in a pinch. Pine nuts, in particular, are high in protein and very filling. Keep a jar of nut butter or a package of cream cheese on hand to spread on ribs of celery for a snack. Or snack on string cheese or other hard cheeses.

# ROASTED MIXED NUTS
*195 calories, 5 g carbs*

| | |
|---|---|
| 1 | cup mixed unsalted pecans, walnuts, and macadamia nuts |
| 1½ | tablespoons apple cider, grape juice, or other fruit juice |
| ½ | teaspoon celery salt and/or curry powder |

Preheat the oven to 350°F.

In a small bowl, combine the nuts, cider or juice, and celery salt and/or curry powder. Toss to coat and spread in a single layer on a baking sheet. Roast until light golden, 4 to 6 minutes. Let cool before serving. These will keep at room temperature, uncovered, for several days.

**Makes 4 servings**

**Per serving:** 195 calories, 4 g protein, 5 g carbohydrates, 20 g fat, 2 g saturated fat, 0 mg cholesterol, 1 mg sodium, 2 g fiber

**Diet Exchanges:** 0 milk, 0 vegetable, 0 fruit, ½ bread, ½ meat, 3½ fat

Flavor Tip

*If humid weather makes the nuts soft, reheat them at 350°F for 1 to 2 minutes.*

# DEVILED EGGS WITH HORSERADISH AND SCALLIONS

*130 calories, 1 g carbs*

| | |
|---|---|
| **4** | **large eggs** |
| **2** | **tablespoons mayonnaise** |
| **1** | **teaspoon Dijon mustard** |
| **1** | **teaspoon prepared horseradish** |
| **1** | **tablespoon finely chopped scallions** |
| **¼** | **teaspoon salt** |
| **⅛** | **teaspoon ground black pepper** |
| **⅛** | **teaspoon paprika (optional)** |

Place eggs in a single layer in a saucepan and cover with cold water by 1". Cover the pan and bring to a boil over high heat. As soon as the water begins to boil, remove the pan from the heat and let it sit, covered, for 15 minutes. Drain, then run cold water over the eggs. Let them sit in the water until completely cooled. To remove the shells, gently tap the eggs all over on a hard surface, roll the eggs between your hands, then peel away the shells.

Cut the eggs in half lengthwise and place the yolks in a small mixing bowl. Mash, adding the mayonnaise and mustard, until a smooth paste forms. Stir in the horseradish, scallions, salt, and pepper. Using a teaspoon, stuff the egg cavities with the yolk mixture and sprinkle with paprika (if using). Serve at room temperature or chilled.

**Makes 4 servings**

**Per serving:** 130 calories, 6 g protein, 1 g carbohydrates, 11 g fat, 3 g saturated fat, 217 mg cholesterol, 279 mg sodium, 0 g fiber

**Diet Exchanges:** 0 milk, 0 vegetable, 0 fruit, 0 bread, 1 meat, 2 fat

## Time-Savers

Make these eggs ahead and keep them in a covered container in the refrigerator for up to 24 hours. To keep them from sliding around, serve on a bed of tossed salad or spinach leaves. If you have leftovers, chop the eggs and roll up in lettuce leaves for a sandwich.

# CRACKED WHEAT SALAD WITH SPINACH

*124 calories, 18 g carbs*

|   |   |
|---|---|
| 1 | cup medium-grind cracked wheat (bulgur) |
| 1½ | cups boiling water |
| 2 | tablespoons olive oil |
| 2 | tablespoons lemon juice |
| 1 | large tomato, chopped |
| 6 | scallions, finely sliced |
| ½ | cup chopped parsley and/or mint |
| ¾ | teaspoon salt |
| ¼ | teaspoon ground black pepper |
|   | Pinch of garlic powder |
|   | Pinch of ground cumin (optional) |

**12–18 spinach leaves**

Combine the cracked wheat and boiling water in a large bowl, cover, and let stand until the wheat is tender, 20 to 30 minutes. Drain off any unabsorbed water.

Add the oil and lemon juice and toss to mix. Stir in the tomato, scallions, parsley and/or mint, salt, pepper, garlic powder, and cumin (if using). Chill for 1 to 2 hours.

Place the spinach leaves on 6 plates and spoon the salad on top.

**Makes 6 servings**

---

**Per serving:** 124 calories, 4 g protein, 18 g carbohydrates, 5 g fat, 1 g saturated fat, 0 mg cholesterol, 316 mg sodium, 4 g fiber

**Diet Exchanges:** 0 milk, ½ vegetable, 0 fruit, 1 bread, 0 meat, 1 fat

## ▶Flavor Tips

Replace ¾ cup of the water with ¾ cup hot vegetable broth. You can also add ½ cup chopped cucumber to the salad. To eat this as an appetizer or sandwich, roll up 1 to 2 tablespoons in very large spinach leaves or Boston lettuce leaves, folding in the ends as you roll. This salad keeps refrigerated for up to 4 days.

*Avocado with Black Bean Salad*

# Avocado with Black Bean Salad
*224 calories, 18 g carbs*

About 1 tablespoon lime juice or vinegar

1½   tablespoons olive oil

1   can (14–19 ounces) black beans, drained

¼   green bell pepper, finely chopped

1   garlic clove, minced

½   teaspoon salt

⅛   teaspoon ground black pepper

⅛   teaspoon ground red pepper (optional)

1½   teaspoons chopped cilantro

1   avocado (8 ounces), quartered

Place the lime juice or vinegar in a large bowl and gradually whisk in the oil. Stir in the beans, bell pepper, garlic, salt, black pepper, and red pepper (if using). Taste and add more lime juice or vinegar if you like. Stir in the cilantro.

Place the avocado, cavities up, on 4 plates. Spoon the bean mixture into the cavities so it overflows onto the plate.

**Makes 4 servings**

**Per serving:** 224 calories, 7 g protein, 18 g carbohydrates, 15 g fat, 2 g saturated fat, 0 mg cholesterol, 602 mg sodium, 8 g fiber

**Diet Exchanges:** 0 milk, 0 vegetable, ½ fruit, 1 bread, ½ meat, 2½ fat

## Time-Saver

Make the bean salad up to 5 days ahead and store it in the refrigerator. Cut the avocado just before serving to minimize the darkening that occurs when avocado is exposed to air.

# WHITE BEANS WITH CHEESE AND BASIL

*91 calories, 11 g carbs*

| | |
|---|---|
| 1½ | **cans (14–19 ounces) cannellini or other white beans, drained, ⅓ cup liquid reserved** |
| 1 | **tablespoon olive oil** |
| ½ | **teaspoon salt** |
| ¼ | **teaspoon garlic powder** |
| ⅛ | **teaspoon ground black pepper** |
| 1½ | **tablespoons chopped fresh basil** |
| 3 | **tablespoons grated Parmesan or Romano cheese** |

Preheat the oven to 425°F.

Place the beans and reserved liquid in a large mixing bowl and partially mash the beans against the side of the bowl with a wooden spoon. Stir in the oil, salt, garlic powder, and pepper. Mix in the basil. Place in a shallow 2- to 3-cup baking dish, and sprinkle with the cheese. Bake until bubbling, 15 to 20 minutes. Serve hot or warm.

**Makes 6 servings**

---

**Per serving:** 91 calories, 4 g protein, 11 g carbohydrates, 4 g fat, 1 g saturated fat, 2 mg cholesterol, 390 mg sodium, 3 g fiber

**Diet Exchanges:** 0 milk, 0 vegetable, 0 fruit, ½ bread, ½ meat, ½ fat

## Time-Saver

*Make this dish whenever you have a minute and store it covered in the refrigerator for up to 4 days. Reheat covered in a 350°F oven for about 20 minutes.*

White Beans with Cheese and Basil

Belgian Endive with Eggplant, Olives, and Pine Nuts

# BELGIAN ENDIVE WITH EGGPLANT, OLIVES, AND PINE NUTS

*75 calories, 10 g carbs*

| | |
|---|---|
| 1 | **small eggplant (8 ounces)** |
| 1½ | **teaspoons walnut or olive oil** |
| 3 | **kalamata or Gaeta olives, chopped** |
| 2 | **teaspoons toasted pine nuts** |
| ¼ | **teaspoon lemon juice (optional)** |
| ¼ | **teaspoon salt** |
| ¼ | **teaspoon ground black pepper** |
| 12 | **Belgian endive leaves** |
| 1 | **teaspoon chopped parsley (optional)** |

Preheat the oven to 425°F. Pierce the eggplant in 4 or 5 places with a fork, and place in a baking pan. Roast until completely soft, 20 to 30 minutes, turning once or twice. Remove from the oven and let cool. Cut the eggplant in half lengthwise and scrape out the pulp, discarding the stem and skin. Finely chop the eggplant and place it in a medium mixing bowl. Gradually add the oil, stirring vigorously, until the eggplant absorbs it. Stir in the olives, pine nuts, lemon juice (if using), salt, and pepper.

Spoon the eggplant onto the wide end of the endive leaves, and sprinkle with parsley (if using).

**Makes 4 servings**

---

**Per serving:** 75 calories, 2 g protein, 10 g carbohydrates, 3 g fat, 0 g saturated fat, 0 mg cholesterol, 205 mg sodium, 5 g fiber

**Diet Exchanges:** 0 milk, 2 vegetable, 0 fruit, 0 bread, 0 meat, ½ fat

## Time-Savers

Roast the eggplant up to 4 days ahead of time and store in a covered container in the refrigerator. Pour off any accumulated liquid before completing the recipe. Or make the entire recipe and store the filled leaves in the refrigerator for up to 3 days. You can also use the filling to roll inside thin slices of turkey or ham for a snack or lunch.

# CRUDITÉS WITH SPICY PEANUT DIPPING SAUCE
*80 calories, 6 g carbs*

⅓    **cup unsweetened peanut butter**

1–2    **small hot chile peppers (¾–1 ounce), seeded and chopped (wear plastic gloves when handling)**

2    **small garlic cloves, minced**

     **About 3 tablespoons mango nectar or apple cider**

¼    **cup lime juice**

2    **tablespoons soy sauce**

¼    **teaspoon salt**

2    **cups assorted raw vegetables**

In a blender, combine the peanut butter, peppers, garlic, nectar or cider, lime juice, soy sauce, and salt. Process until a thick and smooth sauce forms, adding a little more nectar or cider as needed. Serve as a dip with the vegetables.

**Makes 8 servings**

---

**Per serving:** 80 calories, 3 g protein, 6 g carbohydrates, 5 g fat, 1 g saturated fat, 0 mg cholesterol, 331 mg sodium, 1 g fiber

**Diet Exchanges:** 0 milk, ½ vegetable, 0 fruit, 0 bread, ½ meat, 1 fat

## Time-Savers

*Make a double batch of the sauce and use some as a sandwich spread, some as a salad dressing. It's also delicious with apple or jicama slices, crisp whole wheat pita chips, or drizzled over grilled shrimp or catfish. Store in the refrigerator in a covered container for up to 5 days.*

# MINI EGGPLANT PIZZAS
*121 calories, 10 g carbs*

| | |
|---|---|
| 1 | **eggplant, 3" diameter, peeled and cut into 4 slices ½" thick** |
| 4 | **teaspoons olive oil** |
| ½ | **teaspoon salt** |
| ⅛ | **teaspoon ground black pepper** |
| 1 | **large ripe tomato, cut into 4 slices** |
| ½ | **teaspoon dried oregano** |
| ¼ | **teaspoon dried basil** |
| ½ | **teaspoon garlic powder** |
| ½ | **cup (2½ ounces) shredded smoked or regular mozzarella** |

Preheat the oven or toaster oven to 425°F.

Brush both sides of the eggplant with the oil and season with the salt and pepper. Arrange on a baking sheet and bake until browned and almost tender, 6 to 8 minutes, turning once.

Place a tomato slice on each eggplant slice and season with the oregano, basil, and garlic powder. Top with the cheese and bake until the cheese melts, 3 to 5 minutes. Serve hot.

**Makes 4 servings**

---

**Per serving:** 121 calories, 4 g protein, 10 g carbohydrates, 8 g fat, 3 g saturated fat, 11 mg cholesterol, 351 mg sodium, 4 g fiber

**Diet Exchanges:** 0 milk, 2 vegetable, 0 fruit, 0 bread, ½ meat, 1 fat

## Flavor Tip
*You can replace the eggplant with whole wheat mini pita breads, each split to make 2 pizzas.*

# SHRIMP IN MUSTARD-HORSERADISH SAUCE
*126 calories, 2 g carbs*

### SHRIMP

| | |
|---|---|
| 1 | **thin lemon slice** |
| | **Salt to taste** |
| 20 | **large shrimp (1 pound), cleaned and deveined** |

### MUSTARD-HORSERADISH SAUCE

| | |
|---|---|
| 4 | **teaspoons lemon juice** |
| 4 | **teaspoons Dijon mustard** |
| 2½ | **tablespoons olive oil** |
| 1 | **tablespoon prepared horseradish** |
| 2 | **teaspoons sour cream** |
| ¼ | **teaspoon salt** |
| ⅛ | **teaspoon ground black pepper** |
| 2 | **teaspoons finely chopped scallions** |

**To make the shrimp:** In a saucepan, combine 1½ quarts of water, the lemon slice, and salt to taste. Bring to a boil over high heat. Reduce the heat and cook for 5 minutes. Add the shrimp to the lemon water and cook until they are opaque and pink, 2 to 3 minutes. Drain, and discard the lemon slice.

**To make the sauce:** Mix the lemon juice and mustard in a large bowl. Gradually whisk in the oil to make a slightly thickened sauce. Stir in the horseradish, sour cream, salt, and pepper.

Add the shrimp to the sauce and toss to coat. Sprinkle with the scallions. Serve right away at room temperature or chilled.

**Makes 4 servings**

---

**Per serving:** 126 calories, 7 g protein, 2 g carbohydrates, 10 g fat, 2 g saturated fat, 54 mg cholesterol, 330 mg sodium, 0 g fiber

**Diet Exchanges:** 0 milk, 0 vegetable, 0 fruit, 0 bread, 1 meat, 1½ fat

## Time-Saver

Make this recipe up to 3 days ahead and refrigerate in a covered container.

Shrimp in Mustard-Horseradish Sauce

# ZUCCHINI-STUFFED MUSHROOMS

*106 calories, 8 g carbs*

| | |
|---|---|
| 1 | tablespoon olive oil |
| 1 | small onion, finely chopped |
| 1 | celery rib, finely chopped |
| 1 | small zucchini (3–4 ounces), finely chopped |
| 1 | large garlic clove, minced |
| 12 | large mushrooms (14–16 ounces), stems removed and reserved |
| 2 | teaspoons vinegar |
| ½ | teaspoon dried thyme |
| ½ | teaspoon dried oregano |
| ½ | teaspoon paprika (optional) |
| ¼ | cup grated Parmesan cheese |
| ¾ | teaspoon salt |
| ⅛ | teaspoon ground black pepper |
| 3 | tablespoons dry sherry or water |

Preheat the oven to 450°F.

Heat the oil in a large nonstick skillet over low heat. Add the onion, celery, zucchini, and garlic. Finely chop the mushroom stems and add to the skillet. Cook until the mushrooms are tender, 3 to 5 minutes, stirring occasionally. Stir in the vinegar, thyme, and oregano. Cover and cook, stirring occasionally until the celery is crisp-tender, 10 to 15 minutes. Remove to a small bowl and stir in the paprika (if using). Let cool.

Stir in 3 tablespoons of the Parmesan and the salt and pepper. With a teaspoon, fill the mushroom caps, mounding the mixture and firming it slightly with your fingers. Coat a baking dish with cooking spray. Arrange the caps in the dish in a single layer, and sprinkle with the remaining 1 tablespoon cheese. Pour the sherry or water evenly around the bottom of the baking dish. Cover and bake for 5 minutes. Uncover and bake until sizzling, 5 to 7 minutes more. Serve hot.

**Makes 4 servings**

---

**Per serving:** 106 calories, 7 g protein, 8 g carbohydrates, 5 g fat, 2 g saturated fat, 5 mg cholesterol, 568 mg sodium, 2 g fiber

**Diet Exchanges:** 0 milk, 1½ vegetable, 0 fruit, 0 bread, ½ meat, 1 fat

## Time-Savers

To cut down on last-minute preparation, make the stuffing up to 3 days ahead and store it covered in the refrigerator. Or prepare the entire recipe up to 2 days ahead and store in the refrigerator. To reheat: Bring the stuffed mushrooms to room temperature, then sprinkle with the cheese and bake in a 450°F oven for 10 to 12 minutes.

# ICED ORANGE-COCONUT DRINK
*147 calories, 17 g carbs*

- **2** **cups orange juice**
- **1** **cup unsweetened soy milk**
- **1** **cup unsweetened shredded coconut**

Combine half of the orange juice, soy milk, and coconut in a blender and process until the mixture is smooth, 2 to 3 minutes. Repeat with the remaining ingredients. Serve over ice. Store extra servings in the refrigerator for up to 12 hours.

**Makes 4 servings**

**Per serving:** 147 calories, 3 g protein, 17 g carbohydrates, 8 g fat, 6 g saturated fat, 0 mg cholesterol, 13 mg sodium, 3 g fiber

**Diet Exchanges:** 0 milk, 0 vegetable, 1 fruit, 0 bread, meat, 1½ fat

## Flavor Tip

Use pineapple juice in place of 1 cup of the orange juice.

*snacks, appetizers, and beverages*

## Hot Apple Cider with Ginger
*117 calories, 27 g carbs*

| | |
|---|---|
| 1 | **quart apple cider** |
| 4 | **thin slices fresh ginger, unpeeled** |
| ¼ | **teaspoon ground cinnamon** |
| ⅛ | **teaspoon ground nutmeg or cloves (optional)** |

Combine the cider and ginger in a medium saucepan and bring to a simmer over medium heat. Pour into mugs, placing 1 piece of the ginger in each mug. Sprinkle with the cinnamon and nutmeg or cloves (if using).

**Makes 4 servings**

**Per serving:** 117 calories, 0 g protein, 27 g carbohydrates, 0 g fat, 0 g saturated fat, 0 mg cholesterol, 16 mg sodium, 0 g fiber

**Diet Exchanges:** 0 milk, 0 vegetable, 2 fruit, 0 bread, 0 meat, 0 fat

### Time-Saver

Instead of using the stovetop, heat the mixture in a microwave oven on medium power until hot, 2 to 3 minutes. This hot drink travels well in an insulated bottle.

## Strawberry Protein Shake
*149 calories, 22 g carbs*

| | |
|---|---|
| 16 | **large frozen unsweetened strawberries (12 ounces), quartered** |
| 1 | **cup plain yogurt** |
| 2 | **cups cold orange juice or 1½ cups orange juice plus ½ cup seltzer** |
| 1½ | **teaspoons vanilla extract** |
| ¼ | **cup unflavored protein powder** |

Combine half of the berries, yogurt, orange juice, vanilla, and protein powder in a blender and process until smooth, thick, and creamy, 1 to 2 minutes. Repeat with the remaining ingredients. Serve cold.

**Makes 4 servings**

**Per serving:** 149 calories, 8 g protein, 22 g carbohydrates, 3 g fat, 1 g saturated fat, 8 mg cholesterol, 92 mg sodium, 2 g fiber

**Diet Exchanges:** ½ milk, 0 vegetable, 1 fruit, 0 bread, ½ meat, fat

### ▶Flavor Tips

Substitute pear, peach, or mango nectar for the orange juice. Replace the strawberries with blueberries.

# BUTTERMILK FRUIT SHAKE *(photo on page 146)*
*92 calories, 15 g carbs*

| | |
|---|---|
| 2 | **cups frozen unsweetened blueberries or sliced strawberries** |
| 2 | **cups buttermilk** |
| 1 | **teaspoon vanilla extract** |
| ¼–½ | **cup apple cider (optional)** |

Combine half of the berries, buttermilk, and vanilla in a blender and process until smooth. Mix in half the apple cider (if using) to sweeten. Repeat with the remaining ingredients. Serve cold.

**Makes 4 servings**

**Per serving:** 92 calories, 4 g protein, 15 g carbohydrates, 2 g fat, 1 g saturated fat, 4 mg cholesterol, 129 mg sodium, 2 g fiber

**Diet Exchanges:** ½ milk, 0 vegetable, ½ fruit, 0 bread, 0 meat, 0 fat

## SLIMMING BEVERAGE

Sweetened colas and fruit drinks are among the top sources of sugar and calories in the American diet. Flavored teas make a delicious, low-calorie alternative with less sugar. You can infuse regular tea with ginger, lemon, chopped mint, or spices such as cinnamon.

# MINT-INFUSED DARJEELING TEA
*2 calories, 0 g carbs*

| | |
|---|---|
| 1 | **quart water** |
| 3 | **packed tablespoons coarsely chopped fresh mint or 1 tablespoon dried** |
| 3 | **Darjeeling tea bags** |

Boil the water in a saucepan and add the mint and tea bags. Remove from the heat, cover, and steep for 3 to 5 minutes. Strain into mugs.

**Makes 4 servings**

**Per serving:** 2 calories, 0 g protein, 0 g carbohydrates, 0 g fat, 0 g saturated fat, 0 mg cholesterol, 8 mg sodium, 0 g fiber

**Diet Exchanges:** 0 milk, 0 vegetable, 0 fruit, 0 bread, 0 meat, 0 fat

# PEACH-PEAR SMOOTHIE
*114 calories, 24 g carbs*

| | |
|---|---|
| 1 | cup cold peach or mango nectar |
| 2 | pears, peeled and chopped (1½ cups) |
| 1 | cup 2% milk or unsweetened soy milk |
| ⅛ | teaspoon ground nutmeg |

Combine half of the nectar, pears, and milk in a blender and process until very smooth. Pour into glasses and sprinkle with half of the nutmeg. Repeat with the remaining ingredients. Serve cold. Store extra servings in a covered container in the refrigerator for up to 2 days.

**Makes 4 servings**

**Per serving:** 114 calories, 3 g protein, 24 g carbohydrates, 2 g fat, 1 g saturated fat, 5 mg cholesterol, 35 mg sodium, 2 g fiber

**Diet Exchanges:** ½ milk, 0 vegetable, 1½ fruit, 0 bread, 0 meat, 0 fat

## ▶Flavor Tip

*Replace the peach nectar with 1 cup canned peaches in water (drained) and substitute seltzer for all or part of the milk. Serve over ice cubes with a sprig of mint.*

# soups & sandwiches

# WHITE BEAN SOUP WITH SAUSAGE

*218 calories, 17 g carbs*

| | |
|---|---|
| 1 | tablespoon + 1 teaspoon olive oil |
| ½ | pound sweet Italian sausage, casing removed, broken into 1" pieces |
| ½ | large onion, chopped |
| 3 | celery ribs, chopped |
| 2½ | cups (8 ounces) chopped green or red cabbage |
| 1 | cup (8 ounces) dried white beans, soaked overnight and drained |
| 4–5 | cans (14½ ounces each) reduced-sodium chicken broth |
| 1 | can (15 ounces) no-salt-added stewed tomatoes |
| 1 | teaspoon dried Italian seasoning |
| 1 | large bay leaf |
| ¼ | teaspoon ground black pepper |

Heat 1 teaspoon of the oil in a soup pot over medium-low heat. Add the sausage and cook, stirring occasionally, just until cooked through, about 5 minutes. Remove to a plate, cover, and refrigerate.

Pour the remaining 1 tablespoon oil into the same pot over medium heat and stir in the onion, celery, and cabbage. Cook, stirring occasionally, until the vegetables begin to soften, 8 to 10 minutes.

Add the beans, 4 cans of the broth, and the tomatoes to the pot. Bring to a boil and immediately lower the heat, skimming off any froth that comes to the top. Stir in the Italian seasoning and bay leaf. Partially cover, and cook until the beans are tender, 1¼ to 1½ hours depending on the beans, adding more broth if the soup becomes too thick. Stir in the sausage and pepper; simmer for 2 minutes. Discard the bay leaf before serving.

**Makes 8 servings**

---

**Per serving:** 218 calories, 12 g protein, 17 g carbohydrates, 13 g fat, 4 g saturated fat, 26 mg cholesterol, 538 mg sodium, 5 g fiber

**Diet Exchanges:** 0 milk, 1½ vegetable, 0 fruit, ½ bread, 1 meat, 2 fat

## Time-Saver

Make this soup ahead and store it in a covered container in the refrigerator for up to 5 days or in the freezer for up to 2 months. To reheat, thaw the soup in the refrigerator overnight, then cook it in a saucepan over low heat until heated through.

White Bean Soup with Sausage

# HEARTY COUNTRY VEGETABLE SOUP

*126 calories, 18 g carbs*

| | |
|---|---|
| 3 | tablespoons olive oil |
| ½ | large onion, thinly sliced |
| 3 | celery ribs, thinly sliced |
| 1 | small head (1 pound) green cabbage, coarsely chopped |
| 2 | carrots, sliced into ½"-thick rounds |
| 2 | garlic cloves, minced |
| ½ | cup (4 ounces) dried white beans, soaked overnight and drained |
| 2½–3 | cans (14½ ounces each) vegetable broth |
| ½ | teaspoon dried thyme |
| ½ | teaspoon dried savory or sage |
| 8 | ounces green beans, cut into ½" lengths |
| 1 | zucchini (6 ounces), coarsely chopped |
| ½ | teaspoon ground black pepper |
| 2–3 | tablespoons chopped fresh basil or dill (optional) |

Heat the oil in a soup pot over medium-low heat. Stir in the onion, celery, cabbage, carrots, and garlic. Cover the pot and cook, stirring occasionally, until the vegetables soften, 12 to 15 minutes. Add the white beans and 5 cups of the broth; bring to a boil. Reduce the heat to medium-low and stir in the thyme and savory or sage. Cover and cook until the beans are almost tender, 1 to 1½ hours, adding broth if the soup becomes too thick.

Stir in the green beans and zucchini. Partially cover and cook until the beans are tender, 20 to 30 minutes. Season with the pepper and basil or dill (if using). Divide among bowls.

**Makes 8 servings**

---

**Per serving:** 126 calories, 5 g protein, 18 g carbohydrates, 6 g fat, 1 g saturated fat, 0 mg cholesterol, 708 mg sodium, 6 g fiber

**Diet Exchanges:** 0 milk, 2 vegetable, 0 fruit, ½ bread, 0 meat, 1 fat

▶ Flavor Tips

Substitute fennel for all or part of the celery. You can also add ½ cup crushed tomatoes with the white beans. For a nice touch, serve the soup sprinkled with grated Parmesan cheese or a drizzle of extra-virgin olive oil.

# CREAMY BROCCOLI SOUP WITH CHICKEN
*177 calories, 13 g carbs*

| | |
|---|---|
| 2 | **tablespoons butter** |
| 1 | **onion, thinly sliced** |
| 1 | **garlic clove, sliced (optional)** |
| 3 | **tablespoons whole wheat flour** |
| 3 | **cans (14½ ounces each) reduced-sodium chicken broth** |
| 1½ | **bunches (1½ pounds) broccoli, cut into florets, stems peeled and thinly sliced** |
| ¾ | **teaspoon dried sage** |
| 1 | **bay leaf** |
| ¼ | **teaspoon ground black pepper** |
| 1 | **boneless, skinless chicken breast half (½ pound), cut into chunks** |
| ⅓ | **cup half-and-half** |

Melt the butter in a soup pot over low heat. Stir in the onion and garlic (if using). Cover and cook until the onion is almost translucent, 8 to 10 minutes, stirring occasionally. Stir in the flour and cook, stirring frequently, for 1 minute. Gradually stir in the broth, bring the soup to a simmer over medium heat, and add the broccoli, sage, and bay leaf. Cook until the broccoli is tender, 10 to 15 minutes.

Discard the bay leaf. Reserve ½ cup broccoli florets if desired. Ladle the soup into a blender, process until smooth, and return to the pot. Add the pepper, chicken, and half-and-half. Cook just until the chicken is no longer pink, 3 to 4 minutes, stirring once or twice. Top each serving with the reserved broccoli florets (if using).

**Makes 6 servings**

---

**Per serving:** 177 calories, 16 g protein, 13 g carbohydrates, 7 g fat, 4 g saturated fat, 42 mg cholesterol, 190 mg sodium, 4 g fiber

**Diet Exchanges:** 0 milk, 1½ vegetable, 0 fruit, ½ bread, 1 meat, 1 fat

## Time-Saver

Make this soup ahead of time and store it in a covered container in the refrigerator for up to 4 days or freeze it for up to 2 months. To reheat, thaw the soup in the refrigerator overnight, then cook it in a saucepan over low heat until heated through.

Chicken Gumbo

# CHICKEN GUMBO
*214 calories, 10 g carbs*

| | |
|---|---|
| 3 | tablespoons vegetable oil |
| 1 | small onion, chopped |
| 3 | celery ribs, chopped |
| 1 | large green bell pepper, chopped |
| 1 | garlic clove, minced |
| ½ | teaspoon ground black pepper |
| 3½ | tablespoons whole wheat flour |
| 2½–3 | cans (14½ ounces each) reduced-sodium chicken broth |
| ¾ | cup crushed tomatoes |
| ¼ | pound boneless smoked ham, cut into ½" pieces |
| 3 | skinless chicken thighs (¾ pound) |
| 1 | teaspoon dried thyme |
| 1 | bay leaf |
| ⅛ | teaspoon ground red pepper |
| 1 | tablespoon chopped parsley |

Heat the oil in a soup pot over medium heat and add the onion, celery, bell pepper, garlic, and black pepper. Cover and cook just until the vegetables begin to soften, 5 to 6 minutes. Stir in the flour and cook, stirring frequently, for 3 minutes. Gradually stir in 2½ cans of the broth and bring it to a simmer.

Add the tomatoes, ham, chicken, thyme, bay leaf, and ground red pepper. Partially cover, and cook until the chicken is tender, 25 to 35 minutes, adding the remaining broth as necessary if the gumbo is too thick. Remove from the heat, transfer the chicken to a plate, and let cool slightly. Cut into bite-size pieces, discarding the bones, and return to the pot. Reheat briefly and stir in the parsley. Remove the bay leaf before serving.

**Makes 6 servings**

---

**Per serving:** 214 calories, 13 g protein, 10 g carbohydrates, 12 g fat, 2 g saturated fat, 35 mg cholesterol, 340 mg sodium, 2 g fiber

**Diet Exchanges:** 0 milk, 1 vegetable, 0 fruit, ½ bread, 2 meat, 2 fat

## ▶Flavor Tips

*Substitute andouille sausage or kielbasa for the ham. Add 1 box (10 ounces) frozen cut okra along with the chicken.*

# LAMB AND BARLEY SOUP
*194 calories, 17 g carbs*

| | |
|---|---|
| 1 | tablespoon olive oil |
| 1 | pound lamb cubes, cut into bite-size pieces |
| 1 | small onion, chopped |
| 2 | carrots, chopped |
| 4 | celery ribs, chopped |
| 1 | garlic clove, minced |
| 4 | cans (14½ ounces each) reduced-sodium chicken broth |
| 2 | tablespoons tomato paste (optional) |
| ⅔ | cup hulled or regular barley |
| ¾ | teaspoon dried rosemary, crumbled |
| ½ | teaspoon dried oregano |
| ½ | teaspoon ground black pepper |

Heat the oil in a large soup pot over low heat. Add the lamb and cook, stirring frequently, until browned all over, 3 to 5 minutes. Remove to a plate. Stir the onion, carrots, celery, and garlic into the pot. Cover and cook, stirring occasionally, until the vegetables begin to soften, about 10 minutes.

Return the lamb to the pot and add the broth. Bring to a simmer and add the tomato paste (if using), barley, rosemary, oregano, and pepper. Partially cover and cook until the barley is tender-chewy, 45 to 55 minutes. Skim fat from the surface of the soup if necessary.

**Makes 8 servings**

**Per serving:** 194 calories, 17 g protein, 17 g carbohydrates, 7 g fat, 2 g saturated fat, 42 mg cholesterol, 160 mg sodium, 4 g fiber

**Diet Exchanges:** 0 milk, 1 vegetable, 0 fruit, 1 bread, 2 meat, 1 fat

## ▶Flavor Tips

In place of the 4 celery ribs, use 2 celery ribs and ½ fennel bulb. Stir in 2 tablespoons of chopped parsley before serving. You can also replace the lamb with small pieces of stewing beef.

Lamb and Barley Soup

# MUSHROOM AND KASHA SOUP
*112 calories, 11 g carbs*

| | |
|---|---|
| ½ | cup kasha (buckwheat groats) |
| 2 | tablespoons olive oil |
| 20 | ounces mushrooms, coarsely chopped |
| ½ | onion, finely chopped |
| 1 | carrot, finely chopped |
| 1½ | celery ribs, finely chopped |
| ½ | red bell pepper, finely chopped |
| ½ | teaspoon ground black pepper |
| 2¼ | cans (14½ ounces each) chicken or vegetable broth |
| 1 | teaspoon dried dill or thyme |
| 1 | bay leaf |

Toast the kasha in a soup pot over medium heat, stirring, for 2 to 3 minutes. Remove to a bowl.

Heat the oil in the same pot over medium-low heat. Stir in the mushrooms, onion, carrot, celery, bell pepper, and black pepper. Cover and cook, stirring occasionally, for 8 to 10 minutes. Stir in the kasha and broth. Bring to a simmer and add the dill or thyme and the bay leaf. Partially cover, and cook until the kasha is tender, about 10 minutes. Remove the bay leaf before serving.

**Makes 6 servings**

---

**Per serving:** 112 calories, 6 g protein, 11 g carbohydrates, 6 g fat, 1 g saturated fat, 0 mg cholesterol, 687 mg sodium, 3 g fiber

**Diet Exchanges:** 0 milk, 1½ vegetable, 0 fruit, ½ bread, 0 meat, 1 fat

▶Flavor Tips
*Serve sprinkled with chopped scallions. For a vegetarian stew, cook with only 1 cup vegetable broth.*

# LENTIL SOUP WITH CAULIFLOWER AND YOGURT
*128 calories, 19 g carbs*

| | |
|---|---|
| 1½ | tablespoons olive oil |
| 1½ | carrots, finely chopped |
| 1 | onion, finely chopped |
| 1½ | celery ribs, finely chopped |
| 1 | garlic clove, minced |
| ⅓ | cup canned crushed tomatoes |
| 1¼ | cups (9 ounces) lentils, rinsed and drained |
| 4–4½ | cans (14½ ounces each) vegetable broth |
| 1 | bay leaf |
| ½ | head (16 ounces total) cauliflower, cut into bite-size florets |
| 2–3 | tablespoons lemon juice |
| ½ | teaspoon ground black pepper |
| ½ | cup plain low-fat yogurt |

Heat the oil in a soup pot over medium heat. Stir in the carrots, onion, celery, and garlic. Cover and cook until the onion begins to turn translucent, 5 minutes. Stir in the tomatoes, lentils, and 6½ cups of the broth. Bring to a boil and immediately reduce the heat. Skim off any froth that comes to the top and stir in the bay leaf. Cover and cook until the lentils are tender, 40 to 45 minutes, adding broth as needed.

Stir in the cauliflower. Partially cover and cook until the cauliflower is tender, 5 to 8 minutes. Stir in the lemon juice and the pepper. Serve garnished with the yogurt. Discard the bay leaf.

**Makes 8 servings**

**Per serving:** 128 calories, 8 g protein, 19 g carbohydrates, 4 g fat, 1 g saturated fat, 1 mg cholesterol, 950 mg sodium, 5 g fiber

**Diet Exchanges:** 0 milk, 2 vegetable, 0 fruit, ½ bread, 0 meat, 1 fat

## ▶Flavor Tips

*If you don't like cauliflower, you can omit it. To make a thicker soup, puree 1½ cups of the soup (mostly lentils) in a blender, then stir the puree back into the soup. Add ½ teaspoon curry powder.*

Clam Chowder with Greens

# CLAM CHOWDER WITH GREENS
*180 calories, 12 g carbs*

¼ **pound turkey bacon, chopped**

I **tablespoon vegetable oil**

I **onion, finely chopped**

I **garlic clove, minced**

I **small bunch (12 ounces) turnip greens or other greens, coarse stems removed and discarded, leaves chopped**

2 **cans (14½ ounces each) reduced-sodium chicken broth**

2 **cans (10 ounces each) baby clams, juice reserved**

I **cup half-and-half**

2–2½ **tablespoons potato flour (see Flavor Tip)**

¼ **teaspoon ground black pepper**

Cook the turkey bacon in a large saucepan over medium-low heat until crisp. Drain on a paper towel-lined plate. Add the oil to the pan, then add the onion and garlic. Cook, stirring occasionally, until the onion is translucent, 8 to 10 minutes. Add the greens and cook for 2 minutes. Stir in the broth and the reserved clam juice. Bring to a simmer over medium heat and cook for 10 minutes. Stir in the half-and-half and heat through. Sprinkle 2 tablespoons potato flour over the soup and stir in. Add the remaining ½ tablespoon flour for a thicker soup if desired. Stir in the pepper and clams, and cook for 1 to 2 minutes. Sprinkle the turkey bacon over each serving.

**Makes 6 servings**

**Per serving:** 180 calories, 8 g protein, 12 g carbohydrates, 11 g fat, 4 g saturated fat, 42 mg cholesterol, 563 mg sodium, 3 g fiber

**Diet Exchanges:** 0 milk, 1 vegetable, 0 fruit, ½ bread, ½ meat, 2 fat

## ▶Flavor Tip

*Potato flour is used as the thickener in this recipe to lend the characteristic flavor of potatoes without as many carbohydrates. Look for it in the baking aisle of supermarkets or health food stores. Or you can use 1½ tablespoons cornstarch mixed with 2 tablespoons water instead.*

# ITALIAN BEAN SOUP WITH CHARD AND MUSHROOMS

*107 calories, 16 g carbs*

|   |   |
|---|---|
| 2 | tablespoons olive oil |
| ½ | bunch (6 ounces total) chard, chopped |
| ½ | pound mushrooms, chopped |
| 1½ | large red or green bell peppers, chopped |
| 1 | garlic clove, minced |
| 1 | cup (8 ounces) dried white beans, soaked overnight and drained |
| 3 | cans (14½ ounces each) vegetable broth |
| ¾ | teaspoon dried rosemary, crumbled |
| ½ | teaspoon dried sage |
| 6 | scallions, thinly sliced |
| ½ | teaspoon ground black pepper |

Heat the oil in a soup pot over medium heat. Stir in the chard, mushrooms, bell peppers, and garlic. Cover and cook until the vegetables soften, 6 to 8 minutes, stirring occasionally.

Add the beans and broth, bring to a boil, and immediately reduce the heat. Skim off any froth that comes to the top and stir in the rosemary and the sage. Cover and cook until the beans are tender, 1 to 1½ hours.

Stir in the scallions and the black pepper. Cook for 2 to 3 minutes.

**Makes 8 servings**

---

**Per serving:** 107 calories, 7 g protein, 16 g carbohydrates, 4 g fat, 1 g saturated fat, 0 mg cholesterol, 921 mg sodium, 5 g fiber

**Diet Exchanges:** 0 milk, 2 vegetable, 0 fruit, ½ bread, 0 meat, ½ fat

## *Time-Saver*

Make this soup ahead for a quick one-dish meal. Store in a tightly covered container in the refrigerator for up to 5 days or in the freezer for up to 2 months. To reheat, thaw the soup in the refrigerator overnight, then cook it in a saucepan over low heat until heated through.

# CHILLED MELON SOUP WITH BASIL
*68 calories, 17 g carbs*

| | |
|---|---|
| ¾ | large honeydew (4½ pounds) or other melon, cubed |
| 2–3 | tablespoons lime juice |
| 2–3 | tablespoons dry sherry or grape juice |
| ½ | teaspoon salt |
| 1½ | tablespoons sour cream (optional) |
| ¼ | cup chopped fresh basil |

Place half of the melon, 1 tablespoon of the lime juice, and 1 tablespoon of the sherry or grape juice in a blender. Process until very smooth, about 1 minute. Add the salt and up to ½ tablespoon more lime juice or sherry if desired. Repeat with the remaining ingredients, combine the batches in a bowl, and refrigerate until chilled, at least 1 hour.

Top each serving with a dollop of sour cream (if using) and sprinkle with the basil.

**Makes 6 servings**

**Per serving:** 68 calories, 1 g protein, 17 g carbohydrates, 0 g fat, 0 g saturated fat, 0 mg cholesterol, 238 mg sodium, 1 g fiber

**Diet Exchanges:** 0 milk, 0 vegetable, 1 fruit, 0 bread, 0 meat, 0 fat

## ▶Flavor Tip

*The flavor and color of melon soup is best within the first few hours. If you refrigerate the soup for more than 18 hours, refresh it with a little lime juice or sherry before serving.*

# CHILLED CUCUMBER, SCALLION, AND YOGURT SOUP

*236 calories, 16 g carbs*

| | |
|---|---|
| 4½ | **cups plain low-fat yogurt** |
| ⅓ | **cup olive oil** |
| 2 | **tablespoons balsamic vinegar** |
| 4 | **tablespoons cold water** |
| 2–3 | **cucumbers (12 ounces), peeled, seeded, and chopped** |
| 3 | **scallions, finely chopped** |
| ½ | **teaspoon salt** |
| ¼ | **teaspoon ground black pepper** |
| 2 | **tablespoons toasted walnuts (optional)** |
| 1½ | **teaspoons chopped fresh dill** |

Preheat the oven or a toaster oven to 350°F.

Place the yogurt in a large bowl and gradually whisk in the oil. Whisk in the vinegar and enough of the cold water to make a somewhat thick mixture. Stir in half of the cucumbers, the scallions, the salt, and the pepper. Puree in a blender or food processor. Transfer back into the bowl and stir in the remaining cucumbers. Refrigerate until well-chilled, at least 1 hour.

Serve the chilled soup sprinkled with the walnuts (if using) and the dill.

**Makes 6 servings**

---

**Per serving:** 236 calories, 10 g protein, 16 g carbohydrates, 15 g fat, 3 g saturated fat, 11 mg cholesterol, 327 mg sodium, 1 g fiber

**Diet Exchanges:** 1 milk, ½ vegetable, 0 fruit, 0 bread, 0 meat, 3 fat

Flavor Tip

*Just before serving, lightly sprinkle with ground cumin.*

Chilled Cucumber, Scallion, and Yogurt Soup

# MEXICAN-STYLE SUMMER SQUASH SOUP

*86 calories, 9 g carbs*

| | |
|---|---|
| 1½ | tablespoons butter |
| ½ | large onion, thinly sliced |
| 4 | zucchini and/or yellow squash (24 ounces), chopped |
| 2 | garlic cloves, minced |
| ½ | large red bell pepper, chopped |
| ¼ | cup drained, chopped canned tomatoes |
| 2¼ | cans (14½ ounces each) chicken broth |
| ½ | teaspoon ground black pepper |
| ½ | teaspoon dried oregano |
| ¼ | teaspoon ground cumin |
| 1½ | tablespoons cornmeal |

Melt the butter in a medium soup pot over medium heat. Stir in the onion, zucchini or squash, garlic, and bell pepper. Cook, stirring occasionally, until excess liquid from the squash has evaporated, 8 to 10 minutes.

Stir in the tomatoes and broth. Reduce the heat to low and stir in the black pepper, oregano, and cumin. Cook the soup, uncovered, until the vegetables are tender, about 10 minutes.

Stir in the cornmeal and cook until thickened slightly, 5 minutes.

**Makes 6 servings**

---

**Per serving:** 86 calories, 4 g protein, 9 g carbohydrates, 4 g fat, 2 g saturated fat, 8 mg cholesterol, 694 mg sodium, 3 g fiber

**Diet Exchanges:** 0 milk, 1 vegetable, 0 fruit, ½ bread, 0 meat, ½ fat

▶## Flavor Tips

Cook 3 bacon slices in the saucepan until crisp. Drain on a paper towel-lined plate. Use 1½ tablespoons of the drippings in place of the butter to cook the vegetables. Crumble the bacon over each serving. For a thinner soup, omit the cornmeal.

# ROAST BEEF SANDWICH
# WITH MUSTARD-HORSERADISH MAYONNAISE

*349 calories, 22 g carbs*

| | |
|---|---|
| 3 | **tablespoons mayonnaise** |
| 2 | **teaspoons Dijon mustard** |
| 2 | **teaspoons prepared horseradish** |
| 8 | **slices light whole-wheat bread** |
| 12 | **spinach or lettuce leaves** |
| ½ | **cucumber (3 ounces total), peeled and thinly sliced** |
| 12 | **slices roast beef (¾ pound)** |
| ½ | **teaspoon salt** |
| ¼ | **teaspoon ground black pepper** |

In a small bowl, combine the mayonnaise, mustard, and horseradish. Spread over the bread and cover 4 of the slices with the spinach or lettuce. Arrange the cucumber and beef over the spinach or lettuce. Season with the salt and pepper. Top with the remaining bread and cut in half.

**Makes 4 servings**

---

**Per serving:** 349 calories, 30 g protein, 22 g carbohydrates, 17 g fat, 4 g saturated fat, 73 mg cholesterol, 734 mg sodium, 7 g fiber

**Diet Exchanges:** 0 milk, ½ vegetable, 0 fruit, 1½ bread, 3 meat, 1½ fat

▶ Flavor Tips

*Substitute chicken or turkey for the beef. You could also eliminate the bread. Instead, spread the meat with the mayonnaise, top with the cucumber, and wrap in the spinach or lettuce leaves.*

Turkey Sandwich with Swiss Cheese and Apple with Buttermilk Fruit Shake (p. 125)

# TURKEY SANDWICH WITH SWISS CHEESE AND APPLE

*384 calories, 28 g carbs*

| | |
|---|---|
| **3** | **tablespoons macadamia or other nut butter** |
| **8** | **slices light whole-wheat bread, lightly toasted** |
| **4** | **slices (¼ pound) Swiss cheese** |
| **8** | **slices (½ pound) cooked turkey breast** |
| **¼** | **teaspoon salt** |
| **⅛** | **teaspoon ground black pepper (optional)** |
| **1** | **small apple (4 ounces), thinly sliced** |
| **½** | **bunch watercress sprigs or 4 large lettuce leaves** |

Spread the nut butter over the bread. Arrange the cheese on 4 slices, top with the turkey, and season with the salt and pepper (if using). Top with the apple, watercress or lettuce, and the remaining bread. Cut in half.

**Makes 4 servings**

---

**Per serving:** 384 calories, 29 g protein, 28 g carbohydrates, 19 g fat, 5 g saturated fat, 60 mg cholesterol, 714 mg sodium, 2 g fiber

**Diet Exchanges:** 0 milk, 0 vegetable, ½ fruit, 2 bread, 3 meat, 1½ fat

## Time-Saver

This sandwich can be assembled ahead and refrigerated for up to 3 hours.

# I Did It!

## Becky Cleveland

For most of her life, Becky's mother was overweight and led a sedentary lifestyle, which later contributed to numerous medical problems. Becky was determined not to let that happen to herself. After a slew of diet and exercise plans failed, Becky went on a reduced-carbohydrate diet, discovered the joys of cycling, and lost 63 pounds.

before

"I was very slender when I met my husband. However, I started to gain weight immediately after the wedding—maybe it was all that wedding cake! Five years later, when our first child was born, I stayed at home and had little time for exercise. I also enjoyed preparing lots of dishes like pasta, tuna-noodle casserole, and chocolate chip cookies. I now know that these were loaded with refined carbohydrates. My weight continued to climb. After I gave birth to our second child, I gained 40 pounds and

**Weight lost:** 63 pounds
**Time kept off:** 3 years
**Weight-loss strategies:** Lower-carbohydrate diet, exercise, drank lots of water
**Weight-maintenance strategies:** Avoids refined carbohydrates, moderates total carbohydrates, stays active

weighed in at almost 170 pounds. I tried nearly every diet plan out there. Some of them worked for a short time, but then I regained all the weight I had lost—plus more.

"When our kids were a little older, I was able to exercise more, but I never had a formal program. It was when I tipped the scale at 208 pounds that I decided to hire a personal trainer. He developed a customized exercise and diet plan and helped me stick to it. I strengthened my muscles and toned up. I even managed to lose 30 pounds, but I regained 10 of them. Looking back, I think I rationalized that the more I exercised, the more I could eat!

"My real motivation for weight loss came when my mother was told that her sedentary lifestyle and excess weight were severely impacting her health. She became disabled to the point where she was restricted to a wheelchair and bed. I was determined not to let that happen to me if there was any way I could prevent it.

"Gloria, a friend of mine who is a nutritionist, convinced me to make an appointment with her. She reassured me that the reduced-carbohydrate plan she had in mind would be easy to follow, and I would not feel hungry. Gloria and I met on a weekly basis. I have to admit, it was hard adjusting to eating fewer carbohydrates the first week. Then it became easier because I understood why I needed to change my food choices. Gloria taught me how little nutritional value refined carbohydrates had and how important normal insulin levels

were for good health. It wasn't long before I began to enjoy the whole grain substitutes. These dietary changes brought my weight down from about 190 pounds to 145 pounds. I was so happy to get into size 10 or 12 jeans and size 8 or 10 dresses. At one time I was wearing a women's size 20!

"Once my diet improved, I was able to step up the exercise too. Mostly I walked and rode my bike. My son, Adam, who had lost 120 pounds, motivated me further by buying me a new bike. The long bike rides we took were great stress reducers. Now I also swim and do water aerobics for 2 hours 3 days a week.

"These days, the reduced-carbohydrate approach is second nature to me. My family eats out often, but I know to stay away from the huge servings of pasta and heavily breaded foods. I order my salad right away so I'm not tempted to eat the bread and other appetizers. Sure, there are times when I eat foods not on my plan. But I get right back on track instead of waiting until Monday to start choosing foods wisely again.

"I only wish I had listened to an older friend of mine 30 years ago when she told me that I was too young to weigh as much as I did. Losing weight has given me such a wonderful new perspective on life. I just turned 50. And I have more energy and am in better shape physically and mentally than I can ever recall. I even get more compliments today than when I was younger!"

(continued)

*soups and sandwiches*

# I Did It! (cont.)

## BECKY'S TROPICAL CHICKEN SALAD SANDWICHES

*380 calories, 18 g carbs*

- 1 container (6 ounces) low-fat piña colada or coconut yogurt
- ¼ cup light mayonnaise
- 1 can (8 ounces) crushed pineapple, drained
- ½ teaspoon poultry seasoning
- ¼ teaspoon salt
- 1 pound boneless, skinless cooked chicken breast, chopped
- ⅔ cup red or white seedless grapes (about 16), halved
- 1 small celery rib, chopped
- 1 small apple, chopped (optional)
- ½ cup sliced toasted almonds
- 2 tablespoons chopped chives or scallions (optional)
- 8 large Boston lettuce leaves

In a large bowl, combine the yogurt, mayonnaise, pineapple, poultry seasoning, and salt. Stir in the chicken, grapes, celery, apple (if using), almonds, and chives or scallions (if using). Divide the salad among the lettuces leaves and roll up into 8 small sandwiches.

**Makes 4 servings**

**Per serving:** 380 calories, 41 g protein, 18 g carbohydrates, 16 g fat, 3 g saturated fat, 104 mg cholesterol, 390 mg sodium, 2 g fiber

**Diet Exchanges:** 0 milk, 0 vegetable, 1 fruit, 0 bread, 6 meat, 2½ fat

# OPEN-FACE SMOKED SALMON SANDWICHES ON RYE CRISPBREAD

*217 calories, 16 g carbs*

½   **cup + 2 tablespoons whipped cream cheese**

2   **teaspoons capers, drained**

2½  **tablespoons minced red onion**

2   **tablespoons chopped walnuts**

8   **slices rye crispbread**

8   **slices (½ pound) smoked salmon**

¼   **teaspoon ground black pepper**

In a small bowl, mix together the cream cheese, capers, onion, and walnuts. Spread the mixture over the crispbread. Fold the salmon to fit on top of the cream cheese, and sprinkle with the pepper.

**Makes 4 servings**

**Per serving:** 217 calories, 10 g protein, 16 g carbohydrates, 13 g fat, 6 g saturated fat, 35 mg cholesterol, 428 mg sodium, 3 g fiber

**Diet Exchanges:** 0 milk, 0 vegetable, 0 fruit, 1 bread, 1 meat, 2½ fat

## ▶Flavor Tips

Use flavored yogurt cheese (see recipe for Soft Yogurt Cheese on page 107) instead of the cream cheese. Substitute other smoked fish, such as trout, whitefish, or tuna for the salmon, or top with skinless, boneless sardines. Add ½ teaspoon dried dill to the cheese mixture.

## Time-Savers

Make the cream cheese mixture ahead and store it in a covered container in the refrigerator for up to 3 days. You can also store the assembled sandwiches in the refrigerator for up to 4 hours.

# Open-Face Ham Sandwiches on Rye Crispbread

*184 calories, 24 g carbs*

| | |
|---|---|
| 1 | cup **Soft Yogurt Cheese** (page 107) |
| 1 | tablespoon **Dijon mustard** |
| ¾ | teaspoon **dried dillweed** or 2 teaspoons **chopped fresh dill** |
| ¼ | teaspoon **salt** |
| ⅛ | teaspoon **ground black pepper** |
| 8 | slices **rye crispbread** |
| ½ | cup **radishes** or other **sprouts** |
| 2 | **tomatoes,** cut into 8 slices |
| 16 | thin slices (¾ pound) **ham** |

In a small bowl, mix together the yogurt cheese, mustard, dill, salt, and pepper. Spread over the crispbread and cover with the radishes or sprouts. Arrange the tomatoes on top of the sprouts. Fold the ham to fit over the tomatoes.

**Makes 4 servings**

---

**Per serving:** 184 calories, 16 g protein, 24 g carbohydrates, 3 g fat, 1 g saturated fat, 29 mg cholesterol, 352 mg sodium, 4 g fiber

**Diet Exchanges:** ½ milk, 1 vegetable, 0 fruit, 1 bread, 2 meat, 0 fat

## Time-Saver

Make the flavored cheese ahead and store it in a covered container in the refrigerator for up to 5 days.

## HIDDEN ROADBLOCK to weight loss

### ARTIFICIAL SWEETENERS

Many of the people we talked with said that artificial sweeteners have kept them from losing weight. These sweeteners appear to stimulate the desire for real sweets and other foods containing sugar. There is even some preliminary research suggesting that aspartame may increase insulin levels like glucose does. And extra insulin means extra fat storage. Luckily, there are healthy alternatives for those who crave something sweet. See page 57 for sugar substitutes that do not have negative health effects.

# TWO-CHEESE PITA MELT
*230 calories, 19 g carbs*

| | |
|---|---|
| 4 | mini whole wheat pitas, split |
| 4 | teaspoons Dijon mustard |
| 4 | thin slices (3–4 ounces) mozzarella cheese |
| 4 | thin slices (3–4 ounces) Swiss cheese |
| 1⅓ | cups (4 ounces) sliced red or green cabbage |
| ½ | teaspoon dried oregano |
| ½ | teaspoon garlic powder (optional) |
| ¼ | teaspoon salt |
| ¼ | teaspoon ground black pepper |

Preheat the oven to 400°F.

Spread the inside of the pitas with the mustard and arrange the sliced mozzarella and Swiss cheeses inside.

In a bowl, toss the cabbage, oregano, garlic powder (if using), salt, and pepper. Stuff into the pitas. Arrange on a baking sheet and bake until the cheese melts and the edges of the pitas are crisp, 12 to 15 minutes.

**Makes 4 servings**

**Per serving:** 230 calories, 14 g protein, 19 g carbohydrates, 12 g fat, 7 g saturated fat, 36 mg cholesterol, 562 mg sodium, 3 g fiber

**Diet Exchanges:** 0 milk, ½ vegetable, 0 fruit, 1 bread, 1½ meat, 1½ fat

## ▶Flavor Tips

*Replace one of the cheeses with feta or goat cheese. Substitute cooked broccoli for the cabbage.*

# OPEN-FACE BACON-MUSHROOM MELT

*295 calories, 14 g carbs*

| | |
|---|---|
| 8 | strips turkey bacon or pork bacon, halved |
| 4 | slices light whole-wheat bread, toasted |
| 2 | tablespoons mayonnaise |
| 4 | mushrooms (4 ounces), thinly sliced |
| 1/8 | teaspoon salt |
| 1/4 | teaspoon ground black pepper |
| 4 | slices tomato |
| 1/3 | pound Muenster cheese, sliced |
| 1 | cup alfalfa or other sprouts (optional) |

Place a broiler rack farthest from the heat source and preheat the broiler (or a toaster oven).

Arrange the bacon in a large skillet and cook over low heat until crisp, turning occasionally, 5 to 8 minutes. Drain on a paper towel-lined plate.

Spread the bread with the mayonnaise and place on a baking sheet. Top with the mushrooms and season with the salt and pepper. Arrange the tomato over the mushrooms. Cover with slices of cheese and top with the bacon.

Broil until the cheese melts. Top with the sprouts (if using).

**Makes 4 servings**

---

**Per serving:** 295 calories, 16 g protein, 14 g carbohydrates, 20 g fat, 9 g saturated fat, 61 mg cholesterol, 897 mg sodium, 1 g fiber

**Diet Exchanges:** 0 milk, 1 vegetable, 0 fruit, ½ bread, 2 meat, 3½ fat

Flavor Tip

Substitute sliced turkey, chicken, ham, or tuna or salmon salad for the bacon.

Open-Face Bacon-Mushroom Melt

# PESTO CHICKEN SANDWICH WITH ROASTED PEPPERS

*328 calories, 23 g carbs*

| | |
|---|---|
| 4 | **whole wheat tortillas (6" diameter)** |
| ¼ | **cup jarred pesto sauce** |
| ½ | **pound sliced cooked chicken breast, warmed** |
| ¼ | **teaspoon salt** |
| ¼ | **teaspoon ground black pepper** |
| 2 | **jarred roasted red bell peppers (2 ounces), drained and halved** |
| 4 | **thin slices (3–4 ounces) mozzarella cheese** |
| 4 | **romaine lettuce leaves** |

Preheat the oven to 350°F.

Arrange the tortillas on a baking sheet. Spread the pesto evenly over each. Arrange the chicken in a row down the center of each tortilla and sprinkle with the salt and black pepper. Top with the roasted peppers and mozzarella.

Bake just until heated through and the cheese melts. Top with the lettuce, roll into a cylinder, and serve.

**Makes 4 servings**

---

**Per serving:** 328 calories, 29 g protein, 23 g carbohydrates, 16 g fat, 6 g saturated fat, 75 mg cholesterol, 598 mg sodium, 3 g fiber

**Diet Exchanges:** 0 milk, ½ vegetable, 0 fruit, 1½ bread, 3 meat, 2½ fat

## Smart-Carb Insider Tip

### DON'T GO NO-CARB

Carbohydrates are a key element in any healthy diet. But it's important to choose the right ones. Beans, for instance, are higher in carbs than many other foods, but they're also high in fiber and other beneficial nutrients, so there's no reason to avoid them altogether. Also, onions and carrots are slightly higher in carbohydrates than other vegetables. But that doesn't mean you have to substitute onion powder for real onions in your cooking. Doing so would only save you about 1 gram of carbohydrate for an equivalent amount used—and you would sacrifice a lot of delicious flavor! Be smart when making low-carb choices. It's just not practical to eliminate carbohydrates entirely.

Pesto Chicken Sandwich with Roasted Peppers

# Chickpea Pancakes with Spicy Vegetables

*214 calories, 19 g carbs*

| | |
|---|---|
| 1 | **cup chickpea flour** |
| ¾ | **cup + 1–2 tablespoons cold water** |
| 3 | **tablespoons olive oil** |
| 1 | **egg** |
| ¼ | **teaspoon salt** |
| ¼ | **teaspoon ground black pepper** |
| ½ | **small onion, finely chopped** |
| 1 | **zucchini (6 ounces), finely chopped** |
| 2 | **large cauliflower florets (6 ounces), finely chopped** |
| 1 | **teaspoon minced fresh ginger** |
| ⅛ | **teaspoon ground cumin** |
| ⅛ | **teaspoon crushed red pepper flakes** |
| 2 | **tablespoons tomato sauce** |
| 1 | **scallion, thinly sliced** |

Generously coat an 8" nonstick skillet with cooking spray and heat over medium heat. Place the flour in a bowl and gradually whisk in ¾ cup cold water to make a smooth batter the consistency of thin cream (add more water if needed). Whisk in 2 tablespoons of the oil, the egg, ⅛ teaspoon of the salt, and ⅛ teaspoon of the pepper.

Pour 3 tablespoons batter into the skillet and quickly tilt the skillet to coat the bottom with a thin layer of batter. Cook the first side until nicely browned, about 1 minute. Turn the pancake with a spatula and cook the second side for 30 to 45 seconds (it will look spotty). Slide the pancake onto a plate and cook the rest in the same fashion. Cover with foil to keep warm.

Heat the remaining 1 tablespoon oil in another skillet over medium heat. Stir in the onion, zucchini, cauliflower, ginger, cumin, and pepper flakes. Cover and cook, stirring occasionally, for 3 minutes. Stir in the tomato sauce, cover, and cook until the vegetables are tender and the liquid is evaporated, 10 to 15 minutes. Stir in the scallion, the remaining ⅛ teaspoon salt, and the remaining ⅛ teaspoon pepper.

Arrange a pancake, attractive side down, on a plate, and spoon the vegetables in a line one-third of the way from one edge and roll up. Assemble the remaining pancakes in the same manner.

**Makes 8**

---

**Per 2 pancakes:** 214 calories, 7 g protein, 19 g carbohydrates, 13 g fat, 2 g saturated fat, 47 mg cholesterol, 208 mg sodium, 3 g fiber

**Diet Exchanges:** 0 milk, 1 vegetable, 0 fruit, 1 bread, ½ meat, 2 fat

# CRISP TORTILLA WITH AVOCADO, BEANS, AND CHEESE

*347 calories, 24 g carbs*

**4**   corn tortillas (6" diameter)

**I**   can (15 ounces) pinto beans, drained, with 2 tablespoons liquid reserved

**¼**   teaspoon salt

**¼**   teaspoon onion powder

**¼**   teaspoon garlic powder

**I**   avocado, thinly sliced

**I**   jalapeño chile pepper, seeded and chopped (wear plastic gloves when handling)

**¾**   cup (4 ounces) shredded Muenster cheese

Preheat the oven to 350°F.

Arrange the tortillas on a baking sheet in a single layer. Bake, turning occasionally, until golden and crisp, 18 to 20 minutes.

Meanwhile, in a small saucepan over low heat, combine the beans, reserved liquid, ⅛ teaspoon of the salt, the onion powder, and the garlic powder. Cook until hot, 2 to 3 minutes.

Arrange the avocado slices over the tortillas. Season with the remaining ⅛ teaspoon salt and top with the jalapeño pepper. Spoon the beans over the top and cover with the cheese. Bake until the cheese melts, 5 to 8 minutes.

**Makes 4 servings**

---

**Per serving:** 347 calories, 17 g protein, 24 g carbohydrates, 21 g fat, 9 g saturated fat, 41 mg cholesterol, 610 mg sodium, 8 g fiber

**Diet Exchanges:** 0 milk, ½ vegetable, 0 fruit, 1½ bread, 1½ meat, 3 fat

▶ Flavor Tips

*Use jarred, pickled jalapeño peppers or canned, roasted chiles instead of fresh. You could also mash the avocado and spread it over the tortilla instead of slicing. For a soft taco, heat the tortillas just long enough to soften them, then fill and roll without baking.*

# TUNA SALAD IN LETTUCE WRAPPERS

*222 calories, 2 g carbs*

| | |
|---|---|
| 2 | cans (6 ounces each) water-packed tuna, drained |
| ¼ | cup mayonnaise |
| 1 | teaspoon Dijon mustard |
| 1 | tablespoon lemon juice |
| 2 | tablespoons finely chopped red bell pepper or celery |
| 2 | teaspoons capers, drained |
| 2 | scallions, thinly sliced |
| ¼ | teaspoon salt |
| ⅛ | teaspoon ground black pepper |
| 8 | large lettuce leaves, such as Boston or leaf |

In a bowl, flake the tuna with a fork. Stir in the mayonnaise, mustard, and lemon juice. Stir in the bell pepper or celery, capers, scallions, salt, and pepper. Arrange the lettuce on a work surface with the rib end closest to you and the "cup" facing up. Spoon the tuna salad onto the leaf near the rib end and roll to enclose.

**Makes 4 servings**

---

**Per serving:** 222 calories, 21 g protein, 2 g carbohydrates, 14 g fat, 3 g saturated fat, 46 mg cholesterol, 621 mg sodium, 1 g fiber

**Diet Exchanges:** 0 milk, ½ vegetable, 0 fruit, 0 bread, 3½ meat, 2 fat

## ▶Flavor Tips

*Substitute canned or cooked salmon or boneless, skinless sardines for the tuna. Add 1 chopped hard-cooked egg and ½ teaspoon dried dill to the salad. You can also add 3 or 4 thin slices of apple or a slice of Swiss or mozzarella cheese to the wrap.*

# chicken & turkey main dishes

# CHICKEN CUTLETS WITH ROASTED PEPPERS AND THYME

*284 calories, 6 g carbs*

| | |
|---|---|
| 4 | boneless, skinless chicken breast halves (6 ounces each) |
| ½ | teaspoon salt |
| ¼ | teaspoon ground black pepper |
| 2 | tablespoons lemon juice |
| ¼ | cup soy flour |
| 2 | tablespoons olive oil |
| ½ | cup prepared roasted red peppers, chopped |
| 1½ | teaspoons fresh thyme leaves or ½ teaspoon dried |

Arrange the chicken on a platter and season with the salt and black pepper. Drizzle with 1 tablespoon of the lemon juice. Coat with the flour.

Heat 1 tablespoon of the oil in a large nonstick skillet over medium heat. Add the chicken and cook until the first side is golden brown, 2 to 3 minutes. Turn, and brown the other side, 2 to 3 minutes. Reduce the heat to low, and cook until the chicken juices run clear and a meat thermometer registers 170°F, 12 to 15 minutes. Remove to a serving platter.

Add the remaining tablespoon of oil to the skillet and stir in the peppers, thyme, and remaining 1 tablespoon lemon juice. Heat for 30 to 60 seconds, stirring. Spoon over the chicken.

**Makes 4 servings**

---

**Per serving:** 284 calories, 41 g protein, 6 g carbohydrates, 10 g fat, 2 g saturated fat, 99 mg cholesterol, 457 mg sodium, 1 g fiber

**Diet Exchanges:** 0 milk, ½ vegetable, 0 fruit, 0 bread, 6 meat, 1½ fat

## Time-Saver

Make these easy chicken breasts ahead for a future dinner or lunch. They can be refrigerated for up to 2 days. To reheat, arrange in a baking dish and bake at 325°F until heated through, 10 to 15 minutes. Drizzle with a little oil and lemon juice to replace lost moisture.

# CHICKEN CUTLETS IN SHERRY SAUCE WITH GRAPES AND CUCUMBERS

*296 calories, 10 g carbs*

- **4**   **boneless, skinless chicken breast halves (6 ounces each)**
- ½   **teaspoon salt**
- ¼   **teaspoon ground black pepper**
- I   **tablespoon butter**
- **4**   **ounces (about 2 cups) red or green seedless grapes, halved**
- I   **cucumber (6 ounces), peeled, seeded, and finely chopped**
- ¼   **cup dry sherry or chicken broth**
- ⅓   **cup light cream**
- I   **teaspoon chopped fresh dill or ¼ teaspoon dried**

Season the chicken with ¼ teaspoon of the salt and the pepper. Melt the butter in a large nonstick skillet over medium-low heat. Add the chicken and cook, turning once or twice, until the juices run clear and a meat thermometer registers 170°F, 12 to 14 minutes.

Remove to a serving platter and cover with foil to keep warm. Stir the grapes and cucumber into the skillet, and cook for 1 minute. Add the sherry or broth and cream. Increase the heat to high and cook until thick enough to lightly coat the chicken, 3 to 4 minutes. Add the dill and the remaining ¼ teaspoon salt. Pour over the chicken.

**Makes 4 servings**

**Per serving:** 296 calories, 40 g protein, 10 g carbohydrates, 9 g fat, 5 g saturated fat, 119 mg cholesterol, 432 mg sodium, 1 g fiber

**Diet Exchanges:** 0 milk, ½ vegetable, ½ fruit, 0 bread, 5½ meat, 1½ fat

## Time-Saver

To halve grapes easily, line them up in the gutter of a cutting board and slice the whole row with a long knife.

Chicken Cutlets with Mozzarella, Peppers, and Olives

# Chicken Cutlets with Mozzarella, Peppers, and Olives

*411 calories, 4 g carbs*

| | |
|---|---|
| 4 | boneless, skinless chicken breast halves (6 ounces each) |
| 1 | tablespoon fresh basil or ½ teaspoon dried |
| 4 | slices (6 ounces) smoked or regular mozzarella cheese, each ¼" thick |
| ½ | teaspoon salt |
| ¼ | teaspoon ground black pepper |
| 2 | tablespoons olive oil |
| 1 | large green and/or red bell pepper, cut into thin strips |
| ⅓ | cup dry white wine or chicken broth |
| ⅓ | cup (3 ounces) pitted ripe kalamata olives, quartered lengthwise |

Preheat the oven to 350°F.

Make a 3"-long horizontal pocket in each chicken piece (cut through the thicker edge to ½" from the opposite edge). Sprinkle the basil over the cheese slices. Slip a cheese slice into each pocket, folding it as needed to fit. Close the edges and secure with toothpicks. Season with ¼ teaspoon of the salt and the pepper.

Heat the oil in a large oven-safe skillet over medium-low heat. Stir in the bell pepper and season with the remaining ¼ teaspoon salt. Cook, stirring occasionally, until lightly browned and starting to wilt,

4 to 5 minutes. Push the pepper to the edge of the skillet and add the chicken. Cook until lightly browned, 2 to 3 minutes. Turn, and arrange the pepper around the chicken. Add the wine or broth and the olives.

Bake, uncovered, until the chicken juices run clear and a meat thermometer registers 170°F, 12 to 15 minutes, turning once or twice.

Using a slotted spoon, remove the chicken to plates and top with the peppers and olives. There should be about 2 tablespoons of juices in the pan. If more, set the skillet over medium heat and cook until the liquid is reduced, 1 to 3 minutes. Spoon over the chicken.

**Makes 4 servings**

**Per serving:** 411 calories, 48 g protein, 4 g carbohydrates, 20 g fat, 7 g saturated fat, 132 mg cholesterol, 613 mg sodium, 1 g fiber

**Diet Exchanges:** 0 milk, ½ vegetable, 0 fruit, 0 bread, 7 meat, 3½ fat

## Time-Saver

*Prepare extra portions of these stuffed breasts for a quick lunch or supper. Store in a covered container in the refrigerator for up to 2 days. To reheat, arrange the chicken in a baking dish, cover, and bake at 350°F until heated through, 10 to 15 minutes. Drizzle with a little olive oil to replace lost moisture.*

*chicken and turkey main dishes*

# CHICKEN SCALLOPINI WITH SAGE AND CAPERS

*301 calories, 5 g carbs*

¼   **cup dry white wine or chicken broth**

⅓   **cup chicken broth**

1   **tablespoon drained capers**

4   **boneless, skinless chicken breast halves (6 ounces each), pounded to ¼" thick**

½   **teaspoon salt**

¼   **teaspoon ground black pepper**

¾   **teaspoon rubbed sage**

3   **tablespoons whole wheat flour**

4   **teaspoons olive oil**

1   **teaspoon cornstarch**

2   **teaspoons cold water**

1½   **tablespoons cold butter, cut in small pieces**

2   **teaspoons chopped fresh parsley (optional)**

In a small bowl, combine the wine or broth, broth, and capers.

Season the chicken with the salt, pepper, and sage. Lightly coat with the flour, patting off the excess. Heat a large nonstick skillet over high heat and add 2 teaspoons of the olive oil. Add 2 pieces of the chicken and cook until browned, 2 to 3 minutes. Reduce the heat to medium and turn the chicken. Cook until the chicken is no longer pink and the juices run clear, about 2 minutes. Remove to a platter and cover with foil to keep warm.

Add the remaining 2 teaspoons olive oil and cook the remaining chicken in the same fashion. Remove to the platter.

In a small cup, combine the cornstarch and water. Pour the caper mixture into the skillet and heat over medium heat. Bring to a simmer and whisk in the cornstarch mixture. Cook, whisking until thickened, about 15 seconds. Whisk in the butter and spoon the sauce over the chicken. Sprinkle with the parsley (if using).

**Makes 4 servings**

---

**Per serving:** 301 calories, 40 g protein, 5 g carbohydrates, 11 g fat, 4 g saturated fat, 110 mg cholesterol, 593 mg sodium, 1 g fiber

**Diet Exchanges:** 0 milk, 0 vegetable, 0 fruit, ½ bread, 5½ meat, 2 fat

## Time-Saver

Make these scallopini ahead or store the leftovers in a covered container in the refrigerator for up to 2 days. To reheat, arrange the scallopini in a baking dish, cover, and bake at 350°F until heated through, about 15 minutes. Drizzle with a little olive oil to replace lost moisture.

Chicken Scallopini with Sage and Capers

# CHICKEN THIGHS WITH LEMON-PEPPER SAUCE

*111 calories, 2 g carbs*

- **1** **tablespoon + 1 teaspoon lemon juice**
- **1** **tablespoon Worcestershire sauce**
- **2** **teaspoons olive oil**
- **1½** **teaspoons Dijon mustard**
- **¼** **teaspoon ground black pepper**
- **⅛** **teaspoon crushed red pepper flakes**
- **3–4** **tablespoons water**
- **4** **skinless chicken thighs (7 ounces each)**
- **¼** **cup chicken broth**

Preheat the oven to 375°F.

In a small bowl, mix the lemon juice, Worcestershire sauce, oil, mustard, black pepper, crushed pepper flakes, and 2 tablespoons of the water.

Place the chicken in an oven-safe skillet and pour the mustard mixture evenly over the top. Bake until the juices run clear and a meat thermometer registers 180°F, 25 minutes, adding 1 to 2 tablespoons water as necessary. Remove the chicken to a platter and keep warm.

Add the broth to the skillet and cook over medium heat until slightly reduced and thickened, 2 to 4 minutes. Spoon over the chicken.

**Makes 4 servings**

---

**Per serving:** 111 calories, 14 g protein, 2 g carbohydrates, 5 g fat, 1 g saturated fat, 57 mg cholesterol, 211 mg sodium, 0 g fiber

**Diet Exchanges:** 0 milk, 0 vegetable, 0 fruit, 0 bread, 2 meat, 1 fat

## Time-Savers

Make the mustard sauce up to 3 days ahead and store it in a covered container in the refrigerator. Or store the fully prepared chicken in a covered container in the refrigerator for up to 3 days. To reheat, arrange the chicken in a baking dish, cover, and bake at 350°F until heated through, about 15 minutes.

# ROASTED CHICKEN BREASTS WITH LEMON AND MUSTARD

*271 calories, 9 g carbs*

- **4**    **teaspoons Dijon mustard**
- **1**    **tablespoon + 1 teaspoon lemon juice**
- **1**    **large egg**
- **½**    **teaspoon Worcestershire sauce**
- **2**    **teaspoons olive oil**
- **¼**    **teaspoon salt**
- **¼**    **teaspoon ground black pepper**
- **8**    **tablespoons cornmeal**
- **4**    **boneless, skinless chicken breast halves (6 ounces each)**

Place the oven rack in the top position and preheat the oven to 450°F.

In a small bowl, mix 2 teaspoons of the mustard and the lemon juice.

In another small bowl, lightly beat the egg and stir in the Worcestershire sauce, oil, salt, pepper, and remaining 2 teaspoons mustard. Dip the chicken into the egg mixture. Press each piece into the cornmeal and turn to coat both sides. Place on a platter. Refrigerate, uncovered, for 10 to 60 minutes to help the cornmeal mixture stick.

Coat a baking sheet with cooking spray and preheat it on the upper rack of the oven for 5 minutes. Arrange the breasts, thickest side down, on the sheet and cook until golden brown, 8 to 10 minutes. Turn and cook until the juices run clear and a meat thermometer registers 170°F, 4 to 5 minutes. Drizzle with the lemon-mustard sauce.

**Makes 4 servings**

---

**Per serving:** 271 calories, 42 g protein, 9 g carbohydrates, 7 g fat, 1 g saturated fat, 152 mg cholesterol, 408 mg sodium, 1 g fiber

**Diet Exchanges:** 0 milk, 0 vegetable, 0 fruit, ½ bread, 6 meat, 1 fat

## ▶Flavor Tips

*Use 5 tablespoons cornmeal with 3 tablespoons grated Parmesan or Romano cheese. Add 1 teaspoon Dijon mustard to the egg mixture and serve the chicken with lemon wedges instead of the lemon-mustard sauce.*

Curried Chicken with Coconut

# CURRIED CHICKEN WITH COCONUT
*314 calories, 12 g carbs*

| | |
|---|---|
| 2 | teaspoons peanut oil or walnut oil |
| 1 | teaspoon butter |
| ½ | large onion, chopped |
| 2 | garlic cloves, minced |
| ¾ | cup chopped fennel bulb or celery |
| ½ | large green or red bell pepper, chopped |
| 4 | boneless, skinless chicken breast halves (6 ounces each), cut into 1" cubes |
| ½ | teaspoon salt |
| ¼ | teaspoon ground black pepper |
| 1 | tablespoon curry powder |
| ⅔ | cup canned crushed tomatoes |
| ½ | cup chicken broth |
| 3 | tablespoons chopped peanuts |
| 3 | tablespoons shredded unsweetened coconut |

Heat the oil and butter in a pot over medium heat until the butter is melted. Stir in the onion, garlic, fennel or celery, and bell pepper. Cover and cook just until translucent, stirring occasionally, 8 to 10 minutes.

Stir in the chicken, salt, and black pepper. Cook, stirring frequently, until the chicken has lost most of the pink color, 3 to 5 minutes. Sprinkle with the curry powder and cook for 30 seconds, stirring. Add the tomatoes and broth, and bring to a simmer. Cover, reduce the heat to medium-low, and cook until the chicken is tender, about 30 minutes.

Serve with the nuts and coconut for sprinkling on top.

**Makes 4 servings**

---

**Per serving:** 314 calories, 43 g protein, 12 g carbohydrates, 11 g fat, 3 g saturated fat, 101 mg cholesterol, 584 mg sodium, 4 g fiber

**Diet Exchanges:** 0 milk, 1 vegetable, 0 fruit, ½ bread, 5½ meat, 1½ fat

## ▶Flavor Tips

*Substitute turkey for the chicken. For a spicier dish, add ½ small chopped hot chile pepper or ground red pepper. You can also toast the coconut.*

# I Did It!

## Lynne Peters

After she moved to the South, Lynne's diet went steadily downhill. Eventually, she joined a 12-step weight-loss program and lost a few excess pounds. But it wasn't until she lowered her carbohydrate intake that Lynne's dress size shrank dramatically and her energy levels soared.

before

"In my thirties, I consistently gained weight for 5 years before I could admit that it was a problem for me. I had an endless list of excuses for not dealing with the extra pounds. Stress, turning 40, hormonal changes, quitting smoking, relocating to a new house, exercising less often, depression . . . the list went on and on. Although there was some truth in all of these reasons, I knew that they were just excuses.

"I wasn't always overweight.

**Weight lost:** 30 pounds
**Time kept off:** 3 years
**Weight-loss strategies:** Followed low-carbohydrate diet, ate three meals and two snacks a day, maintained support from a structured program
**Weight-maintenance strategies:** Follows low-carbohydrate diet, eats three meals and two snacks a day, maintains support from a structured program, exercises regularly

Throughout my twenties, I was 20 to 30 pounds *underweight* because I hardly ate and I exercised obsessively. In my thirties, I reached a normal weight for the first time in my life. Around that time, I began selling food for a living and—big surprise—eating a lot more. I got to know the best chefs in town and thoroughly enjoyed duplicating their recipes in my own kitchen. Whenever I noticed my clothes getting tight, I would immediately eat less or eat liquid meals. While I enjoyed a normal weight, I was absolutely clueless about what I was consuming in the way of calories and the nutritional balance of my overall diet.

"Then a job transfer took me to the South, and I began to eat what most people call comfort foods. My new diet consisted of heavily breaded, fried foods that were high in fat and starchy foods that were high in carbohydrates—the southern style of cooking.

"I ate fried chicken, fried fish, and fried shrimp. Ham, bacon, and sausage became favorites. I ate tons of pasta and mashed potatoes with gravy. And I loved eating cheese or anything with cheese sauce. I adopted a couch potato lifestyle, too. In no time, I was 50 pounds overweight. It seemed that no matter what I did, the pounds kept adding up. At that time, my lowest weight put me into a loose size 2 and my highest into a tight extra-large.

"During the worst of it, I would wake up in the middle of the night and be unable to go back to sleep unless I ate. That's when I admitted true defeat and turned to a 12-step program for help.

"When I started the program, I was encouraged to cut sugar out of my diet and eat three balanced meals a day. I contacted a nutritionist who gave me a food plan that included three meals and two snacks for a total of 1,700 calories a day. In 3 to 4 months, I lost 17 pounds and fit into a size 12. But the drawback was that I had daily slumps in my energy level—in both the afternoon and the early evening. I know now that refined carbohydrates were probably to blame. Because my energy was so low then, I decided to get a second opinion from another nutritionist. She suggested that I omit enriched flour products and sugar from my diet as well as reduce my overall carbohydrate intake. I began eating mostly low-carbohydrate foods like lean meats, fish, and beans, and eating lots of vegetables. I also avoided anything made with sugar or wheat.

"The difference is amazing. On this reduced-carbohydrate plan, it seems like my energy is boundless. Best of all, I am a size 10 and love it! I'm more active now, too. I do strength training for my legs and abs three times a week at the YMCA and I attend aerobics classes about three times a week. I have such a busy, enjoyable life these days, and my spirit feels alive thanks to eating the foods that are right for my body."

(continued)

chicken and turkey main dishes

# I D★id It! (cont.)

## LYNNE'S ON-THE-GO SKILLET CHICKEN

*378 calories, 14 g carbs*

- **1 pound boneless, skinless chicken pieces**
- **2 cups low-sugar marinara sauce**
- **1 cup (4 ounces) shredded Swiss cheese**
- **½ cup (6 ounces) grated Parmesan cheese**
- **4–5 cups fresh baby spinach or chopped spinach leaves**
- **1 cup water**
- **1 teaspoon dried Italian seasoning**
- **¼ teaspoon salt**

Coat a large, deep skillet or saucepan with cooking spray and heat over medium heat. Add the chicken and cook, turning occasionally, until lightly browned, about 5 minutes. Add the marinara sauce, Swiss, and Parmesan. Cook, stirring, until the cheese melts. Add the spinach, water, seasoning, and salt. Cook for 15 minutes. Serve immediately.

**Makes 4 servings**

---

**Per serving:** 378 calories, 39 g protein, 14 g carbohydrates, 18 g fat, 9 g saturated fat, 127 mg cholesterol, 962 mg sodium, 3 g fiber

**Diet Exchanges:** 0 milk, 0 vegetable, 0 fruit, 1 bread, 5 meat, 3 fat

## ►Flavor Tips

*Serve this over cooked brown rice or whole wheat pasta. For a nice presentation, cook the chicken without the cheese. At the end of cooking, sprinkle the cheese over the entire dish and broil until melted, about 2 minutes.*

# GRILLED ORANGE-ROSEMARY CHICKEN

*307 calories, 5 g carbs*

| | |
|---|---|
| 1 | **large orange** |
| 1 | **tablespoon olive oil** |
| 2 | **tablespoons minced fresh rosemary or 1½ teaspoons dried** |
| 1 | **teaspoon salt** |
| ½ | **teaspoon crushed red pepper flakes** |
| 3½ | **pounds skinless chicken parts** |

Grate the peel from the orange into a large, shallow dish. Squeeze the juice into the dish. Stir in the oil, rosemary, salt, and pepper flakes. Add the chicken and toss to evenly coat. Cover and refrigerate for at least 24 hours or up to 3 days.

Coat a grill rack with cooking spray. Preheat the grill. Arrange the chicken on the rack and cook until nicely browned, turning frequently, until the juices run clear and a meat thermometer registers 170°F for breasts and 180°F for other parts.

**Makes 4 servings**

---

**Per serving:** 307 calories, 47 g protein, 5 g carbohydrates, 10 g fat, 2 g saturated fat, 163 mg cholesterol, 761 mg sodium, 1 g fiber

**Diet Exchanges:** 0 milk, 0 vegetable, ½ fruit, 0 bread, 6½ meat, 1½ fat

## ▶Flavor Tips

*Rub the chicken with a halved garlic clove before marinating. Use chicken breasts only. When chilled, this chicken travels well for a brown-bag lunch.*

## HIDDEN ROADBLOCK to weight loss

### PRESCRIPTION MEDICATIONS

Some medications may hinder weight loss—or even cause you to gain weight. These especially include steroids, birth control pills, and some antidepressant drugs. One teenager we spoke with gained 60 pounds in 1 month when she started on an antidepressant. If you are on any medications, read the package insert or check with your doctor or pharmacist about any weight gain side effects. Don't stop taking your medication. But do discuss possible alternatives with your health care provider.

*chicken and turkey main dishes*

# SAUTÉED CHICKEN WITH SHALLOTS AND WHITE WINE

*353 calories, 4 g carbs*

| | |
|---|---|
| 3½ | **pounds skinless chicken parts** |
| ¾ | **teaspoon salt** |
| ¾ | **teaspoon dried thyme** |
| ¼ | **teaspoon ground black pepper** |
| 1 | **teaspoon olive oil** |
| 1 | **large shallot (2½ ounces), sliced** |
| 1 | **large garlic clove, minced** |
| 2 | **small tomatoes (4 ounces), coarsely chopped** |
| 3 | **tablespoons dry white wine or chicken broth** |
| 2 | **teaspoons cold butter, cut into 2–3 pieces** |
| 2 | **teaspoons chopped parsley** |

Season the chicken with ½ teaspoon of the salt, the thyme, and ⅛ teaspoon of the pepper. Heat the oil in a large nonstick skillet over medium-high heat. Add the chicken, thickest side down, and cook until golden, about 5 minutes. Turn and cook until golden, 3 to 4 minutes.

Reduce the heat to very low, pour off the fat, and arrange the shallot, garlic, and tomatoes around the chicken. Cook for 1 minute. Add the wine or broth, cover, and cook until the breast juices run clear and a meat thermometer registers 170°F, 12 to 15 minutes. Remove the breasts to a platter and cover loosely with foil to keep warm. Cook the remaining chicken, uncovered, until the juices run clear and a meat thermometer registers 180°F, 8 to 10 minutes. Remove to the platter and cover.

There should be about ½ cup of the wine or broth mixture left in the skillet. If there's more, boil it down over high heat, or if there's less, stir in water, wine, or broth to bring it to ½ cup. Bring to a boil over medium heat, and stir in the butter, parsley, the remaining ¼ teaspoon salt, and the remaining ⅛ teaspoon pepper. Pour over the chicken.

**Makes 4 servings**

---

**Per serving:** 353 calories, 40 g protein, 4 g carbohydrates, 18 g fat, 5 g saturated fat, 111 mg cholesterol, 561 mg sodium, 1 g fiber

**Diet Exchanges:** 0 milk, ½ vegetable, 0 fruit, 0 bread, 6 meat, 3 fat

## Time-Saver

*Make this dish ahead and refrigerate it in a covered container for up to 1 day or freeze it for up to 2 months. To reheat, thaw the chicken in the refrigerator overnight, then bake it in a covered baking dish at 375°F until heated through, about 10 minutes. Drizzle with a little olive oil to replace lost moisture.*

Sautéed Chicken with Shallots and White Wine

# Ginger-Soy Chicken Wings
*158 calories, 3 g carbs*

| | |
|---|---|
| 3 | tablespoons low-sodium soy sauce |
| 1 | teaspoon ground ginger |
| ½ | teaspoon garlic powder |
| ½ | teaspoon ground black pepper |
| 3½ | pounds chicken wings, first wing tip trimmed |
| 2 | tablespoons reduced-fat mayonnaise |
| 2 | tablespoons low-fat yogurt |
| 2 | tablespoons chopped fresh basil |
| 1 | teaspoon lime juice |

In a large bowl, mix the soy sauce, ginger, garlic powder, and pepper. Add the chicken and toss to coat. Cover and refrigerate for up to 24 hours.

Place the oven rack in the top position and preheat the oven to 450°F.

Coat a large rimmed baking sheet with cooking spray and preheat in the oven for 5 minutes. Arrange the chicken on the baking sheet, leaving at least ½" between each piece. Cook, turning once or twice, until the chicken is browned, the juices run clear, and a meat thermometer registers 180°F, 20 to 25 minutes.

In a small bowl, combine the mayonnaise, yogurt, basil, and lime juice. Serve with the chicken wings.

**Makes 6 servings**

---

**Per serving:** 158 calories, 20 g protein, 3 g carbohydrates, 7 g fat, 2 g saturated fat, 55 mg cholesterol, 369 mg sodium, 1 g fiber

**Diet Exchanges:** 0 milk, 0 vegetable, 0 fruit, 0 bread, 3 meat, 1 fat

## Time-Saver

Make the wings and sauce ahead and refrigerate them separately in covered containers for up to 2 days. To reheat, place the wings on a baking sheet and bake at 400°F until heated through, about 5 minutes. Serve with the sauce.

# Pan-Fried Chicken with Peppery Cream Gravy
*376 calories, 13 g carbs*

| | |
|---|---|
| 2 | cups buttermilk |
| 3 | large garlic cloves, crushed |
| ½ | teaspoon dried thyme |
| ½ | teaspoon dried marjoram |
| ¾ | teaspoon salt |
| ½ | teaspoon ground black pepper |
| 1 | bay leaf |
| ⅛ | teaspoon crushed red pepper flakes (optional) |
| 3½ | pounds skinless chicken parts, legs separated from thighs, and breasts cut into 2 pieces |
| ¼ | cup vegetable oil |
| ½ | cup + 2 teaspoons whole wheat flour |
| ½ | cup soy flour |
| 1 | cup half-and-half |

Pour the buttermilk into a zip-top bag or a baking dish large enough to hold the chicken in one layer. Stir in the garlic, thyme, marjoram, ¼ teaspoon of the salt, ¼ teaspoon of the black pepper, the bay leaf, and the pepper flakes (if using). Add the chicken pieces and turn to coat. Cover or seal and refrigerate for up to 24 hours.

Heat the oil in a large, heavy skillet over medium-low heat and preheat the oven to 250°F. Cover a baking sheet with a double layer of paper towels.

In a large, shallow bowl, combine ½ cup of the wheat flour, the soy flour, and ¼ teaspoon of the remaining salt. Remove the chicken from the marinade and dredge in the flour mixture. Place on a large platter or baking sheet. Discard the marinade.

When the oil is hot, add the chicken in batches and cook until deep brown on the first side, 6 to 8 minutes. Turn the pieces, cover the skillet loosely with foil, and cook until the chicken is golden, the juices run clear, and a meat thermometer registers 170°F for breasts and 180°F for other parts, 10 to 15 minutes for wings, 15 minutes for breasts, and 20 minutes for thighs and drumsticks. Remove to the lined baking sheet and keep warm in the oven.

Using a slotted spoon, remove most of the loose browned bits from the pan. Stir the remaining 2 teaspoons wheat flour into the oil left in the pan. Cook and stir for 1 minute. Gradually whisk in the half-and-half and cook, stirring, until thickened, 2 to 3 minutes. Season with the remaining ¼ teaspoon salt and remaining ¼ teaspoon pepper. Serve the gravy with the chicken.

**Makes 6 servings**

---

**Per serving:** 376 calories, 37 g protein, 13 g carbohydrates, 19 g fat, 5 g saturated fat, 125 mg cholesterol, 424 mg sodium, 3 g fiber

**Diet Exchanges:** 0 milk, 0 vegetable, 0 fruit, ½ bread, 5 meat, 3 fat

*chicken and turkey main dishes*

# CHICKEN PARMESAN
*366 calories, 16 g carbs*

### SAUCE

| | |
|---|---|
| **1** | **tablespoon olive oil** |
| **2** | **garlic cloves, minced** |
| **1¼** | **cups canned crushed tomatoes** |
| **2** | **tablespoons Italian-style tomato paste** |
| **¼** | **teaspoon salt** |
| **⅛** | **teaspoon ground black pepper** |

### CHICKEN

| | |
|---|---|
| **6** | **slices light whole wheat bread** |
| **2** | **large eggs** |
| **2** | **tablespoons water** |
| **4** | **boneless, skinless chicken breast halves (6 ounces each), pounded to ¼" thickness** |
| **¼** | **teaspoon salt** |
| **½** | **teaspoon ground black pepper** |
| **¼** | **cup soy flour or whole wheat flour** |
| **2** | **teaspoons olive oil** |
| **6** | **ounces shredded part-skim mozzarella cheese** |

**To make the sauce:** Heat the oil in a small saucepan over low heat. Stir in the garlic and cook, stirring frequently, for 30 seconds. Add the tomatoes, tomato paste, oregano, and basil. Cook until thick and rich, 12 to 15 minutes, stirring occasionally. Season with the salt and pepper. Cover and keep warm.

**To make the chicken:** While the sauce is cooking, preheat the oven to 250°F. Place the bread on a baking sheet and bake until completely dry, 10 to 12 minutes. Let cool slightly. Transfer the bread to a food processor and grind to make about 1 cup crumbs. Remove to a large plate. In a shallow bowl, lightly beat the eggs with the water. Season the chicken with the salt and pepper and coat with the flour. Dip into the egg mixture, then press into the crumbs to coat both sides.

Place the broiler rack 4" to 5" from the heat and preheat the broiler.

Heat 1 teaspoon of the oil in a large skillet over medium heat. Add 2 of the coated chicken breasts and cook until golden brown on the first side, 2 to 3 minutes. Turn and cook until no longer pink and the juices run clear, 2 to 3 minutes. Remove to a 13" × 9" baking dish. Repeat with the remaining teaspoon of oil and remaining chicken. Top with the sauce and sprinkle with the cheese. Broil just until the cheese melts, 1 to 2 minutes.

**Makes 6 servings**

**Per serving:** 366 calories, 40 g protein, 16 g carbohydrates, 16 g fat, 5 g saturated fat, 153 mg cholesterol, 572 mg sodium, 2 g fiber

**Diet Exchanges:** 0 milk, ½ vegetable, 0 fruit, 1 bread, 5 meat, 2 fat

Chicken Parmesan

# CHICKEN TETRAZZINI
*325 calories, 18 g carbs*

| | |
|---|---|
| 2 | teaspoons + 1 tablespoon butter |
| 1¼ | cups (4½ ounces) whole wheat rotelle or other short pasta |
| 2¼ | cups chicken broth |
| ¼ | cup dry white wine or chicken broth |
| 1 | bay leaf |
| 4 | boneless, skinless chicken breast halves (6 ounces each), cut crosswise into ¼"-wide strips |
| 6–8 | large mushrooms (8 ounces), sliced |
| ½ | cup heavy cream |
| 2 | tablespoons cornstarch |
| 2 | tablespoons + 1½ teaspoons water |
| ¼ | teaspoon ground black pepper |
| ⅔ | cup grated Parmesan cheese |

Place the oven rack in the top position and preheat the oven to 425°F. Butter an 8" × 8" baking dish with 2 teaspoons of the butter.

Cook the pasta according to package directions. Drain well and remove to a warm, large bowl.

Meanwhile, in a saucepan, combine 1½ cups of the broth, the wine or broth, and bay leaf. Bring to a simmer over medium heat. Add the chicken and cook just until cooked through, 8 minutes, stirring once. Using a slotted spoon, remove the chicken to the pasta bowl. Add the mushrooms to the broth and cook until tender, 3 to 4 minutes. Remove the mushrooms to the pasta bowl. Discard the bay leaf.

Measure the broth left in the pan. If it is more than 1½ cups, boil it until reduced. If it is less than 1½ cups, add more broth. Add the cream and simmer for 1 minute. Increase the heat to medium-high and bring to a boil. In a cup, combine the cornstarch and water. Whisk into the broth mixture and cook, whisking until thickened, 30 to 60 seconds. Season with the pepper and add to the pasta bowl. Toss to mix.

Pour into the prepared baking dish, spreading the mixture evenly. Sprinkle with the cheese, and dot with the remaining 1 tablespoon butter, cut into small pieces. Bake on the top rack until light brown and bubbling, 15 to 20 minutes.

**Makes 6 servings**

**Per serving:** 325 calories, 36 g protein, 18 g carbohydrates, 11 g fat, 6 g saturated fat, 95 mg cholesterol, 364 mg sodium, 2 g fiber

**Diet Exchanges:** 0 milk, 0 vegetable, 0 fruit, 1 bread, 5 meat, 1½ fat

▶Flavor Tips
*Use turkey, fish, or seafood in place of the chicken. Add a fresh herb, such as chopped parsley or basil, or scallions to the pasta mixture.*

# BROILED LEMON-THYME CHICKEN THIGHS
*109 calories, 1 g carbs*

| | |
|---|---|
| 3 | tablespoons lemon juice |
| 1 | tablespoon + 1½ teaspoons brandy or chicken broth |
| 1 | tablespoon chopped fresh thyme or 1 teaspoon dried |
| 1–2 | teaspoons olive oil |
| ¼ | teaspoon ground black pepper |
| 4 | skinless chicken thighs (7 ounces each) |
| ½ | teaspoon salt |

In a large bowl, stir together the lemon juice, brandy or broth, thyme, oil, and pepper. Add the chicken, turning to coat. Cover and refrigerate for up to 24 hours, mixing once or twice.

Place the broiler rack 5" to 6" from the heat source and preheat the broiler.

Coat a broiling pan with cooking spray.

Remove the chicken from the marinade, season with the salt, and arrange, skin side up, on the pan. Cook until well-browned, 8 to 10 minutes. Turn, and cook until the juices run clear and a meat thermometer registers 180°F, 8 to 10 minutes. (If the chicken is browning too much, reduce the oven temperature to 350°F and finish cooking with the oven door slightly ajar.)

**Makes 4 servings**

---

**Per serving:** 109 calories, 14 g protein, 1 g carbohydrates, 4 g fat, 1 g saturated fat, 57 mg cholesterol, 350 mg sodium, 0 g fiber

**Diet Exchanges:** 0 milk, 0 vegetable, 0 fruit, 0 bread, 2 meat, 1 fat

## Time-Savers

Make the chicken ahead and store it in a covered container in the refrigerator for up to 4 days. To reheat, arrange on a baking sheet and bake at 350°F until heated through, 8 to 10 minutes. You can also use extra portions in salads or sandwiches. Dress the salad with oil and vinegar and add chopped, crunchy raw vegetables, such as celery and radishes.

# GRILLED MARINATED CHICKEN KABOBS

*304 calories, 4 g carbs*

| | |
|---|---|
| ¼ | **cup soy sauce** |
| 4 | **teaspoons sesame oil** |
| I | **tablespoon minced fresh ginger** |
| 2 | **teaspoons Japanese mirin or dry sherry (optional)** |
| ¼–½ | **teaspoon hot-pepper sauce** |
| I½ | **pounds boneless, skinless chicken breast, cut into I½" cubes** |
| I | **zucchini (6 ounces), cut into I" pieces** |
| 4 | **large mushrooms (4 ounces), quartered** |

In a large bowl, mix together the soy sauce, sesame oil, ginger, mirin or sherry (if using), and hot-pepper sauce. Add the chicken, zucchini, and mushrooms and toss to coat. Cover and refrigerate for up to 2 hours.

Coat a grill rack with cooking spray. Preheat the grill.

Thread the chicken and vegetables onto skewers. Place on the grill rack and cook, turning occasionally, until browned and the chicken juices run clear, 12 to 15 minutes.

**Makes 4 servings**

**Per serving:** 304 calories, 39 g protein, 4 g carbohydrates, 14 g fat, 3 g saturated fat, 103 mg cholesterol, 630 mg sodium, 1 g fiber

**Diet Exchanges:** 0 milk, ½ vegetable, 0 fruit, 0 bread, 5½ meat, 2 fat

## Time-Savers

Make this dish ahead and store it in a covered container in the refrigerator for up to 3 days. To reheat, arrange the chicken and vegetables on a baking sheet or in a shallow baking dish and bake at 350°F until heated through, about 5 minutes. The chicken also makes a great salad or sandwich filling when tossed with finely chopped celery and apple and dressed with mayonnaise or Soft Yogurt Cheese (page 107).

# CHICKEN DRUMSTICKS ROASTED WITH HERBS

*228 calories, 4 g carbs*

| | |
|---|---|
| 2 | **tablespoons whole wheat flour** |
| 1 | **teaspoon dried oregano** |
| 1 | **teaspoon dried thyme** |
| ¾ | **teaspoon dried dillweed or dill seed** |
| ½ | **teaspoon dried savory or rosemary, crumbled** |
| ½ | **teaspoon paprika** |
| 1 | **teaspoon onion powder** |
| 1 | **teaspoon salt** |
| ½ | **teaspoon ground black pepper** |
| 8 | **skinless chicken drumsticks (about 5 ounces each)** |
| 1 | **tablespoon olive oil** |

Preheat the oven to 425°F. Generously coat a baking sheet with cooking spray.

In a bowl, mix together the flour, oregano, thyme, dill, savory or rosemary, paprika, onion powder, salt, and pepper. Coat the chicken with the oil. Sprinkle with the herbed flour, toss to coat, and press the flour onto the drumsticks.

Preheat the prepared baking sheet for 5 minutes. Arrange the drumsticks on the sheet, leaving at least 1" between each. Roast, turning occasionally, until the chicken is browned and crisp, the juices run clear, and a meat thermometer registers 180°F, 30 to 35 minutes.

**Makes 4 servings**

---

**Per serving:** 228 calories, 30 g protein, 4 g carbohydrates, 10 g fat, 2 g saturated fat, 97 mg cholesterol, 682 mg sodium, 1 g fiber

**Diet Exchanges:** 0 milk, 0 vegetable, 0 fruit, ½ bread, 4 meat, 1½ fat

## ▶Flavor Tips

*Instead of using all whole wheat flour, combine 1 tablespoon soy flour and 1 tablespoon whole wheat flour. Use 4 legs left in one piece or separate the thighs from the drumsticks. Serve with 1 cup tomato sauce.*

# ROAST CHICKEN WITH VEGETABLE-GRITS STUFFING

*448 calories, 16 g carbs*

| | |
|---|---|
| 3 | tablespoons olive oil |
| ½ | cup soy grits |
| 1¼ | cups chicken broth or water |
| 3 | celery ribs, finely chopped |
| ½ | small onion, finely chopped |
| 1 | carrot, finely chopped |
| ½ | large red bell pepper, finely chopped |
| ½ | teaspoon dried thyme |
| ¼ | teaspoon rubbed sage |
| ½ | teaspoon salt |
| ¼ | teaspoon ground black pepper |
| 1 | orange |
| 1 | whole chicken (4 pounds), rinsed and dried |
| 3 | whole sprigs rosemary |

Preheat the oven to 400°F.

Heat 1 tablespoon of the oil in a medium saucepan over medium heat. Add the grits and cook, stirring frequently, until light gold, 2 to 3 minutes. Stir in the broth or water. Cover and cook over low heat until the water is absorbed and the grits are tender, 15 to 20 minutes. Drain excess liquid, and remove to a large bowl.

Wipe out the saucepan. Heat 1½ tablespoons of the remaining oil in the pan over medium-low heat. Stir in the celery, onion, carrot, and bell pepper. Cover and cook until tender, stirring occasionally, about 10 minutes. Add to the grits along with the thyme, sage, ¼ teaspoon of the salt, and ⅛ teaspoon of the black pepper. Transfer to a 1-quart baking dish, cover, and set aside.

Grate the zest from the orange into a small bowl. Cut the orange in half and place inside the chicken cavity. Finely chop 1 of the rosemary sprigs and add to the zest. Place the remaining 2 whole rosemary sprigs inside the chicken cavity. Stir the remaining ¼ teaspoon salt and remaining ⅛ teaspoon pepper into the zest mixture. Carefully lift the skin from the chicken and place the zest mixture evenly underneath. Tie the ends of the legs together with string, and rub the remaining ½ tablespoon oil all over the skin. Place on a rack in a roasting pan and cook for 1 hour.

At the end of the hour, place the grits in the oven. Cook until the grits are heated through, the chicken juices run clear, and a meat thermometer registers 180°F (in the breast), about 15 minutes more. Let stand for 10 minutes before carving. Serve with the pan juices and grits. Remove chicken skin before eating.

**Makes 4 servings**

**Per serving:** 448 calories, 58 g protein, 16 g carbohydrates, 17 g fat, 3 g saturated fat, 145 mg cholesterol, 823 mg sodium, 3 g fiber

**Diet Exchanges:** 0 milk, 1 vegetable, ½ fruit, 0 bread, 7 meat, 3½ fat

# BROILED CHICKEN DIAVOLO
*286 calories, 1 g carbs*

| | |
|---|---|
| 1 | **tablespoon lemon juice** |
| 1 | **tablespoon olive oil** |
| 1 | **teaspoon salt** |
| ¾ | **teaspoon ground black pepper** |
| ¼–½ | **teaspoon ground red pepper** |
| 3½–4 | **pounds skinless chicken parts, legs separated from thighs, and breasts cut into 2 pieces** |

Place the broiler rack 5" to 6" from the heat source and preheat the broiler.

In a large bowl, combine the lemon juice, oil, salt, black pepper, and red pepper. Add the chicken and toss to coat.

Arrange the chicken, skin side up, on a broiling pan. Cook, turning, until the chicken is browned, the juices run clear, and a meat thermometer registers 170°F for breasts, 18 to 20 minutes, and 180°F for thighs and drumsticks, 26 to 30 minutes.

**Makes 4 servings**

**Per serving:** 286 calories, 40 g protein, 1 g carbohydrates, 12 g fat, 3 g saturated fat, 123 mg cholesterol, 683 mg sodium, 0 g fiber

**Diet Exchanges:** 0 milk, 0 vegetable, 0 fruit, 0 bread, 6 meat, 1 fat

## ▶Flavor Tip

*Add 1 teaspoon mixed dried herbs to the marinade, such as thyme, oregano, marjoram, and rosemary.*

## Smart-Carb Insider Tip
### DON'T GO FAT-FREE

We need fat in our diets—especially healthy fats like those found in olive oil, fish, and nuts. Feel free to eat these foods whenever you can. But avoid anything that says "hydrogenated," "partially hydrogenated," or "trans fat"—these terms are found on many processed food labels. Trans fats can be as harmful to your heart as saturated fat. To keep saturated fat low, use oil instead of butter when you can, choose mostly lean cuts of meat, and trim excess visible fat. When possible, microwave meats on high for a minute to drain away excess fat before you start cooking.

*chicken and turkey main dishes*

# GRILLED CHICKEN WITH MANGO SALSA

*259 calories, 11 g carbs*

1 **mango (12 ounces), peeled and finely chopped**

1 **tablespoon lime juice**

1 **tablespoon + 1½ teaspoons orange juice**

¼ **small onion, finely chopped**

¾ **teaspoon salt**

5 **or 6 drops hot-pepper sauce**

2 **teaspoons chopped fresh cilantro**

4 **boneless, skinless chicken breast halves (6 ounces each)**

1 **tablespoon vegetable oil**

½ **teaspoon salt**

¼ **teaspoon ground black pepper**

In a medium bowl, combine the mango, lime juice, orange juice, onion, salt, and pepper sauce. Stir in the cilantro.

Coat a grill rack with cooking spray. Preheat the grill. Rub the chicken with the oil and season with the salt and pepper. Place on the rack and grill, turning once, until the juices run clear and a meat thermometer registers 170°F, 10 to 12 minutes.

Serve topped with the salsa.

**Makes 4 servings**

---

**Per serving:** 259 calories, 40 g protein, 11 g carbohydrates, 6 g fat, 1 g saturated fat, 99 mg cholesterol, 855 mg sodium, 1 g fiber

**Diet Exchanges:** 0 milk, ½ vegetable, ½ fruit, 0 bread, 5½ meat, 1 fat

## ▶Flavor Tips

*Add finely chopped pineapple or papaya to the salsa. You can also cook the chicken in a grill pan. Refrigerate leftover chicken in a covered container for up to 3 days, then cut the chicken into strips and roll up with the salsa in whole wheat tortillas or large lettuce leaves.*

*Grilled Chicken with Mango Salsa*

Turkey Cutlets with Ham and Provolone

# TURKEY CUTLETS WITH HAM AND PROVOLONE
*362 calories, 4 g carbs*

4   turkey cutlets (4 ounces each)

½   teaspoon salt

¼   teaspoon ground black pepper

¼   cup soy flour

1   tablespoon olive oil

4   thin slices (3 ounces) ham, sliced in half

4   thin slices (4 ounces) provolone cheese, sliced in half

4   lemon wedges

Season the turkey with the salt and pepper. Coat in the flour and pat off the excess.

Heat the oil in a large nonstick skillet over high heat. Add the turkey and cook until browned on the first side, 2 to 3 minutes. Turn, reduce the heat to low, and layer the ham and cheese on top. Cover and cook until the turkey juices run clear and the cheese is melted, 2 to 3 minutes. Serve immediately with the lemon wedges for squeezing.

**Makes 4 servings**

**Per serving:** 362 calories, 39 g protein, 4 g carbohydrates, 20 g fat, 8 g saturated fat, 105 mg cholesterol, 479 mg sodium, 1 g fiber

**Diet Exchanges:** 0 milk, 0 vegetable, 0 fruit, ½ bread, 5½ meat, 2½ fat

## ►Flavor Tips

*Substitute Swiss or mozzarella cheese for the provolone and sprinkle the turkey with 1 tablespoon chopped fresh parsley or 1 teaspoon dried thyme. Serve with 2 tablespoons tomato sauce. If your skillet has an oven-safe handle, you can also broil the turkey after adding the ham and cheese.*

# TURKEY DRUMSTICK CURRY
*339 calories, 21 g carbs*

| | |
|---|---|
| 2½ | tablespoons butter |
| 1 | small onion, chopped |
| 1 | large celery rib, thinly sliced |
| 4 | turkey drumsticks (10–12 ounces each) |
| ½ | teaspoon salt |
| ½ | teaspoon ground black pepper |
| 1 | teaspoon minced fresh ginger (optional) |
| 2–3 | teaspoons curry powder |
| 2 | tablespoons whole wheat flour |
| 1 | cup chicken broth |
| 1 | bay leaf |
| 1 | tart apple (7 ounces), peeled and cut into chunks |
| 10 | dried apricots (2 ounces), quartered |

Preheat the oven to 325°F.

Melt the butter in a large pot or deep saucepan with oven-safe handles over low heat. Add the onion and celery. Cover and cook just until soft, about 5 minutes. Add the turkey and sprinkle with the salt, pepper, ginger (if using), curry powder to taste, and flour. Turn the turkey to cook the curry powder and flour, 1 to 2 minutes.

Add the broth and bay leaf, and bring to a simmer. Cover the pot, place in the oven, and cook for 45 minutes, turning the turkey twice. Add the apple and apricots. Cover and cook until the turkey is fork tender, 30 to 45 minutes more. Remove bay leaf before serving.

**Makes 4 servings**

---

**Per serving:** 339 calories, 37 g protein, 21 g carbohydrates, 12 g fat, 7 g saturated fat, 162 mg cholesterol, 729 mg sodium, 41 g fiber

**Diet Exchanges:** 0 milk, ½ vegetable, 1 fruit, ½ bread, 5 meat, 1½ fat

## Time-Saver

Make this curry ahead and keep it in a covered container in the refrigerator for up to 4 days. The flavor improves with age. To reheat, place it in a deep saucepan, cover, and bake at 325°F until heated through, 20 to 25 minutes. If the sauce is too thick, thin it with ¼ cup half-and-half, broth, or water.

# ROAST TURKEY BREAST WITH HERB RUB AND PAN JUICES

*203 calories, 1 g carbs*

- ¾ **teaspoon dried thyme**
- ¾ **teaspoon dried tarragon**
- ½ **teaspoon dried rosemary, crumbled**
- ½ **teaspoon garlic powder**
- ¾ **teaspoon onion powder**
- ¼ **teaspoon ground black pepper**
- 1 **teaspoon salt**
- 2 **teaspoons olive oil or melted butter**
- 1 **whole turkey breast on the bone (6 pounds)**
- ½ **cup dry white wine or chicken broth**
- ½ **cup chicken broth**
- 1½ **teaspoons cornstarch (optional)**
- 2 **teaspoons cold water (optional)**

Preheat the oven to 450°F.

In a small bowl, mix together the thyme, tarragon, rosemary, garlic powder, onion powder, pepper, and ¾ teaspoon of the salt. Rub the oil or butter over the turkey and sprinkle with the herb mixture, pressing it in lightly. Place in a roasting pan and in the oven, immediately reducing the heat to 350°F.

Roast, basting occasionally with the fat in the pan, until a meat thermometer inserted in the thickest part registers 170°F, about 2½ hours. Remove to a platter, reserve the pan juices, and let rest for 15 minutes before carving.

Pour the pan juices into a fat separator or glass measuring cup. Discard the fat that rises to the top and pour the juices (about 2 tablespoons) back into the roasting pan. Add the wine or broth and broth. Bring to a simmer, scraping up the browned bits that are stuck to the bottom of the pan. Cook for 3 minutes, adding any accumulated juices from the platter. Strain if desired, and season with the remaining ¼ teaspoon salt. Whisk the cornstarch with the water. Stir into the pan, cooking until slightly thickened, about 30 seconds.

**Makes 12 servings**

**Per serving:** 203 calories, 41 g protein, 1 g carbohydrates, 2 g fat, 0 g saturated fat, 113 mg cholesterol, 354 mg sodium, 0 g fiber

**Diet Exchanges:** 0 milk, 0 vegetable, 0 fruit, 0 bread, 5 meat, ½ fat

## Time-Saver

Extra portions of this turkey breast are wonderful warm or cold. Store the turkey and gravy in a covered container in the refrigerator for up to 3 days. To reheat, place turkey slices and enough sauce or broth just to cover in a skillet. Cover and heat over very low heat just until heated through, 3 to 4 minutes, without letting the mixture bubble (which would toughen the meat).

# Turkey Loaf
*368 calories, 12 g carbs*

½     **cup chicken broth or water**

¼     **cup quinoa, rinsed until the water runs clear**

I     **large egg**

I     **tablespoon + I½ teaspoons Worcestershire sauce**

I     **tablespoon + I½ teaspoons tomato paste**

I     **tablespoon Dijon mustard**

I     **small garlic clove, minced**

½     **teaspoon salt**

½     **teaspoon dried savory or dill**

½     **teaspoon ground allspice**

¼     **teaspoon ground black pepper**

I½     **pounds ground turkey breast**

2     **tablespoons (⅓ ounce) grated Parmesan cheese**

I     **large shallot (2 ounces) or 5 scallions, white part only, minced**

In a small saucepan, bring the broth or water to a boil over medium heat. Stir in the quinoa. Reduce the heat to low, cover, and cook until the liquid has evaporated and the quinoa is crunchy-tender, 12–15 minutes (if there is liquid left, drain it).

Preheat the oven to 375°F. Coat a baking dish or sheet with cooking spray.

In a large bowl, lightly beat the egg, Worcestershire sauce, tomato paste, mustard, garlic, salt, savory or dill, allspice, and pepper. Stir in the turkey, Parmesan, shallot or scallions, and the quinoa. Using a fork, lightly but thoroughly combine the ingredients. Gently form into a loaf about 7" × 4" and place on the baking sheet. Bake just until cooked through but still juicy and a meat thermometer registers 165°F, 45–50 minutes.

**Makes 4 servings**

**Per serving:** 368 calories, 43 g protein, 12 g carbohydrates, 15 g fat, 4 g saturated fat, 166 mg cholesterol, 757 mg sodium, 1 g fiber

**Diet Exchanges:** 0 milk, 0 vegetable, 0 fruit, 1 bread, 5½ meat, 2 fat

## ▶Flavor Tips

For best results, mix the meat as little as possible; the texture of an overhandled loaf can become mealy. To make a simple sauce, combine ¼ cup yogurt, 2 teaspoons lime juice, and 1 teaspoon honey; serve with the turkey.

Turkey Loaf

# Turkey Burgers Stuffed with Chiles and Cheese

*370 calories, 1 g carbs*

| | |
|---|---|
| 1 | large jalapeño chile pepper (1–1½ ounces); wear plastic gloves when handling |
| 1½ | pounds 7% low-fat ground turkey |
| 4 | slices (¾ ounce each) Muenster cheese |
| 4 | pimiento-stuffed green olives (1 ounce), sliced |
| ¾ | teaspoon salt |
| ¼ | teaspoon ground black pepper |
| 1 | tablespoon vegetable oil |

Place the jalapeño pepper in a small, heavy skillet. Cook over very low heat, turning frequently, until the skin has blistered and blackened slightly, 10 to 15 minutes. Remove from the skillet and let cool. Peel off the skin and cut the pepper in half lengthwise, discarding the stem, seeds, and ribs. Coarsely chop.

Divide the turkey into 8 pieces. Gently press or pat to make rounds about 4" in diameter. Layer the cheese, jalapeño pepper, and olives on the 4 patties. Top with the remaining 4 patties and pinch the edges together to seal. Season with the salt and pepper.

Heat the oil in a large nonstick skillet over medium-high heat. Add the patties and cook until browned on the first side, 3 to 4 minutes. Flip and cook until browned, 2 to 3 minutes more. Reduce the heat to low and cook until the meat is no longer pink but still juicy, 6 to 8 minutes.

**Makes 4 servings**

---

**Per serving:** 370 calories, 41g protein, 1 g carbohydrates, 21 g fat, 7 g saturated fat, 143 mg cholesterol, 799 mg sodium, 0 g fiber

**Diet Exchanges:** 0 milk, ½ vegetable, 0 fruit, 0 bread, 6 meat, 3 fat

## ▶Flavor Tips

Replace the jalapeño pepper with 2 to 3 tablespoons drained, chopped canned green chiles or chopped canned chipotles en adobo (smoked jalapeños in spicy sauce). Or omit the chiles altogether and serve the burgers topped with a tablespoon of hot salsa. Use salsa as the condiment instead of ketchup.

Turkey Burgers Stuffed with Chiles and Cheese

# BREADED TURKEY CUTLETS WITH OREGANO AND LEMON

*392 calories, 7 g carbs*

| | |
|---|---|
| **4** | **turkey cutlets (5–6 ounces each)** |
| **3** | **tablespoons lemon juice** |
| **2** | **tablespoons olive oil** |
| **2** | **tablespoons chopped parsley** |
| **1½** | **teaspoons sweet Hungarian paprika (optional)** |
| **1** | **teaspoon dried oregano** |
| **½** | **teaspoon ground black pepper** |
| **1** | **tablespoon butter** |
| **½** | **teaspoon salt** |
| **¼** | **cup whole wheat pastry flour or soy flour** |
| **2** | **large eggs** |
| **1** | **tablespoon water** |
| **4** | **lemon wedges** |

Drizzle the turkey with the lemon juice and 1 tablespoon of the oil, lightly rubbing to coat. Sprinkle both sides with the parsley, paprika (if using), oregano, and pepper, lightly patting in the seasonings. Cover and refrigerate for 1 hour to 2 hours.

Heat the butter and remaining 1 tablespoon oil in a large nonstick skillet over medium to medium-high heat. Sprinkle the salt over the turkey, and coat with the flour, patting lightly. In a shallow bowl, lightly beat the eggs with the water. Dip the turkey into the egg mixture.

When the butter froths, add the turkey. Cook until browned on the first side, 2 to 3 minutes. Turn, reduce the heat to low, and cook until the turkey juices run clear, 2 to 4 minutes. Serve with the lemon wedges.

**Makes 4 servings**

---

**Per serving:** 392 calories, 46 g protein, 7 g carbohydrates, 19 g fat, 6 g saturated fat, 221 mg cholesterol, 444 mg sodium, 1 g fiber

**Diet Exchanges:** 0 milk, 0 vegetable, 0 fruit, ½ bread, 6 meat, 3 fat

▶ Flavor Tip

*For the best flavor and texture when cooking breaded cutlets, allow the eggs to set before turning the cutlets.*

# beef, pork & lamb main dishes

# Pan-Fried Steak with Mushrooms

*344 calories, 3 g carbs*

| | |
|---|---|
| 1 | **boneless beef skirt steak or other cut (1½ pounds), ½"–¾" thick** |
| ½ | **teaspoon salt** |
| ½ | **teaspoon ground black pepper** |
| 2 | **tablespoons olive oil** |
| 10 | **ounces mushrooms, sliced** |
| 1 | **large garlic clove, minced** |
| 2 | **teaspoons minced fresh rosemary or ½ teaspoon dried and crumbled** |
| 2 | **tablespoons sour cream (optional)** |

Season the beef with ¼ teaspoon of the salt and ¼ teaspoon of the pepper. Heat 1 tablespoon of the oil in a large, heavy skillet over high heat. Add the steak and cook until deeply browned on the first side, 3 to 4 minutes. Turn, and cook until well-browned and a meat thermometer registers 160°F for medium, 5 to 7 minutes. Remove to a platter.

Pour off the excess fat and add the remaining 1 tablespoon oil to the pan. Reduce the heat to medium-low and add the mushrooms and garlic. Cook, stirring occasionally, until the juices start to flow, 2 to 4 minutes. Add the rosemary, the remaining ¼ teaspoon salt, and the remaining ¼ teaspoon pepper. Cook until the mushrooms' juices have evaporated, 2 to 3 minutes more. Remove from the heat. Stir in the sour cream (if using) and beef juices that have accumulated on the platter. Serve the beef with the mushrooms.

**Makes 4 servings**

---

**Per serving:** 344 calories, 38 g protein, 3 g carbohydrates, 19 g fat, 6 g saturated fat, 105 mg cholesterol, 370 mg sodium, 1 g fiber

**Diet Exchanges:** 0 milk, ½ vegetable, 0 fruit, 0 bread, 5 meat, 1 fat

## ▶Flavor Tips

*Choose a heavy skillet for this dish; its ability to hold heat will help create a good crust on the meat and melt the sour cream. You can replace the rosemary with oregano or another dried herb. Or add 1 finely chopped scallion to the mushrooms before serving. If you prefer, broil or grill the beef instead of pan-frying it; rub it with 1 to 2 teaspoons olive oil before cooking.*

# ROAST BEEF WITH ONION PAN JUICES
*329 calories, 3 g carbs*

| | |
|---|---|
| I | tablespoon olive oil |
| I | tablespoon red wine vinegar or apple cider vinegar |
| I | tablespoon Worcestershire sauce |
| ½ | teaspoon dried thyme |
| ¼ | teaspoon ground black pepper |
| | Pinch of ground cloves |
| I | onion, thinly sliced |
| I | bay leaf |
| I | boneless beef sirloin or rib-eye roast (2½ pounds) |
| ¼ | teaspoon salt |
| I | can (14½ ounces) beef broth |

In large glass bowl, mix together the oil, vinegar, Worcestershire sauce, thyme, pepper, and cloves. Stir in the onion and the bay leaf. Add the beef and turn to coat. Cover and refrigerate for at least 5 hours or up to 24 hours, turning the beef once or twice.

Preheat the oven to 500°F. Coat an 8" or 10" roasting pan or heavy, oven-safe skillet with cooking spray. Sprinkle the salt over the beef and place in the pan, fat side up. Roast for 5 minutes. Reduce the heat to 325°F and pour 1½ cups of the broth around the beef.

Cook until a meat thermometer registers 160°F for medium, 1¼–1½ hours, adding more broth if the liquid drops to less than ½". Remove from the oven, discard the bay leaf, and let rest for 15 minutes before carving.

Thinly slice and serve with the onions and pan juices.

**Makes 6 servings**

---

**Per serving:** 329 calories, 44 g protein, 3 g carbohydrates, 14 g fat, 5 g saturated fat, 128 mg cholesterol, 468 mg sodium, 0 g fiber

**Diet Exchanges:** 0 milk, ½ vegetable, 0 fruit, 0 bread, 6½ meat, 2 fat

## ▶Flavor Tips

If you substitute a less costly cut, such as rump or eye round, for the rib eye or sirloin, slice the roast as thinly as possible to avoid toughness. If you have leftovers, refrigerate them for up to 4 days. To reheat, dip thin slices in hot broth for a few seconds and serve immediately. Or serve the meat chilled as part of a main dish salad. You can also chop the meat to use as the basis of a hearty hash.

Grilled Rib-Eye Steak with Mustard Sauce

# GRILLED RIB-EYE STEAK WITH MUSTARD SAUCE

*252 calories, 1 g carbs*

| | |
|---|---|
| **3** | **tablespoons mayonnaise** |
| **1** | **tablespoon + 1½ teaspoons sour cream or plain yogurt** |
| **1** | **scallion, finely chopped** |
| **1** | **teaspoon dry mustard** |
| **¾** | **teaspoon soy sauce** |
| **½** | **teaspoon ground black pepper** |
| **¼** | **teaspoon salt** |
| **1** | **boneless beef rib-eye steak (1½ pounds), 1" thick, fat trimmed** |

In a small bowl, combine the mayonnaise, sour cream or yogurt, scallion, mustard, soy sauce, ¼ teaspoon of the pepper, and ⅛ teaspoon of the salt. Cover and let sit at room temperature.

Meanwhile, coat a grill rack with cooking spray. Preheat the grill. Season the beef with the remaining ¼ teaspoon pepper and the remaining ⅛ teaspoon salt. Grill, turning once, until a meat thermometer registers 160°F for medium, 11 to 13 minutes. Remove to a platter and let rest for 5 minutes.

Slice thinly and serve topped with the mustard sauce.

**Makes 6 servings**

---

**Per serving:** 252 calories, 24 g protein, 1 g carbohydrates, 16 g fat, 5 g saturated fat, 74 mg cholesterol, 230 mg sodium, 0 g fiber

**Diet Exchanges:** 0 milk, 0 vegetable, 0 fruit, 0 bread, 3½ meat, 3 fat

## Time-Savers

Leftovers can be covered and refrigerated for up to 3 days. Add to grain and vegetable salads for a quick main dish. Or serve leftover slices of steak wrapped around slices of Swiss cheese, sprouts, and sliced tomatoes for a sandwich or snack. The sauce can be made ahead and refrigerated for up to 5 days.

# FILET MIGNON WITH TOMATOES AND ROSEMARY

*303 calories, 3 g carbs*

| | |
|---|---|
| 2 | teaspoons soy sauce |
| 1½ | teaspoons Dijon mustard |
| 1½ | teaspoons minced fresh rosemary or ½ teaspoon dried and crumbled |
| ⅛ | teaspoon garlic powder |
| 2 | tomatoes (8 ounces), finely chopped |
| 2 | teaspoons olive oil |
| 4 | filet mignons (6 ounces each), each 1½" thick |
| ¼ | teaspoon salt |
| ½ | teaspoon ground black pepper |

Preheat the oven to 400°F.

In a bowl, combine the soy sauce, mustard, rosemary, and garlic powder. Fold in the tomatoes.

Heat the oil in a large, oven-safe, heavy skillet over high heat. Season the beef with the salt and pepper. Place in the pan and deeply brown the first side, 4 to 5 minutes. Turn and brown the second side for 30 seconds. Place the skillet in the oven and cook until a meat thermometer registers 145°F for medium rare, 12 to 14 minutes. Serve topped with the tomatoes.

**Makes 4 servings**

**Per serving:** 303 calories, 37 g protein, 3 g carbohydrates, 15 g fat, 5 g saturated fat, 105 mg cholesterol, 430 mg sodium, 1 g fiber

**Diet Exchanges:** 0 milk, ½ vegetable, 0 fruit, 0 bread, 5 meat, ½ fat

## ▶Flavor Tips

*Broil or grill the beef instead of pan-searing it; rub the meat with 1 to 2 teaspoons olive oil before cooking. Replace the beef with buffalo or ostrich fillets. Check with your local butcher or supermarket for these meats.*

*beef, pork, and lamb main dishes*

# LONDON BROIL MARINATED IN SOY SAUCE AND MUSTARD

*309 calories, 1 g carbs*

| | |
|---|---|
| 1 | **tablespoon dry mustard** |
| 4 | **teaspoons soy sauce** |
| 2 | **teaspoons red wine vinegar** |
| 1 | **teaspoon onion powder** |
| ¼ | **teaspoon garlic powder** |
| 1 | **tablespoon olive oil** |
| 1 | **top round or sirloin London broil (1½ pounds), 1" thick** |
| ¼ | **teaspoon salt** |
| ¼ | **teaspoon ground black pepper** |

In a small bowl, combine the mustard and soy sauce to make a paste. Stir in the vinegar, onion powder, and garlic powder. Whisk in the olive oil. Place the beef in a glass baking dish. Pour the mustard mixture over the beef and rub lightly to coat all over. Cover and refrigerate for 2 hours or up to 24 hours. Remove from the refrigerator 15 minutes before cooking.

Place the broiler rack 2" to 3" from the heat source and preheat the broiler. Coat a broiling pan with cooking spray.

Transfer the beef to the pan, and sprinkle with the salt and pepper. Broil until the top is browned, 4 to 5 minutes. Turn, and cook the second side until a meat thermometer registers 145°F for medium-rare, 3 to 4 minutes. Remove to a platter and let rest for 5 minutes. Thinly slice diagonally and serve with the juices on the platter.

**Makes 4 servings**

---

**Per serving:** 309 calories, 36 g protein, 1 g carbohydrates, 17 g fat, 6 g saturated fat, 85 mg cholesterol, 560 mg sodium, 0 g fiber

**Diet Exchanges:** 0 milk, 0 vegetable, 0 fruit, 0 bread, 5 meat, 3 fat

## Time-Saver

Refrigerate leftovers in a covered container for up to 3 days. Use them for superfast suppers and lunches. To reheat, slice the beef and dip into simmering beef broth until heated through, 30 to 60 seconds.

beef, pork, and lamb main dishes

# BRAISED SHORT RIBS OF BEEF WITH TURNIPS

*356 calories, 14 g carbs*

| | |
|---|---|
| 8 | pieces bone-in short ribs of beef (6 ounces each) |
| ½ | teaspoon salt |
| ½ | teaspoon ground black pepper |
| 1 | tablespoon olive oil |
| 1 | onion, chopped |
| 1 | small carrot, grated |
| 1 | tablespoon whole wheat flour |
| 1 | can (14½ ounces) beef broth |
| 1 | tablespoon tomato paste |
| ½ | teaspoon dried thyme |
| 1 | bay leaf |
| 2 | large turnips (16 ounces), peeled and cut into 1" cubes |

Preheat the oven to 325°F.

Season the beef with the salt and pepper. Heat the oil in a large pot with oven-safe handles over medium-high heat. Working in 2 batches, add the beef and cook until browned on all sides, turning often, 6 to 8 minutes. Remove to a plate.

Reduce the heat to medium-low and add the onion and carrot. Cover, and cook for 3 minutes, stirring occasionally. Stir in the flour and cook, stirring almost continuously, for 1 minute. Gradually stir in the broth to make a smooth sauce. Add the tomato paste, thyme, and bay leaf. Return the beef, along with any juices on the plate, to the pot. Bring to a simmer.

Cover, and bake until almost tender, 1¾ to 2 hours. Stir in the turnips, cover, and cook until both the turnips and the beef are tender, 20 to 30 minutes. Remove the beef and turnips to a platter. Skim the fat from the surface of the liquid. Discard the bay leaf. Return the beef and turnips to the pan and serve.

**Makes 4 servings**

**Per serving:** 356 calories, 30 g protein, 14 g carbohydrates, 20 g fat, 7 g saturated fat, 82 mg cholesterol, 780 mg sodium, 4 g fiber

**Diet Exchanges:** 0 milk, ½ vegetable, 0 fruit, 0 bread, 7 meat, 2 fat

## Time-Savers

Use 1¾ to 2 pounds of boneless stewing beef instead of the ribs and cook for about 1½ hours total. Store leftover ribs in a covered container in the refrigerator for up to 4 days or in the freezer for up to 2 months. To reheat, thaw the ribs in the refrigerator. Cook them in a pot (with oven-safe handles) over low heat for 2 to 3 minutes, then bake in the same pot at 325°F until heated through, 30 to 40 minutes.

Braised Short Ribs of Beef with Turnips

# CUBAN-STYLE BEEF PICADILLO
*340 calories, 17 g carbs*

| | |
|---|---|
| 1½ | **pounds extra-lean ground beef chuck** |
| 1 | **green bell pepper, finely chopped** |
| 4 | **scallions, finely chopped** |
| 10 | **pimiento-stuffed green olives, chopped** |
| 1¼ | **cups tomato sauce** |
| ¼ | **cup raisins** |
| 2 | **tablespoons drained capers** |
| 3 | **garlic cloves, minced** |
| 1½ | **teaspoons ground cumin** |
| 1 | **teaspoon dried oregano** |
| 2 | **tablespoons olive oil** |
| ¼ | **teaspoon salt** |
| ¼ | **teaspoon ground black pepper** |

In a large bowl, combine the beef, bell pepper, scallions, olives, tomato sauce, raisins, capers, garlic, cumin, and oregano. Cover, and set aside for 20 minutes.

Heat the oil in a large, deep skillet over medium heat. Add the beef mixture and cook, breaking it up with a spoon, until the beef is no longer pink, 3 to 4 minutes. Season with the salt and black pepper and cook, stirring occasionally, until it starts to brown in the pan, 25 to 30 minutes.

**Makes 4 servings**

---

**Per serving:** 340 calories, 35 g protein, 17 g carbohydrates, 17 g fat, 4 g saturated fat, 90 mg cholesterol, 1,040 mg sodium, 3 g fiber

**Diet Exchanges:** 0 milk, 1½ vegetable, ½ fruit, 0 bread, 5 meat, 2½ fat

▶**Flavor Tips**

*Serve the ground meat mixture in prepared, crisp taco shells or over cooked brown rice with hot sauce. You could also serve the mixture with warmed corn tortillas to make soft, rolled tacos. Or make a casserole out of the cooked picadillo by mixing it with cooked brown rice or tortilla chips; top with 1 to 1½ cups grated Muenster cheese and bake at 375°F until the cheese melts, about 5 minutes.*

# SPICY MEATBALLS WITH COCONUT MILK
*213 calories, 2 g carbs*

| | |
|---|---|
| 1½ | **pounds extra-lean ground beef chuck** |
| 3 | **scallions, finely chopped** |
| 1 | **large egg, lightly beaten** |
| 5 | **tablespoons + ½ cup coconut milk** |
| 2 | **tablespoons soy sauce** |
| 1½ | **teaspoons ground cumin** |
| ¾ | **teaspoon ground coriander seed** |
| ½ | **teaspoon crushed red pepper flakes** |

Place the broiler rack 3" to 4" from the heat source and preheat the broiler. Coat a large broiling pan with cooking spray.

In a large bowl, combine the beef, scallions, egg, 5 tablespoons of the coconut milk, 1½ tablespoons of the soy sauce, the cumin, coriander, and red pepper flakes.

Gently form into 1½"-diameter meatballs and arrange on the prepared pan, placing at least ½" apart. Broil (without turning) just until browned on the top, no longer pink inside, and the juices run clear. Remove to a serving dish and discard the fat drippings in the pan. Pour the remaining ½ cup coconut milk into the pan and scrape up the browned bits, stirring until dissolved. Season with the remaining ½ tablespoon soy sauce and pour over the meatballs.

**Makes 6 servings**

---

**Per serving:** 213 calories, 24 g protein, 2 g carbohydrates, 12 g fat, 8 g saturated fat, 95 mg cholesterol, 389 mg sodium, 1 g fiber

**Diet Exchanges:** 0 milk, 0 vegetable, 0 fruit, 0 bread, 4 meat, 2 fat

## ▶Flavor Tips

*Spoon over a bed of whole wheat couscous, brown rice, or buckwheat noodles (soba). Or tuck sliced meatballs into a sandwich. Sprinkle with 1 tablespoon chopped fresh cilantro just before serving.*

*Beef Kabobs with Yogurt and Spices*

# BEEF KABOBS WITH YOGURT AND SPICES
*356 calories, 14 g carbs*

½  cup low-fat plain yogurt

1  tablespoon soy sauce

1  tablespoon lemon juice

1  teaspoon ground ginger

1  teaspoon ground cumin

¼  teaspoon ground black pepper

1½  pounds boneless beef sirloin, fat trimmed, cut into 1½" cubes

2  small red and/or green bell peppers (6 ounces), cut into 1½" squares

In a large bowl, combine the yogurt, soy sauce, lemon juice, ginger, cumin, and black pepper. Add the beef, tossing to coat. Cover and refrigerate for 6 to 8 hours.

Coat a grill rack with cooking spray. Preheat the grill. Thread the beef onto skewers, alternating with the bell peppers. Place the skewers on the grill rack and cook, turning to brown all sides, until no longer pink and a meat thermometer registers 145° for medium rare, 12 to 15 minutes.

**Makes 4 servings**

---

**Per serving:** 356 calories, 30 g protein, 14 g carbohydrates, 20 g fat, 8 g saturated fat, 82 mg cholesterol, 780 mg sodium, 4 g fiber

**Diet Exchanges:** 0 milk, 2 vegetable, 0 fruit, 0 bread, 4 meat, 3½ fat

## Time-Savers

Make extra portions of this dish for a speedy supper or lunch later in the week. Store in a covered container in the refrigerator for up to 4 days. To reheat, arrange on a baking sheet or in a shallow baking dish and bake at 400°F until heated through, about 5 minutes. Serve with a little steak sauce to replace lost moisture. To make sandwiches, tuck the beef into whole wheat pitas or roll into tortillas.

beef, pork, and lamb main dishes

# MEAT LOAF WITH WALNUTS
*222 calories, 7 g carbs*

| | |
|---|---|
| I | large egg, lightly beaten |
| 2 | tablespoons Worcestershire sauce |
| ¼ | cup tomato paste |
| ½ | teaspoon dried thyme |
| ½ | teaspoon salt |
| ½ | teaspoon ground black pepper |
| ½ | onion, finely chopped |
| I | large garlic clove, minced |
| ⅔ | cup (1½ ounces) ground walnuts |
| I½ | pounds extra-lean ground beef chuck |
| ½ | cup tomato sauce |

Preheat the oven to 375°F.

In a large bowl, combine the egg, Worcestershire sauce, tomato paste, thyme, salt, and pepper. Add the onion, garlic, walnuts, and beef. Using a fork, gently combine the meat with the seasonings. Form into a loaf and place in a 9" × 5" × 3" loaf pan. Spread the tomato sauce evenly over the top. Bake until the juices run clear and a meat thermometer registers 160°F, 50 to 55 minutes. Pour off the fat in the pan and slice the loaf.

**Makes 6 servings**

---

**Per serving:** 222 calories, 26 g protein, 7 g carbohydrates, 11 g fat, 3 g saturated fat, 95 mg cholesterol, 430 mg sodium, 1 g fiber

**Diet Exchanges:** 0 milk, 1 vegetable, 0 fruit, 0 bread, 4 meat, 1½ fat

## Time-Savers

*A rotary hand cheese grater is excellent for grinding nuts. Store leftover meat loaf in a covered container in the refrigerator for up to 3 days. To reheat, slice the meat loaf and arrange it in a baking dish. Add a few tablespoons of broth, cover, and bake at 350°F until heated through, 8 to 12 minutes.*

# ITALIAN-STYLE BEEF BURGERS
*252 calories, 2 g carbs*

| | |
|---|---|
| 1½ | **pounds extra-lean ground beef chuck** |
| 5 | **tablespoons (1 ounce) grated Romano cheese** |
| 2 | **tablespoons (1 ounce) pine nuts, toasted and finely chopped** |
| ½ | **teaspoon salt** |
| 1 | **teaspoon dried oregano** |
| ¾ | **teaspoon garlic powder** |
| ¼ | **teaspoon ground black pepper** |

Place the broiler rack 2" to 3" from the heat source and preheat the broiler.

Place the beef in a large bowl and break into pieces. Add the Romano, nuts, salt, oregano, garlic powder, and pepper. Using a fork, gently combine the beef and seasonings. Divide the meat into 4 even pieces and gently form into burgers approximately 4" in diameter and 1" thick.

Place on a broiling pan, and cook until the top is browned, 4 to 6 minutes. Turn, and cook until done and a meat thermometer registers 160°F for medium, 4 to 6 minutes.

**Makes 4 servings**

---

**Per serving:** 252 calories, 37 g protein, 2 g carbohydrates, 12 g fat, 5 g saturated fat, 98 mg cholesterol, 482 mg sodium, 0 g fiber

**Diet Exchanges:** 0 milk, 0 vegetable, 0 fruit, 0 bread, 5 meat, 1½ fat

## ▶Flavor Tips

*For burgers with the best texture, handle the ground meat as little as possible. You can grill or pan-fry the burgers instead of broiling them. Top with a slice of mozzarella cheese during the last minute of cooking if desired. Serve with 1 cup of tomato sauce. To make an easy meat sauce for whole wheat pasta, break the burgers into pieces and cook them in 3 cups tomato sauce for 3 to 5 minutes.*

# BOLOGNESE SAUCE FOR PASTA

*216 calories, 9 g carbs*

| | |
|---|---|
| 2 | tablespoons olive oil |
| 1 | celery rib, finely chopped |
| 1 | small carrot, finely chopped |
| 1 | small onion, finely chopped |
| 2 | garlic cloves, minced |
| ¾ | pound extra-lean ground beef chuck |
| ¼ | pound ground pork |
| ¾ | cup dry red wine or beef broth |
| 1 | cup crushed tomatoes |
| 1 | cup beef broth |
| 2 | tablespoons tomato paste |
| 1 | teaspoon dried oregano |
| ½ | teaspoon salt |
| ¼ | teaspoon ground black pepper |
| 2 | tablespoons chopped basil or parsley (optional) |

Heat the oil in a saucepan over medium-low heat. Stir in the celery, carrot, onion, and garlic, and cook until the celery and onion are soft, 4 to 6 minutes. Add the ground beef and ground pork, increase the heat to medium-high, and cook, stirring and breaking the meat up, until the meat is no longer pink, 3 to 5 minutes. Add the wine or broth and reduce the heat to medium so that the wine or broth simmers. Cook until reduced to about ⅓ cup liquid, 12 to 15 minutes.

Stir in the tomatoes, broth, tomato paste, and oregano. Partially cover and cook until thick, 40 to 45 minutes. Season with the salt, pepper, and basil or parsley (if using).

**Makes 6 servings**

**Per serving:** 216 calories, 16 g protein, 9 g carbohydrates, 11 g fat, 3 g saturated fat, 44 mg cholesterol, 455 mg sodium, 2 g fiber

**Diet Exchanges:** 0 milk, 2 vegetable, 0 fruit, 0 bread, 2 meat, 2 fat

## ▶Flavor Tips

*Replace the pork with sweet or hot Italian sausage. Serve this wonderfully rich sauce with 2 to 3 ounces of quinoa pasta or whole wheat pasta per person, tossing half of it with the pasta, and spooning the other half on top. Top each serving with 1 tablespoon grated Parmesan cheese per person.*

# PORK SCALLOPINI WITH LEMON-CAPER SAUCE AND DILL
*291 calories, 5 g carbs*

8–12 **pieces (2–3 ounces each) pork scallopini, each ¼" thick**

¼ **teaspoon salt**

½ **teaspoon ground black pepper**

½ **cup soy flour**

1 **tablespoon olive oil**

2 **tablespoons butter, cut into small pieces**

½ **cup chicken broth**

2 **tablespoons lemon or lime juice**

1 **tablespoon capers, drained**

1 **tablespoon chopped fresh dill or 1 teaspoon dried dillweed**

Season the pork with the salt and pepper. Coat with the flour, patting off the excess.

Heat 1½ teaspoons of the oil and 1½ teaspoons of the butter in a large skillet over medium heat. When the butter froths, add as much of the pork as will fit in the skillet without crowding. Cook until browned on the first side, 1 to 2 minutes. Turn, and cook the second side just until the juices run clear, 2 to 3 minutes. Remove to a platter. Use the remaining 1½ teaspoons oil and 1½ teaspoons of the remaining butter to cook the remaining pork in the same manner. Cover loosely with foil to keep warm.

Reduce the heat to medium and add the broth, lemon or lime juice, and capers to the pan. Cook the sauce until reduced to about ¼ cup, 3 to 4 minutes. Stir in the remaining 1 tablespoon butter and pour over the scallopini. Sprinkle with the dill or dillweed.

**Makes 4 servings**

---

**Per serving:** 291 calories, 28 g protein, 5 g carbohydrates, 18 g fat, 7 g saturated fat, 92 mg cholesterol, 439 mg sodium, 2 g fiber

**Diet Exchanges:** 0 milk, 0 vegetable, 0 fruit, ½ bread, 4 meat, 3 fat

## Time-Saver

Make a double batch for later use. Store extras in a covered container in the refrigerator for up to 3 days. To reheat, arrange on a baking sheet coated with cooking spray and top with slices of mozzarella cheese. Bake at 375°F until heated through and the cheese melts, 5 to 10 minutes.

# PORK CHOPS WITH APPLE CIDER, WALNUTS, AND PRUNES

*296 calories, 11 g carbs*

| | |
|---|---|
| 4 | pork chops (6–8 ounces each), each ¾" thick |
| ½ | teaspoon salt |
| ½ | teaspoon ground rubbed sage |
| ¼ | teaspoon ground black pepper |
| 1 | tablespoon walnut oil or olive oil |
| 6 | pitted prunes (2–3 ounces), chopped |
| ½ | cup apple cider |
| ¼ | cup dry white wine or apple cider |
| 2 | tablespoons chopped walnuts |

Season the pork with the salt, sage, and pepper. Heat the oil in a large skillet over medium-high heat. Add the pork and cook until browned on the first side, 4 to 5 minutes. Hold the chops on the edges and cook the edges until browned if desired, 1 to 2 minutes. Turn and cook until the second side is browned, about 1 minute. Reduce the heat to low and pour off any fat in the skillet. Add the prunes, cider, and wine or cider, and cook until the juices run clear and a meat thermometer registers 155°F, turning once or twice, 12 to 15 minutes.

Remove to plates and spoon the prunes on top. There should be about 2 tablespoons juices left in the pan. If more, cook over low to medium heat until reduced. Spoon the juices over the pork and sprinkle with the walnuts.

**Makes 4 servings**

---

**Per serving:** 296 calories, 22 g protein, 11 g carbohydrates, 17 g fat, 5 g saturated fat, 60 mg cholesterol, 342 mg sodium, 1 g fiber

**Diet Exchanges:** 0 milk, 0 vegetable, 1 fruit, 0 bread, 3 meat, 2 fat

## Time-Saver

Leftovers of these chops make for quick suppers and lunches. Store the leftovers in a covered container in the refrigerator for up to 3 days. To reheat, arrange in a baking dish and drizzle with apple cider to replace lost moisture. Cover and bake at 375°F until heated through, about 15 minutes.

Pork Chops with *Apple Cider, Walnuts, and Prunes*

# SMOKED PORK CHOPS IN MUSTARD-WINE SAUCE

*363 calories, 8 g carbs*

| | |
|---|---|
| 1 | cup apple cider |
| ⅓ | cup Madeira, Marsala, port wine, or apple cider |
| 1 | tablespoon Dijon mustard |
| 1 | teaspoon dried thyme |
| 1 | teaspoon vegetable oil |
| 4 | smoked pork chops (6–8 ounces each), each ¾"–1" thick |
| ⅛ | teaspoon ground black pepper |

In a small bowl, mix the cider, wine or cider, mustard, and thyme.

Heat the oil in a large skillet over medium-high heat. Add the pork and cook until browned on the first side, about 2 minutes. Turn and cook until browned on the second side, about 1 minute. Pour off any fat in the skillet, reduce the heat to low, and pour the cider mixture over the pork.

Cook, turning once, until the juices run clear and a meat thermometer registers 160°F, 5 to 7 minutes. There should be about 2 tablespoons of lightly thickened juices in the pan. If there is more, remove the pork to a platter and cook the pan juices over medium heat until reduced to 2 tablespoons, 5 to 7 minutes. Pour the juices over the chops and sprinkle with the pepper.

**Makes 4 servings**

**Per serving:** 363 calories, 43 g protein, 8 g carbohydrates, 14 g fat, 4 g saturated fat, 82 mg cholesterol, 2,196 mg sodium, 0 g fiber

**Diet Exchanges:** 0 milk, 0 vegetable, ½ fruit, 0 bread, 6 meat, 2½ fat

## ▶Flavor Tips

*Stir 2 teaspoons finely chopped scallions into the sauce before pouring over the chops. Substitute a thick ham steak for the smoked pork chops. To reduce sodium, use 4 center rib pork chops in place of the smoked chops.*

# BROILED BONELESS PORK CHOPS WITH SPICY LENTILS

*500 calories, 23 g carbs*

| | |
|---|---|
| 1 | **tablespoon olive oil** |
| ½ | **onion, chopped** |
| 1 | **small green bell pepper, chopped** |
| ½ | **cup (4 ounces) brown lentils, rinsed and drained** |
| 1¼ | **cups vegetable broth or chicken broth** |
| 2 | **tablespoons raisins** |
| ¼ | **teaspoon ground black pepper** |
| ⅛ | **teaspoon ground red pepper** |
| 4 | **boneless pork chops (6 ounces each), each ¾" thick** |
| ½ | **teaspoon paprika** |
| ¼ | **teaspoon salt** |

Heat 1 teaspoon of the oil in a saucepan over medium heat. Add the onion and bell pepper and cook, stirring occasionally, for 4 minutes. Stir in the lentils. Add the broth and bring to a simmer. Cover and cook, without stirring, until the lentils are tender but still retain their shape, 35 to 40 minutes. Drain any excess liquid. Fold in the raisins, a pinch of the black pepper, and the red pepper. Cover and keep warm.

Place the broiler rack 3" to 4" from the heat source and preheat the broiler. Coat a broiler pan with cooking spray. Rub the pork with the remaining 2 teaspoons oil, and season with the paprika, salt, and remaining black pepper. Arrange on the prepared pan. Broil, turning once, until lightly browned and a meat thermometer registers 160°F for medium, 12 to 14 minutes. Arrange on a bed of lentils and serve hot.

**Makes 4 servings**

---

**Per serving:** 500 calories, 62 g protein, 23 g carbohydrates, 17 g fat, 5 g saturated fat, 136 mg cholesterol, 573 mg sodium, 9 g fiber

**Diet Exchanges:** 0 milk, 0 vegetable, ½ fruit, 1 bread, 8 meat, 2½ fat

▶Flavor Tips

*Substitute bone-in pork chops or lamb chops. Use currants or other dried fruit instead of the raisins. Garnish with 1 tablespoon chopped parsley or fresh mint.*

Roast Pork Tenderloin with Sherry, Cream, and Almonds

# ROAST PORK TENDERLOIN WITH SHERRY, CREAM, AND ALMONDS

*330 calories, 5 g carbs*

| | |
|---|---|
| 1 | **pork tenderloin (1½–1¾ pounds)** |
| ¾ | **teaspoon paprika** |
| ½ | **teaspoon ground black pepper** |
| ¼ | **teaspoon salt** |
| 1 | **tablespoon whole wheat flour** |
| 1 | **tablespoon olive oil** |
| 2 | **large shallots or ¾ onion, sliced** |
| ⅓ | **cup dry sherry or chicken broth** |
| ⅓ | **cup + 1–2 tablespoons chicken broth** |
| ¼ | **cup half-and-half** |
| 2 | **tablespoons (1 ounce) sliced almonds or 24 whole almonds, toasted** |

Preheat the oven to 350°F.

Season the pork with the paprika, pepper, and salt. Coat with the flour.

Heat the oil in a 13" × 8" heavy roasting pan or a large, heavy oven-safe skillet over medium heat. Add the pork and cook until lightly browned on all sides, 4 to 5 minutes. Scatter the shallots or onion in the pan and cook, stirring once or twice, for 1 minute. Pour the sherry or broth and ⅓ cup of the broth around the meat.

Roast, turning once or twice, until the juices run clear and a meat thermometer registers 155°F for medium, 25 to 30 minutes. If the pan juices appear to be less than 3 to 4 tablespoons, add 1 to 2 tablespoons more broth.

Remove to a platter and let rest for 10 minutes. Place the pan of juices over medium-low heat and stir in the half-and-half. Cook until slightly thickened, 1 to 2 minutes, stirring once or twice. Slice the pork on a slight diagonal and sprinkle with the almonds. Serve the cream sauce on the side.

**Makes 4 servings**

**Per serving:** 330 calories, 37 g protein, 5 g carbohydrates, 16 g fat, 5 g saturated fat, 120 mg cholesterol, 322 mg sodium, 1 g fiber

**Diet Exchanges:** 0 milk, 0 vegetable, 0 fruit, ½ bread, 4½ meat, 1½ fat

# BARBECUED COUNTRY SPARERIBS

*304 calories, 5 g carbs*

| | |
|---|---|
| 2 | **cans (6 ounces each) tomato juice** |
| ⅓ | **cup apple cider or peach nectar** |
| 2 | **tablespoons Worcestershire sauce** |
| 1½ | **tablespoons apple cider vinegar** |
| 2 | **teaspoons Dijon mustard** |
| ¾ | **teaspoon ground black pepper** |
| ½ | **teaspoon chili powder** |
| ¼ | **teaspoon salt** |
| ¼ | **teaspoon garlic powder** |
| 8 | **boneless pork country spareribs (3½ ounces each), fat trimmed** |

Preheat the oven to 350°F.

In a roasting pan or baking dish, combine the tomato juice, cider or nectar, Worcestershire sauce, vinegar, mustard, pepper, chili powder, salt, and garlic powder. Add the pork and coat completely.

Cover with foil and bake, turning once, until very tender, 1¾ to 2 hours. If the sauce thickens too much, thin it with a little hot water.

**Makes 6 servings**

---

**Per serving:** 304 calories, 32 g protein, 5 g carbohydrates, 16 g fat, 6 g saturated fat, 102 mg cholesterol, 488 mg sodium, 0 g fiber

**Diet Exchanges:** 0 milk, ½ vegetable, 0 fruit, 0 bread, 4½ meat, 1 fat

## Time-Saver

*These flavorful ribs can be made ahead of time. Store them in a covered container in the refrigerator for up to 4 days or in the freezer for up to 2 months. To reheat, thaw the ribs in the refrigerator overnight, then arrange them in a shallow baking dish. Add a small amount of water and bake at 325°F until heated through, about 20 minutes.*

# PORK STEW WITH CABBAGE
*361 calories, 15 g carbs*

1½    **pounds boneless pork stew meat, cut into 1½" cubes**

½    **teaspoon ground black pepper**

2    **tablespoons olive oil**

1    **small onion, chopped**

1    **garlic clove, minced**

1½    **tablespoons red wine or apple cider vinegar**

1    **tablespoon whole wheat flour**

1    **can (14½ ounces) beef broth**

1    **can (14½ ounces) crushed tomatoes**

1    **teaspoon dried thyme**

1    **teaspoon dried oregano**

1    **bay leaf**

½    **head green cabbage (10 ounces total), cored and cut into 1" pieces**

Preheat the oven to 350°F.

Season the pork with the pepper. Heat 1½ tablespoons of the oil in a heavy pot with oven-safe handles over medium-high heat. Working in batches, add the pork and cook until browned on all sides, 5 to 6 minutes, removing the pieces to a plate when they are done.

Reduce the heat to medium and add the remaining ½ tablespoon oil. Stir in the onion and garlic. Cover and cook, stirring occasionally, until the vegetables begin to soften, about 5 minutes. Stir in the wine or vinegar, return the meat to the pot, and stir in the flour. Cook, stirring frequently, for 1 minute. Add the broth, tomatoes, thyme, oregano, and bay leaf. Bring to a simmer, cover the pot, and transfer to the oven. Bake for 1 hour. Stir in the cabbage and bake for another 20 to 30 minutes, or until the pork is fork-tender. Discard the bay leaf before serving.

**Makes 4 servings**

**Per serving:** 361 calories, 40 g protein, 15 g carbohydrates, 15 g fat, 4 g saturated fat, 107 mg cholesterol, 725 mg sodium, 4 g fiber

**Diet Exchanges:** 0 milk, 3 vegetable, 0 fruit, 0 bread, 5 meat, 2½ fat

## ▶Flavor Tips

*Add ½ teaspoon dried dillweed to the seasonings or sprinkle with ½ teaspoon caraway seeds or 2 teaspoons chopped fresh dill when serving. Use lamb instead of pork. Use tomato juice or tomato sauce instead of crushed tomatoes.*

# ROAST PORK LOIN WITH ORANGE JUICE AND WHITE WINE

*344 calories, 6 g carbs*

¾    teaspoon paprika

¾    teaspoon garlic powder

½    teaspoon onion powder

½    teaspoon dried oregano

½    teaspoon salt

¼    teaspoon ground black pepper

I    center cut loin of pork on the bone (2½–2¾ pounds), trimmed of visible fat

¾    cup orange juice

¾    cup white wine or nonalcoholic white wine

Preheat the oven to 450°F.

In a small bowl, combine the paprika, garlic powder, onion powder, oregano, salt, and pepper. Pat over the top of the pork and place in a small, heavy roasting pan or heavy, oven-safe skillet.

Roast for 10 minutes. Reduce the heat to 325°F and pour the orange juice and wine around the pork (not over). Roast until the juices run clear and a meat thermometer registers 160°F for medium, 1 to 1¼ hours.

Remove from oven and let rest for 15 minutes in the pan. There should be about ⅓ cup juices left in the pan. If there is more, remove the pork to a platter and cook over medium-low heat until the juices are reduced to ⅓ cup. Thinly slice the pork and spoon the pan juices over the top.

**Makes 4 servings**

---

**Per serving:** 344 calories, 41 g protein, 6 g carbohydrates, 13 g fat, 5 g saturated fat, 115 mg cholesterol, 390 mg sodium, 0 g fiber

**Diet Exchanges:** 0 milk, 0 vegetable, ½ fruit, 0 bread, 5½ meat, 2½ fat

*beef, pork, and lamb main dishes*

# PEPPERED VENISON FILLETS
*315 calories, 7 g carbs*

| | |
|---|---|
| 1½ | teaspoons butter, softened |
| 1 | tablespoon whole wheat flour |
| 8 | venison loin medallions (3 ounces each), each ¾"–1" thick |
| 1½ | teaspoons ground black pepper |
| ¼ | teaspoon salt |
| 2–3 | tablespoons vegetable oil or walnut oil |
| 1 | can (14½ ounces) beef broth or mushroom broth |
| 2 | tablespoons plum or red currant fruit spread, at room temperature (optional) |

In a small bowl, cream the butter and flour to make a paste.

Season the venison with the pepper and the salt. Heat 1 tablespoon of the vegetable or walnut oil in a large, heavy skillet over medium-high heat. Slip in as much venison as will fit without crowding. Cook until browned on the first side, 3 to 4 minutes. Turn, reduce the heat to medium, and cook until a meat thermometer registers 145° for medium-rare, 3 to 4 minutes, turning once. If necessary to prevent sticking, add up to ½ tablespoon additional oil during cooking. Remove to a platter. Cook the remaining venison with the remaining oil and remove to the platter. Cover with foil to keep warm.

There should be about ⅔ cup liquid in the pan. If there is more, cook until reduced to ⅔ cup. Reduce the heat to low and add the broth (it should boil from the heat of the pan). Using a wooden spoon or spatula, scrape up the browned bits stuck to the bottom. Whisk in the butter-flour paste to make a smooth sauce and cook until slightly thickened, 30 to 60 seconds (if too thin, cook 1 to 2 minutes more). Whisk in the fruit spread (if using). Serve over the venison.

**Makes 4 servings**

---

**Per serving:** 315 calories, 40 g protein, 7 g carbo-hydrates, 13 g fat, 3 g saturated fat, 148 mg choles-terol, 621 mg sodium, 0 g fiber

**Diet Exchanges:** 0 milk, 0 vegetable, 0 fruit, ½ bread, 5½ meat, 2 fat

Flavor Tip

*Use beef tenderloin instead of venison.*

# LAMB CUBES WITH GARLIC AND MUSHROOMS

*308 calories, 5 g carbs*

| | |
|---|---|
| 1½ | **pounds lamb cubes** |
| ½ | **teaspoon salt** |
| ½ | **teaspoon ground black pepper** |
| 2 | **tablespoons olive oil** |
| 1¼ | **pounds mushrooms, sliced** |
| 4 | **cloves garlic, minced** |
| ¼ | **teaspoon crushed hot-pepper flakes** |
| 1 | **cup red wine or beef broth** |
| 1 | **can (14½ ounces) beef broth** |
| 3 | **tablespoons sour cream** |
| 1 | **tablespoon chopped parsley (optional)** |

Season the lamb with the salt and pepper. Heat the oil in a large, oven-safe skillet over medium-high heat. Add the lamb and cook, stirring frequently, until lightly browned, 2 to 3 minutes. Stir in the mushrooms, garlic, and pepper flakes. Cook until the mushrooms begin to lose their liquid, 3 to 4 minutes. Add the wine or broth and the broth and bring to a boil. Reduce the heat to medium-low and simmer until the lamb is tender, 1 to 1¼ hours.

Remove from the heat and stir in the sour cream until evenly distributed. Sprinkle with the parsley (if using).

**Makes 4 servings**

---

**Per serving:** 308 calories, 27 g protein, 5 g carbohydrates, 17 g fat, 6 g saturated fat, 85 mg cholesterol, 502 mg sodium, 1 g fiber

**Diet Exchanges:** 0 milk, 1 vegetable, 0 fruit, 0 bread, 3½ meat, 3½ fat

## ▶Flavor Tips

*You could easily add more vegetables to this dish. Add 1 sliced celery rib and 2 sliced carrots along with the mushrooms. Garnish with chopped fresh basil instead of the parsley.*

# LAMB KABOBS WITH MUSHROOMS AND TOMATOES
*261 calories, 3 g carbs*

| | |
|---|---|
| **2** | **tablespoons + 1½ teaspoons soy sauce** |
| **¾** | **teaspoon sesame oil** |
| **½** | **teaspoon dry mustard** |
| **¼** | **teaspoon garlic powder** |
| **½** | **teaspoon ground ginger** |
| **1½** | **pounds lamb cubes** |

**12–16 cherry tomatoes (6 ounces)**

**12–16 small mushrooms (4 ounces)**

In a bowl, combine the soy sauce, oil, mustard, garlic powder, and ginger. Add the lamb, tomatoes, and mushrooms, tossing to coat. Cover and refrigerate for up to 10 hours, tossing once or twice.

Coat a grill rack with cooking spray. Preheat the grill. Thread the lamb, tomatoes, and mushrooms onto skewers. Place on the rack and cook, turning to brown all sides, until a meat thermometer registers 160°F for medium, 10 to 14 minutes.

**Makes 4 servings**

**Per serving:** 261 calories, 38 g protein, 3 g carbohydrates, 10 g fat, 3 g saturated fat, 112 mg cholesterol, 689 mg sodium, 1 g fiber

**Diet Exchanges:** 0 milk, ½ vegetable, 0 fruit, 0 bread, 5 meat, 1½ fat

## ▶ Flavor Tips

*Broil instead of grilling. For color, add thick zucchini slices along with the tomatoes and mushrooms. Top each serving with a tablespoon of low-fat plain yogurt. Serve over cooked whole wheat couscous or brown rice.*

## Smart-Carb Insider Tip
### LOOK YOUR BEST

As you shrink out of them, donate your clothes to a charity or have them altered. As you reach weight-loss milestones, treat yourself to new wardrobe accessories. It's important to look your best each day. If you look good, you will feel good about yourself.

Lamb Chops with Olives

# Lamb Chops with Olives

*334 calories, 2 g carbs*

| | |
|---|---|
| 8 | rib lamb chops (about 3½ ounces each), each 1" thick |
| ½ | teaspoon salt |
| 1 | tablespoon chopped fresh oregano or 1 teaspoon dried |
| ¼ | teaspoon ground black pepper |
| 2 | tablespoons olive oil |
| 8 | pitted ripe kalamata olives, chopped |
| 2 | tablespoons balsamic vinegar |
| ⅛ | teaspoon crushed red pepper flakes |

Season the lamb with the salt, oregano, and pepper. Heat 1 tablespoon of the oil in a large, heavy skillet over medium-high heat. Add the lamb and cook until browned on both sides and a meat thermometer registers 160°F for medium-rare, 4 to 6 minutes. (If necessary, cook in 2 batches, removing the first batch to a platter and covering loosely with foil while cooking the second.) Remove to a platter.

Pour off the fat. Add the olives, vinegar, pepper flakes, and the remaining 1 tablespoon oil. Bring to a simmer over medium heat, stirring and scraping up the browned bits stuck on the bottom of the skillet. Pour over the lamb.

**Makes 4 servings**

---

**Per serving:** 334 calories, 30 g protein, 2 g carbohydrates, 22 g fat, 6 g saturated fat, 98 mg cholesterol, 183 mg sodium, 1 g fiber

**Diet Exchanges:** 0 milk, 0 vegetable, 0 fruit, 0 bread, 4½ meat, 1½ fat

## ▶Flavor Tips

*For evenly browned chops, choose a heavy skillet, such as cast iron or heavy-gauge aluminum. You can use loin lamb chops or a 1"-thick lamb steak cut from the leg instead of the rib chops. Or use veal or pork chops.*

# LAMB BURGERS WITH TOMATOES AND FETA CHEESE

*329 calories, 5 g carbs*

| | |
|---|---|
| 1¼ | **pounds ground lamb** |
| 2 | **garlic cloves, minced** |
| 1 | **tablespoon fresh chopped rosemary or 1 teaspoon dried and crumbled** |
| ½ | **teaspoon ground black pepper** |
| ¼ | **teaspoon salt** |
| 1 | **cup canned crushed tomatoes** |
| | **Pinch of salt** |
| ⅓ | **cup crumbled feta cheese, at room temperature** |

In a large bowl, combine the lamb, garlic, rosemary, pepper, and salt. Using a fork, break up the meat and mix in the seasonings. Form 4 patties approximately 4" in diameter and 1" thick.

Heat a large, heavy skillet over medium-high heat until drops of water skip over the surface. Add the patties. Cook until the first side has a brown crust, 4 to 5 minutes. Turn and cook until the second side is lightly browned, 1 to 2 minutes. Pour off fat, reduce the heat to low, and pour the tomatoes around the patties (the tomatoes will boil briefly). Cook until a meat thermometer registers 160°F for medium, about 10 minutes, turning once more. Season the tomatoes with a pinch of salt and spoon over the burgers. Sprinkle with the cheese.

**Makes 4 servings**

---

**Per serving:** 329 calories, 27 g protein, 5 g carbohydrates, 22 g fat, 10 g saturated fat, 105 mg cholesterol, 512 mg sodium, 1 g fiber

**Diet Exchanges:** 0 milk, 1 vegetable, 0 fruit, 0 bread, 3½ meat, 2½ fat

## HIDDEN ROADBLOCK to weight loss

### LACK OF ACTIVITY

It's no secret that exercise can help you get more fit. But here's why. Increased physical activity helps you maintain or improve your metabolic rate. That means that the more active you are, the more efficient your body becomes at burning calories. Strength training or other muscle-building activities are especially helpful. Your body will burn additional calories to sustain its increased muscle mass. Keep in mind that if you are weight training, you may not see much change in your weight. That's because muscle weighs more than fat does. However, you should notice a significant difference in your body definition and size. If exercise isn't currently in your life, try to get a little more active each week.

# fish & shellfish main dishes

# BAKED COD WITH LEMON AND OLIVE OIL
*174 calories, 1 g carbs*

| | |
|---|---|
| 4 | cod fillets (6 ounces each), each 1" thick |
| 1½ | tablespoons lemon juice |
| 1 | tablespoon olive oil |
| 2 | garlic cloves, minced, or ¼ teaspoon garlic powder |
| ½ | teaspoon dried thyme |
| | Pinch of salt |
| ⅛ | teaspoon ground black pepper |
| ¼ | teaspoon sweet Hungarian paprika (optional) |

Preheat the oven to 400°F.

Arrange the fillets in a 13" × 9" baking dish. Drizzle with the lemon juice and oil, and sprinkle with the garlic, thyme, salt, and pepper. Sprinkle with the paprika (if using), and lightly rub it in. Bake until the flesh is completely opaque but still juicy, 15 to 20 minutes. Serve with the pan juices spooned over the top.

**Makes 4 servings**

---

**Per serving:** 174 calories, 30 g protein, 1 g carbohydrates, 5 g fat, 1 g saturated fat, 73 mg cholesterol, 185 mg sodium, 0 g fiber

**Diet Exchanges:** 0 milk, 0 vegetable, 0 fruit, 0 bread, 4½ meat, ½ fat

## ▶Flavor Tips

*Use the mild white fish that is most fresh at your market. You can use haddock, hake, red snapper, or sole instead of cod. Serve this dish over a bed of whole grains or noodles to soak up the milky juices. Bake with 2 tablespoons chopped roasted red peppers or serve sprinkled with 1 tablespoon chopped fresh basil.*

Baked Cod with Lemon and Olive Oil

# BREADED BAKED COD WITH TARTAR SAUCE

*268 calories, 14 g carbs*

TARTAR SAUCE

½    **cup reduced-fat mayonnaise**

1½    **tablespoons lemon juice**

1    **tablespoon finely chopped dill or sweet pickles**

2    **teaspoons mustard**

2    **teaspoons capers, drained and chopped**

2    **teaspoons chopped parsley (optional)**

FISH

2    **slices whole wheat bread, torn**

2    **eggs**

1    **tablespoon water**

1¼    **pounds cod or scrod fillet, cut into 1"–1½" pieces**

½    **teaspoon salt**

¼    **teaspoon ground black pepper**

**To make the tartar sauce:** In a small bowl, combine the mayonnaise, lemon juice, pickles, mustard, capers, and parsley (if using). Cover and refrigerate.

**To make the fish:** Preheat the oven to 400°F. Coat a baking sheet with cooking spray.

Place the bread in a food processor and process into fine crumbs. Place in a shallow bowl. In another bowl, beat the eggs with the water. Season the fish with the salt and pepper. Dip into the eggs, then into the bread crumbs. Place on the prepared baking sheet. Generously coat the breaded fish with cooking spray. Bake until opaque inside, 10 minutes.

Serve with the tartar sauce.

**Makes 4 servings**

---

**Per serving:** 268 calories, 30 g protein, 14 g carbohydrates, 10 g fat, 2 g saturated fat, 174 mg cholesterol, 734 mg sodium, 1 g fiber

**Diet Exchanges:** 0 milk, 0 vegetable, 0 fruit, 1 bread, 3½ meat, ½ fat

## Time-Savers

*Cook a few extra pieces of fish, as the leftovers make quick hot or cold meals. Store extra portions in a covered container in the refrigerator for up to 3 days. To reheat, arrange on a baking sheet and bake at 400°F until heated through, 3 to 5 minutes. Or to serve cold, make a sandwich by wrapping the fried fish in lettuce leaves or whole wheat pitas spread with tartar sauce. The tartar sauce can be stored in a covered container in the refrigerator for up to a week.*

# BAKED SEA BASS WITH SOY SAUCE AND SESAME OIL

*201 calories, 2 g carbs*

2    **tablespoons soy sauce**

1    **tablespoon rice vinegar**

2    **teaspoons sesame oil**

4    **Chilean sea bass fillets (6 ounces each), each 1" thick**

⅛    **teaspoon ground black pepper**

2    **scallions, thinly sliced on a bias**

Preheat the oven to 400°F.

In a small bowl, combine the soy sauce, vinegar, and oil. Arrange the fish in a baking dish that's large enough to fit the fish comfortably in a single layer. Pour the soy sauce mixture over the fish and turn to coat. Sprinkle with the pepper. Cover and bake until opaque throughout, 18 to 20 minutes.

Serve topped with the pan juices and scallions.

**Makes 4 servings**

**Per serving:** 201 calories, 32 g protein, 2 g carbohydrates, 6 g fat, 1 g saturated fat, 70 mg cholesterol, 577 mg sodium, 0 g fiber

**Diet Exchanges:** 0 milk, 0 vegetable, 0 fruit, 0 bread, 4½ meat, 1 fat

## ▶Flavor Tips

*Serve the fish over a bed of brown rice to capture the brothy juices. Substitute black sea bass, flounder, or orange roughy for the sea bass. These varieties are thinner and will cook in 12 to 15 minutes. You can also replace the chopped tomatoes with crushed tomatoes or tomato sauce.*

## Smart-Carb Insider Tip

### LEAN ON A FRIEND

Find a friend, relative, or coworker with whom you can share your triumphs and setbacks. Better still, find someone else ready to lose some pounds along with you and support each other. It's fun to share recipes, food tips, and other slimming ideas.

# I D★id It!

## Betty Carlucci

Betty reached menopause and started to put on pounds. She adopted a new eating plan, made a commitment to exercise, and woke up to a renewed zest for life.

before

"My weight was never much of a problem for me until I reached menopause. During the 10 or so years of perimenopause, I thought that the 10- to 15-pound fluctuations I experienced were due to fluid retention. But I kept having strong cravings for sugar. It seemed that if I ate anything with even a little sugar in it, I got more and more hungry. And this really put on the pounds . . . 40 of them! My clothes got tighter, and I felt like I was losing control of my food choices. This made it a lot harder to cope with the hormonal changes I was going through.

"I tried all kinds of diets. But I knew that to keep my weight off for good, I would have to make long-term changes in my eating habits. After looking closely at

**Weight lost:** 40 pounds
**Time kept off:** 3 years
**Weight-loss strategies:**
 Avoided refined carbohydrates, ate more vegetables, began exercising again
**Weight-maintenance strategies:** Maintains lower carbohydrate intake, does weight-bearing exercise 3 to 5 times a week

my diet, I realized how high my total carbohydrate intake had been. I started avoiding all sweets. I also replaced white flour, refined cereals, and regular pasta with

*fish and shellfish main dishes*

whole grain versions. I concentrated on eating lots of vegetables; getting protein from lean sources like soy foods, eggs, beans, and fish; and enjoying fresh fruit now and then. I cut back on dairy products, too, because they seemed to inhibit my weight loss. I supplemented my diet with a multivitamin high in calcium and magnesium.

"My other commitment was to get to the gym for a 1-hour workout three times a week. My exercise was as important to me as my obligation to go to work. After a while, I discovered that the exercise actually gave me *more* energy; and it is impossible to describe how much better I felt mentally.

"The best thing about my lifestyle now is that I feel good in my clothes again, I have the stamina to play with my young grandchildren, and I enjoy my food more. I'm truly enjoying the commitment and discipline of taking care of myself. I thank God for my good health at the age of 60 and ask for his blessings and guidance."

# BETTY'S BAKED FISH WITH MUSHROOMS AND SCALLIONS

*246 calories, 6 g carbs*

- **3 tablespoons butter or olive oil**
- **1 pound (4 cups) sliced mushrooms**
- **8 scallions, chopped**
- **⅓ cup white wine or white wine vinegar**
- **1½ pounds mild white fish fillets (orange roughy, flounder, or cod)**
- **2 tablespoons chopped fresh tarragon or 1 teaspoon dried**
- **¼ teaspoon salt**
- **¼ teaspoon paprika**

Preheat the oven to 350°F. Coat a 13" × 9" baking dish with cooking spray.

Warm the butter or oil in a large skillet over medium heat. Add the mushrooms and scallions, and cook until the mushrooms begin to release their liquid, about 5 minutes. Add the wine or vinegar and cook until the mushrooms are tender, about 5 minutes more.

Place the fish in the prepared baking dish. Stir the tarragon into the mushrooms and spread the mixture over the fish. Sprinkle with the salt and paprika. Bake until the fish just flakes easily when tested with a fork, 15 to 20 minutes.

**Makes 4 servings**

---

**Per serving:** 246 calories, 29 g protein, 6 g carbohydrates, 10 g fat, 5 g saturated fat, 57 mg cholesterol, 347 mg sodium, 2 g fiber

**Diet Exchanges:** 0 milk, 1 vegetable, 0 fruit, 0 bread, 4 meat, 2 fat

*fish and shellfish main dishes*

# BLUEFISH BAKED WITH PEPPERS AND CAPERS

*300 calories, 6 g carbs*

2 tablespoons olive oil

2 large red and/or green bell peppers, thinly sliced

½ small jalapeño chile pepper, seeded and finely chopped (optional); wear plastic gloves when handling

¼ teaspoon salt

¼ teaspoon ground black pepper

2 tablespoons dry white wine or white wine vinegar

2 teaspoons drained capers

1½ teaspoons chopped fresh thyme or ½ teaspoon dried

4 bluefish fillets (6 ounces each), each ½" thick

Preheat the oven to 400°F.

Heat the oil in a skillet over medium heat. Add the bell peppers, jalapeño pepper (if using), ⅛ teaspoon of the salt, and ⅛ teaspoon of the black pepper. Cook, stirring occasionally, until the peppers start to soften, 5 to 6 minutes. Stir in the wine or vinegar, capers, and thyme, and remove from the heat.

Place the fillets in a baking dish that's large enough to fit the fish comfortably in a single layer and season with the remaining ⅛ teaspoon salt and ⅛ teaspoon black pepper. Spoon the bell pepper mixture around and over the fillets, scraping the juices from the skillet with a rubber spatula. Cover the dish and bake until the fish is opaque throughout, 12 to 15 minutes.

Serve topped with the peppers and pan juices.

**Makes 4 servings**

**Per serving:** 300 calories, 35 g protein, 6 g carbohydrates, 14 g fat, 3 g saturated fat, 100 mg cholesterol, 292 mg sodium, 2 g fiber

**Diet Exchanges:** 0 milk, 1 vegetable, 0 fruit, 0 bread, 5 meat, 2 fat

▶ **Flavor Tips**

*Substitute other fillets, such as bass, red snapper, trout, or salmon for the bluefish. Use red wine instead of white wine.*

# POACHED HALIBUT WITH HERBED OLIVE OIL
*319 calories, 2 g carbs*

| | |
|---|---|
| 1 | **lemon, halved** |
| 3–4 | **cups water** |
| 2½ | **cups 2% milk** |
| 1 | **bay leaf** |
| ¼ | **teaspoon + 1 pinch of salt** |
| 4 | **halibut steaks or fillets (8 ounces each), each 1"–1¼" thick** |
| 2 | **tablespoons extra-virgin olive oil** |
| 2 | **tablespoons chopped fresh herbs (such as thyme and tarragon) or 2 teaspoons dried** |
| ⅛ | **teaspoon ground black pepper** |

Cut 3 thin slices from one lemon half. In a deep skillet that is large enough to hold the fish in a single layer, combine 3 cups of the water, the milk, the lemon slices, the bay leaf, and ¼ teaspoon salt. Bring to a simmer over medium-low heat and cook gently for 5 minutes to blend flavors. Carefully slide in the fish. (The fish should be just covered by liquid; if not, add just enough hot tap water to cover.) Cook at a gentle simmer until the fish is opaque throughout, 15 to 18 minutes.

Meanwhile, in a small bowl, combine the oil, herbs, and the pinch of salt.

Using a slotted spoon, carefully remove the fish to plates. Discard the bay leaf. Sprinkle the fish with the pepper. Drizzle with the herbed olive oil. Cut 4 wedges of lemon and serve with the fish.

**Makes 4 servings**

---

**Per serving:** 319 calories, 47 g protein, 2 g carbohydrates, 12 g fat, 2 g saturated fat, 73 mg cholesterol, 275 mg sodium, 0 g fiber

**Diet Exchanges:** 0 milk, 0 vegetable, 0 fruit, 0 bread, 7 meat, 1½ fat

## ▶Flavor Tips

*Use a fruity extra-virgin olive oil for the best flavor. You can substitute cod or haddock for the halibut steaks. Or substitute salmon steaks or fillets, omitting the milk and using all water.*

*fish and shellfish main dishes*

Baked Halibut Wrapped in Lettuce Leaves

# BAKED HALIBUT WRAPPED IN LETTUCE LEAVES

*249 calories, 2 g carbs*

| | |
|---|---|
| 8 | large Boston or other soft lettuce leaves |
| 4 | skinless halibut fillets (6 ounces each), each ½"–¾" thick |
| 1½ | teaspoons chopped fresh thyme or ¾ teaspoon dried |
| ½ | teaspoon salt |
| ¼ | teaspoon ground black pepper |
| ¼ | cup half-and-half |
| 3 | tablespoons dry white wine or nonalcoholic white wine |
| 1 | tablespoon butter |
| 1 | cucumber (6 ounces), peeled, seeded, and chopped |

Preheat the oven to 400°F. Coat a large, shallow baking dish (large enough to hold the fillets in 1 layer) with cooking spray.

Lay 4 lettuce leaves on the bottom of the prepared baking dish. Season the halibut with the thyme, ¼ teaspoon of the salt, and the pepper. Place 1 fillet on each lettuce leaf and top with the remaining 4 leaves. Drizzle with the half-and-half and wine. Dot with the butter.

Bake until the fish is opaque, 15 to 20 minutes. Remove to plates, reserving the pan juices. Pour the juices into a small saucepan. Stir in the cucumber and cook over low heat until slightly thickened and reduced to about ¼ cup, about 2 minutes. Season with the remaining ¼ teaspoon salt and spoon over the fish.

**Makes 4 servings**

---

**Per serving:** 249 calories, 36 g protein, 2 g carbohydrates, 8 g fat, 3 g saturated fat, 70 mg cholesterol, 419 mg sodium, 1 g fiber

**Diet Exchanges:** 0 milk, ½ vegetable, 0 fruit, 0 bread, 5 meat, 1 fat

## Time-Savers

To speed prep time, omit the lettuce. For quick-fixing lunches or suppers, store leftover fillets in a covered container in the refrigerator for up to 2 days. To reheat, arrange the fillets in a baking dish, cover, and bake at 350°F until heated through, 5 to 8 minutes.

*fish and shellfish main dishes*

# BROILED MACKEREL WITH LEMON-MINT BUTTER

*284 calories, 1 g carbs*

| | |
|---|---|
| **2** | **tablespoons butter, softened** |
| **1** | **tablespoon chopped fresh mint or 1 teaspoon dried** |
| **1½** | **teaspoons lemon juice** |
| **½** | **teaspoon ground black pepper** |
| **4** | **skinless mackerel fillets (6 ounces each), each ½" thick** |
| **¼** | **teaspoon salt** |

Place the broiler rack 2" to 3" from the heat source and preheat the broiler.

In a small bowl, combine the butter, mint, lemon juice, and ¼ teaspoon of the pepper.

Season the fish with the salt and the remaining ¼ teaspoon pepper. Lightly coat a broiling pan with cooking spray and arrange the fish on it. Broil, without turning, until the top is lightly browned and the flesh is completely opaque, 5 to 6 minutes. Spread the lemon-mint butter evenly over the fish and serve.

**Makes 4 servings**

**Per serving:** 284 calories, 35 g protein, 1 g carbo-hydrates, 15 g fat, 6 g saturated fat, 120 mg choles-terol, 300 mg sodium, 0 g fiber

**Diet Exchanges:** 0 milk, 0 vegetable, 0 fruit, 0 bread, 5 meat, 2½ fat

## Time-Savers

Make the lemon butter ahead. It keeps well in a covered container in the refrigerator for up to 1 week or in the freezer for up to 2 months. Thaw in the refrigerator before using. To store extra portions of the fish, refrigerate in a covered container for up to 2 days. To reheat, arrange the fish in a baking dish, cover, and bake at 375° until heated through, 5 to 6 minutes.

# Grilled Catfish with Scallion-Anchovy Vinaigrette
*341 calories, 1 g carbs*

| | |
|---|---|
| 5 | **anchovy fillets, drained, patted dry, and finely chopped** |
| 2 | **scallions, finely chopped** |
| 2 | **teaspoons lemon juice** |
| 2 | **teaspoons red wine vinegar** |
| 1 | **teaspoon Dijon mustard** |
| 3 | **tablespoons extra-virgin olive oil** |
| ¼ | **teaspoon ground black pepper** |
| 4 | **catfish fillets (6 ounces each)** |
| ¼ | **teaspoon salt** |

In a small bowl, combine the anchovies, scallions, lemon juice, vinegar, mustard, 2 tablespoons of the oil, and ⅛ teaspoon of the pepper.

Brush the remaining 1 tablespoon oil over the fish, and season with the salt and the remaining ⅛ teaspoon pepper.

Generously coat a grill rack with cooking spray. Preheat the grill. Place the catfish, round side down, on the rack and cook until golden, 5 to 6 minutes. Turn and cook until the flesh is completely opaque but still juicy, 2 to 4 minutes more. Serve topped with the scallion-anchovy vinaigrette.

**Makes 4 servings**

---

**Per serving:** 341 calories, 28 g protein, 1 g carbohydrates, 24 g fat, 5 g saturated fat, 84 mg cholesterol, 452 mg sodium, 0 g fiber

**Diet Exchanges:** 0 milk, 0 vegetable, 0 fruit, 0 bread, 4 meat, 3 fat

▶ ## Flavor Tips

*Broil the catfish instead of grilling. Or substitute grouper fillets for the catfish. Stir 1 small minced garlic clove (or ¼ teaspoon garlic powder) into the anchovy vinaigrette.*

# GRILLED GROUPER WITH CHILI-LIME BUTTER

*235 calories, 1 g carbs*

| | |
|---|---|
| 3 | tablespoons butter, softened |
| | Grated peel of 1 lime |
| 1 | teaspoon chili powder |
| ¼ | teaspoon salt |
| 4 | grouper fillets (6 ounces each), each ¾" thick |
| 2 | teaspoons chopped fresh cilantro (optional) |

Place the butter, lime peel, chili powder, and salt in a small microwaveable bowl. Microwave on medium power until the butter is melted, 1 minute.

Coat a grill rack with cooking spray. Preheat the grill. Brush the fish on both sides with the chili-lime butter. Sprinkle with the cilantro (if using).

Place on the rack, round side down, and grill until golden, 5 to 6 minutes. Turn and brush again with the butter. Cook until the flesh is completely opaque but still juicy, 3 to 4 minutes more. Drizzle any remaining butter evenly over the fish.

**Makes 4 servings**

---

**Per serving:** 235 calories, 33 g protein, 1 g carbohydrates, 10 g fat, 6 g saturated fat, 86 mg cholesterol, 330 mg sodium, 0 g fiber

**Diet Exchanges:** 0 milk, 0 vegetable, 0 fruit, 0 bread, 4½ meat, 1½ fat

## HIDDEN ROADBLOCK to weight loss

### GENETICS

When all else fails, perhaps you can blame it on your genes. There is a well-known familial relationship to weight management as well as to body fat distribution. If most of your ancestors had the same body build as you do, it is unlikely that you will be able to change your body shape by changing the foods you eat. That doesn't mean, however, that you should throw in the towel. A study at the University of Utah School of Medicine found that physical activity and environmental factors in the home may be closely related to weight management despite similar genes among siblings. Researchers studied 145 sets of siblings raised under the same roof. In each set of siblings, daily caloric intake differed by more than 350 calories, and there was a difference in energy expenditure. It's no surprise that the obese sibling ate more and was less active. The bottom line is that by eating less and exercising more, you can overcome your genetics and lose weight.

# SAUTÉED TROUT WITH ALMOND BUTTER SAUCE

*398 calories, 10 g carbs*

| | |
|---|---|
| 5 | tablespoons 2% milk or unsweetened soy milk |
| 2 | tablespoons lemon juice |
| 1½ | tablespoons almond butter |
| ½ | teaspoon salt |
| ¼ | teaspoon ground black pepper |
| 1 | large egg |
| ⅓ | cup whole wheat flour |
| 4 | trout fillets (6 ounces each), each ½" thick |
| 2 | tablespoons vegetable oil |
| 4 | lemon wedges (optional) |

In a bowl, combine 3 tablespoons of the milk, the lemon juice, the almond butter, ¼ teaspoon of the salt, and ⅛ teaspoon of the pepper.

Preheat the oven to 250°F. In a shallow bowl, lightly beat the egg and the remaining 2 tablespoons milk. In another shallow bowl, combine the flour, the remaining ¼ teaspoon salt, and the remaining ⅛ teaspoon pepper. Dip the fish into the egg mixture, then into the flour, lightly pressing so the flour sticks.

In a large nonstick skillet, heat 1 tablespoon of the oil over medium heat. Add the fish in batches, skin side up, and cook until the first side is browned, 2 to 3 minutes. Turn, and cook the second side until the flesh is opaque, 3 to 4 minutes more. Remove to the baking sheet and keep warm in the oven. Before adding the next batch of fish, add the remaining 1 tablespoon oil.

Serve with the almond-butter mixture and lemon wedges for squeezing (if using).

**Makes 4 servings**

---

**Per serving:** 398 calories, 40 g protein, 10 g carbohydrates, 21 g fat, 4 g saturated fat, 155 mg cholesterol, 377 mg sodium, 2 g fiber

**Diet Exchanges:** 0 milk, 0 vegetable, 0 fruit, ½ bread, 5 meat, 3½ fat

## ▶Flavor Tips

*A variety of nut butters are available in health food stores and supermarkets. Use another nut butter such as macadamia or cashew. You can also replace all or half of the wheat flour with soy flour. When buying trout, pick what's most fresh. The more pink-fleshed steelhead trout and the more white-fleshed rainbow trout are good choices.*

# PAN-FRIED PERCH IN CORNMEAL WITH BACON
*362 calories, 15 g carbs*

| | |
|---|---|
| 2 | bacon strips |
| I | egg |
| I | tablespoon water |
| ½ | cup cornmeal |
| ¼ | teaspoon salt |
| ¼ | teaspoon ground black pepper |
| 4 | skinless fresh perch fillets (about 5 ounces each), each about ½" thick, or I package (I pound) frozen and thawed fillets |
| ¼ | cup soy flour |
| 2 | tablespoons vegetable oil |
| 4 | lemon wedges |

Cook the bacon in a large, heavy skillet over low heat until crisp, 10 to 14 minutes, turning once or twice. Drain on a paper towel-lined plate, reserving no more than 1 tablespoon of the fat in the pan.

In a small bowl, lightly beat the egg and water. In another bowl, combine the cornmeal, salt, and pepper. Coat the fish with the flour, then dip into the egg mixture and coat with the cornmeal, lightly pressing to help the coating stick. Arrange in a single layer on a large plate and refrigerate for at least 15 minutes or up to 60 minutes to help the coating adhere.

Heat the oil in the same skillet with the bacon fat over medium heat. Add the fish, round side down, without crowding. Cook until golden brown and crisp on the outside, 3 to 4 minutes. Turn and cook until browned on the outside and opaque inside, 2 to 4 minutes more. (If necessary cook in two batches, keeping the first batch warm in a 250°F oven on a baking sheet lined with paper towels.)

Crumble the bacon over the top and serve with the lemon wedges for squeezing.

**Makes 4 servings**

---

**Per serving:** 362 calories, 33 g protein, 15 g carbohydrates, 19 g fat, 4 g saturated fat, 120 mg cholesterol, 360 mg sodium, 2 g fiber

**Diet Exchanges:** 0 milk, 0 vegetable, 0 fruit, 1 bread, 4 meat, 3 fat

▶Flavor Tip

*For an easy lunch dish, tuck a fillet (hot or cold) between crisp leaves of romaine lettuce spread with tartar sauce.*

# SHARK BRAISED IN RED WINE WITH TOMATO AND ANCHOVY

*327 calories, 6 g carbs*

| | |
|---|---|
| 2 | tablespoons olive oil |
| 1 | small red onion, thinly sliced |
| ½ | cup chopped drained canned tomatoes |
| 1–2 | anchovy fillets, finely chopped |
| ¼ | teaspoon dried oregano |
| ½ | cup dry red wine or nonalcoholic red wine |
| 4 | shark steaks (6 ounces each), each ¾" thick |
| ¼ | teaspoon salt |
| ¼ | teaspoon ground black pepper |
| 2 | tablespoons whole wheat flour |

Preheat the oven to 350°F.

In a large skillet with oven-safe handles, heat 1 tablespoon of the oil over medium heat. Add the onion and cook, stirring occasionally, until lightly browned, 2 to 3 minutes. Add the tomatoes, the anchovies, and the oregano. Cook for 30 seconds, stirring. Pour in the wine, cook for 30 seconds, and remove to a bowl.

Season the shark steaks with the salt and pepper. Coat with the flour and pat off the excess.

Heat the remaining 1 tablespoon olive oil in the same skillet over medium-high heat. Add the fish and cook until browned on the first side, 3 to 4 minutes. Turn and cook until browned on the second side, 3 to 4 minutes. Remove from the heat and pour the tomato-wine mixture over and around the fish. (The liquid will spatter and boil.) Cover and bake until the fish is opaque throughout, 10 to 12 minutes.

**Makes 4 servings**

---

**Per serving:** 327 calories, 37 g protein, 6 g carbohydrates, 15 g fat, 3 g saturated fat, 88 mg cholesterol, 321 mg sodium, 1 g fiber

**Diet Exchanges:** 0 milk, ½ vegetable, 0 fruit, 0 bread, 5 meat, 3 fat

▶Flavor Tips

*Substitute tuna, salmon, or swordfish for the shark. Replace the chopped tomatoes with crushed tomatoes or tomato sauce.*

# SAUTÉED TUNA STEAKS WITH GARLIC SAUCE

*295 calories, 1 g carbs*

2     large garlic cloves, minced

1     tablespoon + 1½ teaspoons olive oil

1     tablespoon balsamic vinegar

¼     teaspoon salt

⅛     teaspoon ground black pepper

4     tuna steaks (6 ounces each), each 1" thick

1½    teaspoons chopped fresh parsley or basil

In a large, heavy nonstick skillet, cook the garlic in 1 tablespoon of the oil over very low heat, until the garlic's aroma is apparent, 30 to 60 seconds, stirring. Immediately add the vinegar, ⅛ teaspoon of the salt, and half of the pepper. Remove to a bowl and cover with foil to keep warm.

Season the fish with the remaining ⅛ teaspoon salt and the remaining pepper. Heat the remaining 1½ teaspoon oil in the same skillet over medium heat. Add the fish and cook until browned on the first side, 4 to 5 minutes. Turn and cook until the fish is just opaque throughout, 3 to 4 minutes. Serve topped with the garlic sauce and parsley or basil.

**Makes 4 servings**

**Per serving:** 295 calories, 40 g protein, 1 g carbohydrates, 13 g fat, 3 g saturated fat, 65 mg cholesterol, 214 mg sodium, 0 g fiber

**Diet Exchanges:** 0 milk, 0 vegetable, 0 fruit, 0 bread, 5½ meat, 2 fat

## ▶Flavor Tips

Substitute swordfish, salmon, or shark for the tuna. If there are leftovers, store them in a covered container in the refrigerator for up to 3 days. For a quick and delicious tuna salad, break the fish into large flakes and toss with a yogurt or mayonnaise dressing.

Sautéed Tuna Steaks with Garlic Sauce

# BAKED SALMON WITH OREGANO

*290 calories, 1 g carbs*

| | |
|---|---|
| 2 | **teaspoons olive oil** |
| 4 | **skinless salmon fillets (6 ounces each), each 1" thick** |
| 1 | **tablespoon + 1½ teaspoons lemon juice** |
| 1 | **teaspoon dried oregano** |
| ½ | **teaspoon salt** |
| ¼ | **teaspoon ground black pepper** |
| 1 | **tablespoon butter, cut into small pieces** |
| 1 | **teaspoon chopped fresh parsley (optional)** |

Preheat the oven to 375°F.

Use the oil to grease a shallow baking dish that is large enough to fit the fillets in a single layer. Arrange the fish in the dish and turn to coat with the oil. Sprinkle with the lemon juice, oregano, salt, and pepper. Dot with the butter and cover with foil.

Bake until the flesh is cooked through but still very juicy, 20 to 24 minutes. Serve topped with the pan juices and parsley (if using).

**Makes 4 servings**

---

**Per serving:** 290 calories, 34 g protein, 1 g carbohydrates, 16 g fat, 4 g saturated fat, 101 mg cholesterol, 395 mg sodium, 0 g fiber

**Diet Exchanges:** 0 milk, 0 vegetable, 0 fruit, 0 bread, 4 meat, 1 fat

## Time-Savers

Make this dish ahead or make extras for fast meals. Store extra portions in a covered container in the refrigerator for up to 3 days. To reheat, arrange the fillets in a baking dish, cover, and bake at 350°F until heated through, 5 to 8 minutes. Or serve the fillets cold or at room temperature mixed with vinegar and oil for a fish salad.

# SALMON SALAD WITH FRESH GINGER

*279 calories, 3 g carbs*

| | |
|---|---|
| 1 | **skinless salmon fillet (1½ pounds), 1" thick** |
| 2 | **teaspoons peanut oil or vegetable oil** |
| ⅛ | **teaspoon salt** |
| ⅛ | **teaspoon ground black pepper** |
| 2 | **large scallions, very thinly sliced** |
| 1 | **tablespoon grated fresh ginger** |
| 2 | **tablespoons soy sauce** |
| 2 | **teaspoons rice vinegar or apple cider vinegar** |
| 4 | **large Boston or red leaf lettuce leaves (optional)** |
| 1 | **cup (3 ounces) fresh bean sprouts** |

Preheat the oven to 375°F.

Rub the salmon with 1 teaspoon of the oil and season with the salt and pepper. Place in a shallow baking dish, cover, and bake just until cooked through but still very juicy, 20 to 25 minutes. Let cool 5 to 10 minutes.

Meanwhile, in a large bowl, combine the scallions, ginger, soy sauce, vinegar, and remaining 1 teaspoon oil. Flake the salmon into large pieces and add to the bowl. Gently toss to coat.

Arrange the lettuce leaves (if using) on plates and top with the salmon and bean sprouts. Serve immediately.

**Makes 4 servings**

---

**Per serving:** 279 calories, 35 g protein, 3 g carbohydrates, 13 g fat, 2 g saturated fat, 94 mg cholesterol, 632 mg sodium, 1 g fiber

**Diet Exchanges:** 0 milk, ½ vegetable, 0 fruit, 0 bread, 4½ meat, ½ fat

## Time-Saver

Make the fish for this main-dish salad ahead if you can. Keep the fish (undressed) in a covered container in the refrigerator for up to 2 days. Don't flake and toss with the sauce until just before serving.

Grilled Salmon with Mint-Cilantro Yogurt

# GRILLED SALMON WITH MINT-CILANTRO YOGURT
*333 calories, 2 g carbs*

¼ **cup + 2 tablespoons low-fat plain yogurt**

2 **tablespoons sour cream**

1 **tablespoon chopped fresh cilantro**

2 **teaspoons chopped fresh mint**

¼ **teaspoon salt**

¼ **teaspoon ground black pepper**

**Pinch of ground red pepper (optional)**

4 **salmon steaks or fillets (7 ounces each), each ¾"–1" thick**

2 **teaspoons vegetable oil**

In a small bowl, combine the yogurt, sour cream, cilantro, mint, salt, ⅛ teaspoon of the black pepper, and the red pepper (if using).

Coat a grill rack with cooking spray. Preheat the grill. Brush the fish with the oil, and season with the remaining ⅛ teaspoon black pepper.

Place the salmon on the rack and cook until golden, 5 to 6 minutes. Turn and cook until the flesh is completely opaque but still juicy, 3 to 4 minutes more. Serve topped with the mint-cilantro yogurt.

**Makes 4 servings**

**Per serving:** 333 calories, 41 g protein, 2 g carbohydrates, 17 g fat, 3 g saturated fat, 114 mg cholesterol, 253 mg sodium, 0 g fiber

**Diet Exchanges:** 0 milk, 0 vegetable, 0 fruit, 0 bread, 5½ meat, ½ fat

## ▶Flavor Tips

*Broil the salmon instead of grilling it. Substitute red snapper, bass, or flounder for the salmon. Eliminate the sour cream and add 2 tablespoons more yogurt. Add ¼ of a peeled, seeded, and finely chopped small cucumber (1½ ounces) to the sauce.*

# SALMON AND COUSCOUS SALAD WITH VEGETABLES

*397 calories, 28 g carbs*

| | |
|---|---|
| 1 | skinless salmon fillet (1 pound), 1" thick |
| 3 | tablespoons + 1 teaspoon olive oil |
| ¾ | teaspoon salt |
| ¼ | teaspoon ground black pepper |
| 20 | spears (10 ounces) fresh or frozen thin asparagus, thawed if frozen and cut into ½" lengths |
| 1 | zucchini (6 ounces), halved lengthwise and thinly sliced |
| 1 | garlic clove, minced |
| ¾ | cup water |
| ⅔ | cup whole wheat couscous |
| 2–3 | teaspoons red wine vinegar or lemon juice |

Preheat the oven to 375°F. Rub the salmon with 1 teaspoon of the olive oil and season with ¼ teaspoon of the salt and ⅛ teaspoon of the pepper. Arrange in a shallow baking dish and bake just until the salmon is cooked through but still juicy, 20 to 25 minutes. Let cool until easy to handle, 5 to 10 minutes. Break into large flakes.

Heat the remaining 3 tablespoons olive oil in a large saucepan over medium heat. Add the asparagus, zucchini, and garlic. Cook, stirring occasionally, until crisp-tender, 3 to 5 minutes. Add the water, the remaining ½ teaspoon salt, and the remaining ⅛ teaspoon pepper. Simmer for 2 to 3 minutes over medium heat. Bring to a boil and stir in the couscous. Cover, remove from the heat, and let sit 5 minutes.

Fluff the couscous with a fork, remove to a large bowl, and season with the vinegar or lemon juice. Cool slightly and fold in the salmon. Serve warm, at room temperature, or chilled.

**Makes 4 servings**

**Per serving:** 397 calories, 29 g protein, 28 g carbohydrates, 19 g fat, 3 g saturated fat, 62 mg cholesterol, 543 mg sodium, 3 g fiber

**Diet Exchanges:** 0 milk, 1 vegetable, 0 fruit, 1½ bread, 3 meat, 2 fat

## Time-Saver

Replace the fresh salmon with 2 cups of canned salmon. You can also make this salad up to 3 days ahead and store it in a covered container in the refrigerator.

# SHRIMP SALAD WITH DILL AND ORANGES
*170 calories, 11 g carbs*

- 1½ **pounds (50–60 pieces) medium shrimp, peeled and deveined**
- ¼ **cup reduced-fat mayonnaise**
- 1 **celery rib, finely chopped**
- 2 **tablespoons low-fat plain yogurt**
- 1 **tablespoon minced red onion**
- 1 **tablespoon chopped fresh dill or ½ teaspoon dried**
- 1 **teaspoon lemon juice**
- ¼ **teaspoon salt**
- ¼ **teaspoon ground black pepper**
- 2 **navel oranges, peeled and segmented**

Bring a large pot of water to a boil over high heat. Add the shrimp, reduce the heat to medium, and cook until curled and opaque, 2 to 3 minutes. Drain and cool under cold running water. Cut into ½" pieces.

In a large bowl, combine the mayonnaise, celery, yogurt, onion, dill, lemon juice, salt, and pepper. Add the shrimp and toss to coat well. Spoon onto plates and garnish with the oranges. Or chill for 1 to 2 hours before garnishing and serving.

**Makes 4 servings**

---

**Per serving:** 170 calories, 17 g protein, 11 g carbohydrates, 6 g fat, 1 g saturated fat, 120 mg cholesterol, 391 mg sodium, 2 g fiber

**Diet Exchanges:** 0 milk, 0 vegetable, 1 fruit, 0 bread, 2½ meat, 1 fat

## ▶Flavor Tips

*Sprinkle 1 tablespoon drained capers over the salad when serving. Serve on a bed of fresh spinach leaves. Substitute 1 large grapefruit, peeled and segmented, for the oranges. You could also leave the shrimp whole if you prefer.*

*fish and shellfish main dishes*

# GRILLED SHRIMP WITH SPICY CABBAGE SLAW

*201 calories, 8 g carbs*

| | |
|---|---|
| 3 | tablespoons extra-virgin olive oil or walnut oil |
| 1 | tablespoon apple cider vinegar or distilled white vinegar |
| 1 | teaspoon Dijon mustard |
| ½ | teaspoon hot-pepper sauce |
| ½ | teaspoon salt |
| ¼ | teaspoon ground black pepper |
| ½ | head (12 ounces total) green cabbage, finely shredded |
| 1 | small carrot, grated |
| 1½ | pounds large shrimp (40–45 pieces), peeled and deveined |

In a large bowl, combine 2 tablespoons of the oil, the vinegar, mustard, pepper sauce, salt, and ⅛ teaspoon of the pepper. Add the cabbage and carrot, and toss to coat.

In a medium bowl, combine the remaining 1 tablespoon oil and remaining ⅛ teaspoon pepper. Add the shrimp and toss to coat.

Coat a grill rack with cooking spray. Preheat the grill. Thread the shrimp onto skewers by pushing the skewer through the back at the thickest part and then through the tail section. Grill the shrimp, turning once, until firm and opaque throughout when cut with a knife, 4 to 6 minutes. Serve over the cabbage slaw.

**Makes 4 servings**

---

**Per serving:** 201 calories, 16 g protein, 8 g carbohydrates, 12 g fat, 2 g saturated fat, 106 mg cholesterol, 467 mg sodium, 3 g fiber

**Diet Exchanges:** 0 milk, 1½ vegetable, 0 fruit, 0 bread, 2 meat, 2 fat

## Time-Saver

Make this salad ahead and store the shrimp in a covered container in the refrigerator for up to 3 days. Keep the slaw in a separate covered container in the refrigerator for up to 4 days. Sprinkle with 1 tablespoon chopped fresh parsley or dill if desired.

# Spicy Sautéed Shrimp with Garlic
*125 calories, 2 g carbs*

| | |
|---|---|
| 1 | tablespoon olive oil |
| 2 | teaspoons butter |
| 1½ | pounds large shrimp (40–45 pieces), peeled and deveined |
| ⅛ | teaspoon salt |
| ⅛ | teaspoon ground black pepper |
| 2–3 | large garlic cloves, finely slivered or chopped |
| ¼ | teaspoon crushed red pepper flakes |
| 1 | tablespoon lemon juice |
| 1 | tablespoon chopped parsley or basil (optional) |

Heat the oil and butter in a large skillet over medium-high heat until the butter is melted. Add the shrimp, salt, and black pepper. Cook, stirring frequently, until just slightly translucent inside, 2 to 3 minutes.

Stir in the garlic and pepper flakes and cook, stirring frequently, until the shrimp are opaque throughout, 1 to 2 minutes more, lowering the heat if the garlic begins to color. Remove from the heat and stir in the lemon juice. Serve sprinkled with parsley or basil (if using).

**Makes 4 servings**

---

**Per serving:** 125 calories, 14 g protein, 2 g carbohydrates, 7 g fat, 2 g saturated fat, 112 mg cholesterol, 217 mg sodium, 0 g fiber

**Diet Exchanges:** 0 milk, 0 vegetable, 0 fruit, 0 bread, 2 meat, 1 fat

## Time-Saver

Save any leftovers for quick meals. Refrigerate the shrimp in a covered container for up to 3 days. To reheat, cook the shrimp in a skillet over low heat until heated through, stirring frequently, 1 to 2 minutes. Serve over brown rice or whole wheat spaghetti if desired.

# CREOLE-STYLE STEAMED CLAMS

*123 calories, 10 g carbs*

| | |
|---|---|
| 1 | **tablespoon butter or olive oil** |
| 5 | **scallions, white part only, finely chopped** |
| 1 | **small green and/or red bell pepper, finely chopped** |
| ½ | **celery rib, finely chopped** |
| 2 | **garlic cloves, minced** |
| 1 | **can (14½ ounces) chopped tomatoes, with juice** |
| ¼ | **cup white wine or water** |
| | **Pinch of ground red pepper** |
| 2 | **pounds littleneck or cherrystone clams, scrubbed** |

Melt the butter or oil in a large pot (twice the volume of the clams) over medium heat. Stir in the scallions, bell pepper, celery, and garlic. Cook just until the vegetables soften, 6 to 8 minutes, stirring occasionally. Stir in the tomatoes (with juice), wine or water, and red pepper. Add the clams, raise the heat to medium-high, cover, and steam until they open, 5 to 8 minutes. Discard any clams that don't open.

With a slotted spoon or tongs, remove the clams to serving bowls and ladle the vegetables and broth on top.

**Makes 4 servings**

**Per serving:** 123 calories, 11 g protein, 10 g carbohydrates, 4 g fat, 2 g saturated fat, 32 mg cholesterol, 87 mg sodium, 2 g fiber

**Diet Exchanges:** 0 milk, 1½ vegetable, 0 fruit, 0 bread, 1½ meat, 1 fat

## Flavor Tips

*Sprinkle with 1 tablespoon chopped parsley and 1 tablespoon grated Parmesan before serving. Serve over whole wheat noodles or brown rice to soak up the flavorful juices.*

# SCALLOPS IN TARRAGON CREAM
*201 calories, 5 g carbs*

| | |
|---|---|
| 1 | tablespoon butter, softened |
| 1½ | pounds fresh or thawed frozen sea scallops, rinsed |
| 1½ | teaspoons chopped fresh tarragon or ½ teaspoon dried |
| ¼ | teaspoon ground black pepper |
| ¼ | cup half-and-half |
| 1 | tablespoon Pernod or 2 tablespoons dry sherry (optional) |
| 2 | tablespoons lemon juice |
| 1 | tablespoon chopped fresh parsley |

Melt the butter in a large skillet over medium-high heat. When the butter foams, add the scallops, tarragon, and pepper. Cook for 2 to 3 minutes, stirring constantly.

Stir in the half-and-half, Pernod or sherry (if using), and lemon juice. Reduce the heat to medium-low and cook until the scallops look opaque throughout and feel slightly springy when lightly pressed, 1 to 2 minutes. Stir in the parsley.

**Makes 4 servings**

---

**Per serving:** 201 calories, 29 g protein, 5 g carbo-hydrates, 6 g fat, 3 g saturated fat, 71 mg cholesterol, 312 mg sodium, 0 g fiber

**Diet Exchanges:** 0 milk, 0 vegetable, 0 fruit, 0 bread, 4 meat, 1 fat

## ▶Flavor Tips

*Both frozen and fresh scallops can have a briny flavor, so don't add salt until you've tasted them. If the sauce in the pan is too thin for your taste, remove the scallops and cook the sauce over medium heat until slightly reduced. Pour over the scallops.*

# BAKED SCALLOPS WITH HERBS AND WHITE WINE

*229 calories, 4 g carbs*

| | |
|---|---|
| 3 | tablespoons butter, softened |
| 1½ | pounds fresh or thawed frozen bay scallops, rinsed |
| 1 | tablespoon dry white wine or nonalcoholic white wine |
| ¼ | teaspoon ground black pepper |
| 1 | tablespoon chopped fresh parsley |
| 1 | tablespoon chopped fresh dill |

Preheat the oven to 500°F. Grease a shallow baking dish with 1 tablespoon of the butter and add the scallops. Sprinkle with the wine and the pepper. Dot with the remaining 2 tablespoons butter.

Bake just until the scallops look opaque throughout and are slightly springy when lightly pressed, 5 to 7 minutes. Remove from the oven and stir in the parsley and dill. Serve immediately with the pan juices.

**Makes 4 servings**

---

**Per serving:** 229 calories, 29 g protein, 4 g carbohydrates, 10 g fat, 6 g saturated fat, 79 mg cholesterol, 363 mg sodium, 0 g fiber

**Diet Exchanges:** 0 milk, 0 vegetable, 0 fruit, 0 bread, 4 meat, 2 fat

▶Flavor Tips

*Use 1 teaspoon chopped fresh basil or tarragon with 2 teaspoons parsley. Add ¼ cup chopped or crushed canned tomatoes along with the scallops. To take advantage of the buttery pan juices, serve the scallops over brown rice, whole wheat couscous, or another whole grain.*

## HIDDEN ROADBLOCK to weight loss

### FLUID RETENTION

Excess water weight may be preventing you from dropping those last few pounds. Many people retain fluids if they use too much table salt or eat foods that are high in sodium, especially snack foods. Plus, when the body burns fat, it produces water. And if you don't drink enough water, your body will retain even more water. The bottom line for weight loss is that drinking water helps you lose weight—even water weight. Drink at least 64 ounces (8 glasses) of water a day to help flush excess water out of your system. If you think you are retaining fluids, use less table salt and cut back on salty foods such as pickles, mustard, canned fish, commercial salad dressings, broth, bouillon, and soy sauce. You can also choose vegetables with natural diuretic properties, such as celery, cucumbers, asparagus, and cabbage to help you naturally shed some fluid.

Baked Scallops with Herbs and White Wine

# STEAMED MUSSELS WITH ROASTED PEPPERS AND CAPERS

*146 calories, 7 g carbs*

| | |
|---|---|
| **2** | **tablespoons olive oil** |
| **1** | **small onion, finely chopped** |
| **2** | **garlic cloves, minced** |
| **½** | **cup chopped prepared roasted red peppers** |
| **½** | **teaspoon dried thyme or oregano** |
| **⅓** | **cup white wine or nonalcoholic white wine** |
| **3½** | **pounds cultivated mussels, scrubbed, beards trimmed if necessary** |
| **⅓** | **cup chopped fresh parsley and/or basil** |
| **1** | **tablespoon drained capers** |
| **¼** | **teaspoon ground black pepper** |

Heat the oil in a large pot (twice the volume of the mussels) over medium-low heat. Add the onion and garlic and cook, stirring occasionally, until the onion is almost tender, 6 to 8 minutes. Stir in the roasted peppers and the thyme or oregano and cook for 1 minute. Add the white wine.

Add the mussels, cover, raise the heat to high, and cook until the mussels open, 3 to 6 minutes. Discard any mussels that don't open. With a slotted spoon, remove the mussels to serving bowls. Stir the parsley and/or basil, capers, and pepper into the broth. Ladle over the mussels.

**Makes 4 servings**

---

**Per serving:** 146 calories, 8 g protein, 7 g carbohydrates, 8 g fat, 1 g saturated fat, 16 mg cholesterol, 383 mg sodium, 1 g fiber

**Diet Exchanges:** 0 milk, 1 vegetable, 0 fruit, 0 bread, 1 meat, 1½ fat

## Time-Savers

To trim mussel beards easily, use scissors. To reduce trimming and cleaning, look for Prince Edward Island mussels, which are practically beardless and require only a rinse under cold water. You could also replace the mussels with 4 dozen littleneck clams.

# casseroles
# &one-dish
# dinners

# STIR-FRIED CHICKEN AND BROCCOLI
*321 calories, 18 g carbs*

½   **cup chicken broth**

3   **tablespoons Chinese oyster sauce**

2   **tablespoons orange juice**

1   **tablespoon + 1½ teaspoons soy sauce**

2   **cloves garlic, minced**

2   **teaspoons minced fresh ginger**

1   **teaspoon sesame oil**

¼   **teaspoon hot-pepper sauce (optional)**

1   **tablespoon cornstarch**

1   **tablespoon + 1½ teaspoons cold water**

3   **tablespoons vegetable oil**

1   **pound boneless, skinless chicken breasts, cut into thin strips**

1   **large bunch (2 pounds) broccoli, cut into small florets**

5   **scallions, sliced**

1   **teaspoon toasted sesame seeds (optional)**

In a small bowl, combine the broth, oyster sauce, orange juice, soy sauce, garlic, ginger, sesame oil, and hot-pepper sauce (if using).

In a cup, dissolve the cornstarch in the cold water.

Heat the oil in a large wok or skillet over high heat until the oil just starts to smoke. Add the chicken and cook, stirring continually until no longer pink on the surface, about 30 seconds. Stir in the broccoli and cook, stirring continually, until it turns bright green and the chicken is half-cooked, about 2 minutes. Pour in the broth mixture and cook, stirring frequently, for 2 minutes. Stir in the scallions and cornstarch mixture. Cook, stirring, until the sauce comes to a boil, thickens, and the chicken is cooked through, about 1 minute. Sprinkle with the sesame seeds (if using).

**Makes 4 servings**

**Per serving:** 321 calories, 34 g protein, 18 g carbohydrates, 14 g fat, 1 g saturated fat, 66 mg cholesterol, 692 mg sodium, 8 g fiber

**Diet Exchanges:** 0 milk, 3 vegetable, 0 fruit, 0 bread, 4 meat, 2½ fat

## ▶Flavor Tips
*Replace half of the broccoli with ½ bunch sliced bok choy or 2 cups string beans. Replace the chicken with small shrimp or slivered pork.*

# CHICKEN AND HAM JAMBALAYA
*282 calories, 25 g carbs*

½  **teaspoon dried thyme**

½  **teaspoon ground black pepper**

¼  **teaspoon salt**

⅛–¼  **teaspoon ground red pepper**

2  **tablespoons butter**

1  **smoked ham steak (6 ounces), chopped**

5  **skinless, boneless chicken thighs (about 5 ounces each), each cut into eighths**

1½  **large onions, chopped**

1  **large green bell pepper, chopped**

3  **cloves garlic, minced**

1  **cup canned crushed tomatoes**

1½  **cups chicken broth**

¾  **cup long-grain brown rice**

Preheat the oven to 350°F.

In a small bowl, combine the thyme, black pepper, salt, and red pepper.

Melt the butter in a large pot with oven-safe handles over high heat. Add the ham and chicken and cook until lightly browned, stirring occasionally, about 5 minutes. Sprinkle the spice mixture over the meat and stir to combine. Add the onions, bell pepper, and garlic. Reduce the heat to medium and cook, stirring frequently, until the vegetables start to soften, about 5 minutes. Stir in the tomatoes and cook for 1 minute. Stir in the broth and rice. Bring to a simmer and cover. Bake for 45 minutes until the rice is tender, the liquid has been absorbed, and the chicken is tender.

**Makes 6 servings**

**Per serving:** 282 calories, 18 g protein, 25 g carbohydrates, 9 g fat, 4 g saturated fat, 72 mg cholesterol, 751 mg sodium, 2 g fiber

**Diet Exchanges:** 0 milk, 1 vegetable, 0 fruit, 1½ bread, 2 meat, 1½ fat

## Time-Saver

You can make this dish up to 4 days ahead. Keep it in a covered container in the refrigerator. To reheat, remove from the refrigerator about 45 minutes before cooking, then place in a baking dish, cover, and bake at 350°F until heated through, 20 to 30 minutes.

# CHICKEN POT PIE WITH BUTTERMILK BISCUITS
*566 calories, 37 g carbs*

| | |
|---|---|
| 3 | **cans (14½ ounces each) reduced-sodium chicken broth** |
| 2 | **bay leaves** |
| 2½ | **pounds boneless skinless chicken breasts** |
| 3 | **parsnips or turnips (12 ounces), chopped** |
| 3 | **large carrots (1 pound), chopped** |
| 2 | **large celery ribs, sliced** |
| 1 | **cup drained canned pearl onions** |
| 1 | **cup light cream** |
| 1 | **teaspoon dried thyme** |
| 5 | **tablespoons butter, softened** |
| ½ | **cup whole wheat pastry flour** |
| 1½ | **teaspoons Worcestershire sauce** |
| ¼ | **teaspoon ground black pepper** |
| 1 | **package (10 ounces) frozen peas** |
| | **Dough from Sesame Buttermilk Biscuits (page 101)** |

In a large skillet over medium heat, bring the broth and bay leaves to a simmer. Add the chicken and cook until no longer pink inside, 12 to 14 minutes. Using a slotted spoon, remove the chicken to a platter and let cool. Cut into bite-size cubes.

Increase the heat to medium-high and add the parsnips or turnips, carrots, and celery. Cook until tender-firm, 8 to 10 minutes, adding the onions during the last 2 minutes. Using a slotted spoon, remove to a colander. Discard the bay leaves. If there is more than 3 cups of broth in the pan, increase the heat to medium-high and boil until reduced. Reduce the heat to medium and stir in the cream and thyme. Cook until bubbling.

In a small bowl, combine the butter and flour. Gradually whisk into the broth mixture, increasing the heat slightly, until it boils. Remove from the heat and season with the Worcestershire sauce and pepper.

Preheat the oven to 425°F.

In a large bowl, toss together the chicken, peas, carrot mixture, and sauce. Pour into a 4-quart baking dish. Cover with plastic wrap, pressing it against the filling.

Prepare the biscuits and cut them out. Remove the plastic wrap from the baking dish and place the cut biscuits on top of the filling, about an inch apart.

Bake until the biscuits are lightly browned and the filling is bubbling, 25 to 30 minutes.

**Makes 8 servings**

---

**Per serving:** 566 calories, 45 g protein, 37 g carbohydrates, 27 g fat, 16 g saturated fat, 147 mg cholesterol, 633 mg sodium, 7 g fiber

**Diet Exchanges:** ½ milk, 1½ vegetable, 0 fruit, 1½ bread, 5 meat, 4 fat

Chicken Pot Pie with Buttermilk Biscuits

# CHICKEN BRUNSWICK STEW WITH CORN AND LIMA BEANS

*469 calories, 21 g carbs*

| | |
|---|---|
| **3** | **bacon strips, cut into 1" pieces** |
| **4** | **pounds skinless bone-in chicken parts** |
| **½** | **teaspoon ground black pepper** |
| **¼** | **teaspoon salt** |
| **2** | **tablespoons whole wheat flour** |
| **3** | **tablespoons butter** |
| **1** | **large onion, chopped** |
| **1** | **large green bell pepper, chopped** |
| **½** | **teaspoon dried thyme** |
| **½** | **teaspoon dried sage or marjoram** |
| **1** | **can (15½ ounces) crushed tomatoes** |
| **1** | **can (14½ ounces) chicken broth** |
| **1** | **package (10 ounces) frozen succotash (corn and lima beans), thawed** |

Preheat the oven to 350°F. Cook the bacon in a large, heavy skillet over medium-low heat until crisp, 4 to 5 minutes. Remove to a paper towel-lined plate. Discard all but 1 tablespoon of the fat in the skillet.

Season the chicken with the black pepper and salt and coat with the flour. Melt the butter in the same skillet with the rendered fat over medium-high heat. Add the chicken in batches and cook until browned, about 12 minutes. Place, meat side up, in a baking dish.

Add the onion, bell pepper, thyme, and sage or marjoram to the skillet. Reduce the heat to medium and cook, stirring occasionally, until slightly softened, 6 to 8 minutes. Stir in the tomatoes and broth. Bring to a simmer. Pour over the chicken, cover, and bake until the chicken is almost cooked through, about 30 minutes. Stir in the succotash. Cover and cook until the chicken is tender and a meat thermometer registers 180°F, 10 to 15 minutes.

Serve with the bacon crumbled over top.

**Makes 6 servings**

---

**Per serving:** 469 calories, 48 g protein, 21 g carbohydrates, 22 g fat, 9 g saturated fat, 150 mg cholesterol, 762 mg sodium, 5 g fiber

**Diet Exchanges:** 0 milk, 4 vegetable, 0 fruit, 0 bread, 6 meat, 3½ fat

## ▶Flavor Tips

*Replace the succotash with 1 cup of trimmed, sliced okra, adding it during the last 10 minutes of cooking. Stir in 2 teaspoons of lemon juice right before serving. Serve over brown rice or another whole grain to soak up the flavorful sauce.*

# Beef and Barley Casserole
*387 calories, 25 g carbs*

| | |
|---|---|
| 2 | tablespoons olive oil |
| 1½ | pounds boneless stew beef, cut into cubes |
| ¼ | teaspoon salt |
| ¼ | teaspoon ground black pepper |
| 1 | onion, chopped |
| 1 | large red or green bell pepper, chopped |
| 2 | cans (14½ ounces each) beef broth |
| ¾ | cup pearl barley |
| ½ | cup canned crushed tomatoes |
| 1 | teaspoon ground coriander |
| 1 | bay leaf (optional) |
| ½ | cup toasted walnuts, chopped |
| | Grated peel of 1 large lemon (optional) |

Preheat the oven to 350°F.

Heat the oil in a large, deep skillet with oven-safe handles over medium-high heat. Add the meat and cook, seasoning with the salt and pepper, until browned, 10 to 12 minutes (work in batches if necessary and remove pieces to a plate as they're done). Reduce the heat to medium.

Return the meat to the pot and add the onion and bell pepper. Cook until the vegetables begin to soften, 7 to 8 minutes, stirring occasionally. Stir in 1½ cans of the broth, the barley, tomatoes, coriander, and bay leaf (if using). Bring to a simmer. Cover and bake until the beef and barley are tender and the broth is absorbed, 1¼ to 1½ hours. Add up to ¼ cup broth as necessary to prevent the mixture from drying out. Stir in the nuts and lemon peel (if using). Discard the bay leaf before serving.

**Makes 4 servings**

---

**Per serving:** 387 calories, 31 g protein, 25 g carbohydrates, 18 g fat, 4 g saturated fat, 75 mg cholesterol, 648 mg sodium, 6 g fiber

**Diet Exchanges:** 0 milk, 1 vegetable, 0 fruit, 1 bread, 3½ meat, 2 fat

## ▶ Flavor Tips

*Substitute 1 cup of brown rice for the barley and stir in 1 or 2 cloves of garlic, minced, along with the onion and pepper just as the vegetables start to soften. Add ⅛ to ¼ teaspoon ground red pepper right before baking. Add ½ cup raisins along with the tomatoes. Top each serving with 1 tablespoon chopped fresh cilantro, 3 chopped scallions, or ⅓ cup grated Parmesan cheese.*

# Skillet Scramble with Beef, Eggs, and Greens

*279 calories, 7 g carbs*

| | |
|---|---|
| 1 | large bunch (1¼ pounds) Swiss chard, stemmed and chopped |
| 2 | tablespoons olive oil |
| 1 | small onion, chopped |
| 1 | garlic clove, minced |
| 12 | ounces ground beef chuck |
| ¼ | teaspoon salt |
| ¼ | teaspoon ground black pepper |
| ¼ | teaspoon ground allspice |
| 3 | large eggs, at room temperature |
| 4–5 | drops hot-pepper sauce |
| ¼ | cup (1 ounce) grated Parmesan cheese or ½ cup (2 ounces) shredded Swiss cheese |

Bring a large pot of salted water to a boil. Add the chard and cook just until tender, about 3 minutes. Drain and cool under cold running water. Squeeze dry.

Heat the oil in a large skillet over medium heat. Add the onion and cook, stirring occasionally, until lightly browned and soft, 8 to 9 minutes. Stir in the garlic and cook, stirring, for 30 seconds. Add the meat and cook, stirring to crumble, just until browned, 5 to 6 minutes. Stir in the chard, salt, pepper, and allspice. Cook, stirring frequently, until the meat is no longer pink, 5 to 6 minutes. Reduce the heat to low.

In a small bowl, lightly beat the eggs and hot-pepper sauce. Stir into the beef mixture. Cook, stirring, until the eggs are set but still creamy, 4 to 6 minutes. Remove to a platter and sprinkle with the cheese.

**Makes 4 servings**

---

**Per serving:** 279 calories, 27 g protein, 7 g carbohydrates, 17 g fat, 5 g saturated fat, 209 mg cholesterol, 706 mg sodium, 2 g fiber

**Diet Exchanges:** 0 milk, 1 vegetable, 0 fruit, 0 bread, 3½ meat, 2½ fat

Flavor Tip

*Substitute kale, broccoli rabe, broccoli, or cabbage for the chard.*

# TEXAS BURRITO
*603 calories, 48 g carbs*

| | |
|---|---|
| 3 | tablespoons vegetable oil |
| 1½ | pounds boneless stew beef, cut into ½" cubes |
| 1 | onion, chopped |
| 2 | garlic cloves, minced |
| 1–1½ | small jalapeño chile peppers, seeded and finely chopped (wear plastic gloves when handling) |
| 1 | tablespoon + 1½ teaspoons chili powder |
| 2 | teaspoons ground cumin |
| ½ | teaspoon salt |
| ¼ | teaspoon ground black pepper |
| 1 | tablespoon tomato paste |
| 1¼ | cups hot water or beef broth |
| 8 | whole wheat tortillas (6") |
| 1 | cup (4 ounces) shredded Monterey Jack cheese |
| 4 | large lettuce leaves, shredded (optional) |
| 1 | large ripe tomato, finely chopped |

Heat the oil in a saucepan over medium-high heat. Working in batches, add the beef and cook, stirring, until browned, 5 to 8 minutes. Remove to a plate. Reduce the heat to medium. Return the beef to the pan and stir in the onion, garlic, and jalapeño peppers. Cook, stirring occasionally, until the vegetables start to soften, about 5 minutes.

Stir in the chili powder, cumin, salt, and black pepper.

In a cup, combine the tomato paste and water or broth. Stir into the beef mixture. Reduce the heat to low. Cover and cook, stirring occasionally, for 1 hour. Remove the lid and cook until the beef is tender, 30 minutes.

Meanwhile, preheat the oven to 375°F and wrap the tortillas in foil. Bake until steaming and pliable, 5 to 10 minutes.

To assemble each burrito, place a tortilla on a work surface and arrange a line of cheese down the center. Top with the beef mixture, lettuce (if using), and tomato. Fold two opposite sides over the filling, then fold one of the remaining sides over to enclose.

**Makes 4 servings (8 burritos )**

**Per serving:** 603 calories, 50 g protein, 48 g carbohydrates, 28 g fat, 9 g saturated fat, 129 mg cholesterol, 897 mg sodium, 6 g fiber

**Diet Exchanges:** 0 milk, 1½ vegetable, 0 fruit, 2 bread, 6 meat, 4 fat

## Time-Saver

*Make a double batch of the filling and refrigerate or freeze it. Store in a covered container in the refrigerator for up to 5 days or in the freezer for up to 2 months. To reheat, thaw in the refrigerator, then cook in a saucepan over low heat, stirring occasionally, until heated through, about 10 minutes.*

# Eggplant Stuffed with Savory Beef

*372 calories, 22 g carbs*

2 eggplants (16 ounces each)

3 tablespoons olive oil

1 large onion, chopped

1 red bell pepper, chopped

2 garlic cloves, minced

1 pound extra-lean ground beef chuck

1½ teaspoons dried oregano

1 tablespoon + 1½ teaspoons tomato paste

2 anchovy fillets, finely chopped (optional)

1 tablespoon capers, drained and coarsely chopped (optional)

½ cup (2 ounces) shredded or grated Parmesan cheese

¼ teaspoon salt

¼ teaspoon ground black pepper

Preheat the oven to 400°F. Pierce the eggplants in 2 or 3 places and place on a baking sheet. Roast, turning once or twice, just until tender when pierced with a fork, 20 to 25 minutes. Let cool enough to handle. Halve lengthwise. Scoop out the pulp, leaving a ½" to ¾" shell. Chop the pulp and let drain in a colander in the sink.

Heat 2 tablespoons of the oil in a large skillet over medium heat. Add the onion and bell pepper and cook, stirring occasionally, until tender, 8 to 10 minutes. Add the garlic and beef. Cook, stirring to crumble the beef, until no longer pink, 5 to 6 minutes. Stir in the eggplant pulp, oregano, tomato paste, anchovies (if using), and capers (if using). Reduce the heat to low and cook, stirring occasionally, until thick, 15 to 20 minutes. Stir in ¼ cup of the Parmesan, the salt, and black pepper.

Place the eggplant shells on a baking sheet and divide the beef mixture among them. Sprinkle with the remaining ¼ cup cheese and drizzle with the remaining 1 tablespoon oil. Roast until lightly browned on top, 15 to 20 minutes.

**Makes 4 servings**

**Per serving:** 372 calories, 31 g protein, 22 g carbohydrates, 20 g fat, 6 g saturated fat, 74 mg cholesterol, 380 mg sodium, 8 g fiber

**Diet Exchanges:** 0 milk, 4 vegetable, 0 fruit, 0 bread, 4 meat, 3 fat

▶Flavor Tip

*Replace the beef with lamb.*

Eggplant Stuffed with Savory Beef

# Beef and Cabbage Casserole with Tomato Sauce

*373 calories, 31 g carbs*

| | |
|---|---|
| 2 | tablespoons olive oil |
| 1 | large onion, chopped |
| ½ | small head (12 ounces total) green cabbage, shredded |
| 4 | garlic cloves, minced |
| 2 | pounds extra-lean ground beef chuck or pork |
| 1 | can (14½ ounces) beef broth |
| ⅓ | cup pimiento-stuffed green olives, chopped |
| ¾ | teaspoon dried oregano |
| ¼–½ | teaspoon mace (optional) |
| ½ | cup whole wheat couscous |
| ½ | teaspoon ground black pepper |
| ¼ | teaspoon salt |
| 1 | large red bell pepper, coarsely chopped |
| 1 | can (28 ounces) chopped tomatoes (with juice) |
| ⅓ | cup (1½ ounces) grated Parmesan cheese |

Preheat the oven to 375°F and coat an 8" × 8" baking dish with cooking spray.

Heat 1 tablespoon oil in a large, deep skillet over medium heat. Stir in the onion and cabbage and cook, stirring occasionally, until almost tender, 8 to 10 minutes. Add 2 of the garlic cloves and the meat, stirring, until the meat is crumbled and browned, 5 to 6 minutes. Stir in 1½ cups of the broth, the olives, oregano, and mace (if using). Bring to a boil and stir in the couscous, ¼ teaspoon of the black pepper, and ⅛ teaspoon of the salt. Immediately reduce the heat to low. Cover and cook for 10 minutes. Uncover, increase the heat to medium-high, and cook until the liquid has evaporated, 5 to 6 minutes. Spread the meat mixture in the prepared baking dish and cover to keep warm.

Wipe out the skillet, add the remaining 1 tablespoon oil, and heat over medium heat. Stir in the bell pepper and cook, stirring occasionally, until soft, 8 to 10 minutes. Stir in the remaining 2 garlic cloves and cook, stirring frequently, for 30 seconds. Stir in the tomatoes (with juice) and season with the remaining ¼ teaspoon pepper and ⅛ teaspoon salt. Cook until thickened, 12 to 15 minutes, stirring occasionally.

Spoon the tomato sauce on top of the beef, cover with foil, and bake for 25 minutes. Uncover and top with the Parmesan. Cut into squares and serve.

**Makes 6 servings**

**Per serving:** 373 calories, 36 g protein, 31 g carbohydrates, 13 g fat, 4 g saturated fat, 82 mg cholesterol, 759 mg sodium, 7 g fiber

**Diet Exchanges:** 0 milk, 3 vegetable, 0 fruit, 1 bread, 4 meat, 1½ fat

# NEW ENGLAND BOILED DINNER
*554 calories, 23 g carbs*

| | |
|---|---|
| 3 | whole cloves |
| 1 | large onion |
| 1 | corned beef brisket (about 4 pounds) |
| ½ | bunch parsley, tied with string |
| 1 | celery rib, halved |
| ½ | teaspoon whole peppercorns (optional) |
| 2 | bay leaves |
| 3 | turnips (8 ounces), peeled and halved |
| 3 | parsnips (8 ounces), halved lengthwise |
| 3 | carrots (6 ounces), peeled and cut into thirds crosswise, or 1 cup baby carrots |
| 1 | small head (1½ pounds) green cabbage, cut into 6 wedges |
| ⅔ | cup Mustard-Horseradish Sauce (p. 120) |

Insert the cloves into the onion. Place the beef in a large pot and add water to cover by 2 to 3 inches. Add the onion, parsley, celery, peppercorns (if using), and bay leaves.

Bring to a boil over high heat. Immediately reduce the heat to low and skim the foam from the surface. Partially cover the pot and cook until almost tender, 2½ to 2¾ hours.

Discard the onion, celery, and parsley. Add the turnips, parsnips, carrots, and cabbage. Partially cover, and cook until the vegetables are tender, about 15 minutes. Discard the bay leaves. Thinly slice the beef across the grain and serve with the vegetables and the sauce.

**Makes 6 servings**

**Per serving:** 554 calories, 37 g protein, 23 g carbohydrates, 34 g fat, 11 g saturated fat, 122 mg cholesterol, 492 mg sodium, 7 g fiber

**Diet Exchanges:** 0 milk, 3 vegetable, 0 fruit, ½ bread, 5 meat, 4 fat

## Flavor Tip
*Omit the bay leaves, peppercorns, and parsley and use the flavoring packet that comes with the meat.*

Chili-Cornbread Pie

# CHILI-CORNBREAD PIE
*394 calories, 39 g carbs*

| | |
|---|---|
| 2 | **tablespoons vegetable oil** |
| 1 | **onion, chopped** |
| 3 | **garlic cloves, minced** |
| ½ | **small jalapeño chile pepper, seeded and minced (wear plastic gloves when handling)** |
| 1 | **pound extra-lean ground beef chuck** |
| 1 | **can (14½ ounces) stewed tomatoes or 2 cups crushed** |
| 2–3 | **tablespoons chili powder** |
| ¼ | **teaspoon salt** |
| ¼ | **teaspoon ground black pepper** |
| ¼ | **teaspoon ground cumin (optional)** |
| 1 | **can (15–19 ounces) pinto beans, rinsed and drained** |
| 1 | **cup yellow cornmeal** |
| ½ | **cup whole wheat pastry flour** |
| 1½ | **teaspoons baking powder** |
| ¼ | **teaspoon salt** |
| 1 | **large egg, at room temperature** |
| 1 | **cup 2% milk, at room temperature** |
| 3 | **tablespoons melted butter** |

Heat the oil in a large skillet over medium heat. Add the onion, garlic, and jalapeño pepper. Cook until soft, stirring occasionally, 8 to 10 minutes. Add the beef and cook, stirring, until crumbled and browned, 5 to 6 minutes. Stir in the tomatoes, chili powder, salt, black pepper, and cumin (if using). Reduce the heat to low and cook for 30 minutes, stirring occasionally. Stir in the beans and cook for 15 minutes. Transfer to an 8" × 8" baking dish.

Preheat the oven to 400°F.

In a large bowl, combine the cornmeal, flour, baking powder, and salt.

In a small bowl, lightly beat the egg, milk, and butter. Stir into the cornmeal mixture until smooth. Pour over the meat mixture and spread evenly. Bake until a toothpick inserted in the center of the cornbread comes out clean, 20 to 30 minutes.

**Makes 6 servings**

---

**Per serving:** 394 calories, 24 g protein, 39 g carbohydrates, 17 g fat, 7 g saturated fat, 93 mg cholesterol, 632 mg sodium, 7 g fiber

**Diet Exchanges:** 0 milk, 1½ vegetable, 0 fruit, 2 bread, 2½ meat, 2½ fat

## *Time-Saver*

Make this dish ahead and keep it on hand for quick, satisfying meals. Store it in a covered container in the refrigerator for up to 4 days or in the freezer for up to 2 months. To reheat, thaw in the refrigerator for 12 hours if frozen, then place in a baking dish and bake at 350°F until heated through, 25 to 30 minutes.

# SMOTHERED POT ROAST

*417 calories, 8 g carbs*

| | |
|---|---|
| 1 | tablespoon + 1½ teaspoons olive oil |
| 1 | onion, cut into small wedges |
| 2 | garlic cloves, minced |
| 1 | boneless beef chuck (about 2 pounds) |
| ¼ | teaspoon salt |
| ½ | teaspoon ground black pepper |
| 1½ | teaspoons whole wheat flour |
| 1 | can (14½ ounces) beef broth |
| 1 | can (6 ounces) vegetable cocktail juice |
| 1 | teaspoon Worcestershire sauce |
| ½ | teaspoon dried thyme |

Preheat the oven to 350°F.

Heat 1 tablespoon of the oil in a large, heavy pot with oven-safe handles over medium heat. Add the onion and garlic. Cover and cook, stirring occasionally, until the onion begins to brown and turn translucent, 5 to 8 minutes. Remove to a plate. Remove the pot from the heat.

Season the meat with the salt and pepper and sprinkle all over with the flour, rubbing it in lightly. Heat the remaining 1½ teaspoons oil in the pot over high heat. Add the meat and cook until browned, 3 to 5 minutes. Reduce the heat to low and return the vegetables to the pot, scattering them over and around the meat. Add the broth, juice, Worcestershire sauce, and thyme. Bring to a simmer and cover. Bake until fork-tender, 2 to 2½ hours. Remove the beef and vegetables to a platter. Pour the pan juices into a fat separator or glass cup and discard the fat that rises to the surface. Pour the juices over the meat and serve.

**Makes 4 servings**

**Per serving:** 417 calories, 53 g protein, 8 g carbohydrates, 18 g fat, 6 g saturated fat, 155 mg cholesterol, 738 mg sodium, 1 g fiber

**Diet Exchanges:** 0 milk, 1 vegetable, 0 fruit, 0 bread, 6½ meat, 1 fat

## ▶Flavor Tips

*Substitute tomato juice for the vegetable cocktail juice and add 1 celery rib, quartered. Add 10 ounces of sliced mushrooms during the last 45 minutes of cooking. Serve with a side dish of couscous or quinoa to soak up the juices.*

# BRAISED BEEF WITH MUSHROOMS
*337 calories, 9 g carbs*

| | |
|---|---|
| ¼ | **ounce (2 tablespoons) dried wild mushrooms** |
| ½ | **cup boiling water** |
| 2 | **pounds boneless beef stew meat, cut into 1½" cubes** |
| ½ | **teaspoon salt** |
| ¼ | **teaspoon ground black pepper** |
| ⅛ | **teaspoon ground allspice (optional)** |
| 2 | **tablespoons olive oil** |
| 10 | **ounces mushrooms, quartered** |
| 1 | **onion, chopped** |
| 1 | **garlic clove, minced** |
| 2 | **tablespoons whole wheat flour** |
| 1¼ | **cups dry red wine or beef broth** |
| ½–1 | **cup water** |
| 1 | **tablespoon tomato paste** |
| ½ | **teaspoon dried thyme or oregano** |

Preheat the oven to 350°F.

In a bowl, soak the dried mushrooms in ½ cup boiling water until softened, about 20 minutes. Using tongs, pluck out the mushrooms and reserve the soaking water. Trim away any dirty sections from the mushrooms and chop any large pieces. Set aside.

Season the meat with the salt, pepper, and allspice (if using). Heat the oil in a large, heavy pot with oven-safe handles over medium-high heat. Working in batches, add the meat and cook until browned, 12 to 15 minutes, removing pieces to a plate as they are done.

Reduce the heat to medium and add the fresh mushrooms, rehydrated mushrooms, onion, and garlic. Cook, stirring, for 2 minutes. Return the meat to the pot, sprinkle with the flour, and cook, stirring, for 1 minute. Carefully pour in the mushroom soaking liquid, leaving behind any grit that has settled to the bottom of the bowl. Add the wine or broth, ½ cup of the water, and the tomato paste. If the mixture is too thick, add up to ½ cup more water. Bring to a boil and add the thyme or oregano. Cover, and bake until the meat is tender, about 1½ hours.

**Makes 6 servings**

---

**Per serving:** 337 calories, 37 g protein, 9 g carbohydrates, 13 g fat, 4 g saturated fat, 100 mg cholesterol, 276 mg sodium, 2 g fiber

**Diet Exchanges:** 0 milk, 1 vegetable, 0 fruit, 0 bread, 4 meat, 2 fat

## Time-Saver

*Make this richly flavored dish whenever you have time. Store it in a covered container in the refrigerator for up to 5 days or in the freezer for up to 2 months. To reheat, thaw in the refrigerator for 12 hours if frozen, then place in a pot over low heat, cover, and cook until heated through, stirring frequently, for 15 to 30 minutes.*

# CINCINNATI-STYLE TURKEY CHILI

*306 calories, 29 g carbs*

| | |
|---|---|
| 1 | tablespoon + 1½ teaspoons vegetable oil |
| 1 | large onion, chopped |
| 1 | large green bell pepper, chopped |
| 2 | garlic cloves, chopped |
| 1⅓ | pounds ground turkey |
| 1¾ | cups chicken broth |
| 3 | tablespoons tomato paste |
| 2–3 | tablespoons chili powder |
| 1½ | teaspoons dried oregano |
| 1 | teaspoon ground coriander |
| ¼ | teaspoon salt |
| ½ | teaspoon ground cumin |
| ¼ | teaspoon ground cinnamon |
| 1 | can (15 ounces) red kidney beans (with juice) |
| 6 | ounces whole wheat spaghetti, broken into short pieces |
| ½ | cup (2 ounces) shredded Monterey Jack or Muenster cheese |

Heat the oil in a large, heavy pot over medium heat. Add the onion, bell pepper, and garlic. Cook, stirring occasionally, until the onion starts to brown, 8 to 10 minutes. Add the turkey and cook, stirring to coarsely crumble until no longer pink, 8 to 10 minutes. Stir in the broth, tomato paste, chili powder, oregano, coriander, salt, cumin, and cinnamon. Bring to a simmer. Partially cover and cook, stirring occasionally, until the meat is tender and the broth is slightly thickened, about 30 minutes.

Meanwhile, pour the beans (with juice) into a microwaveable bowl. Microwave on high power for 1 to 2 minutes or until heated through. Drain and cover to keep warm.

Cook the pasta according to the package directions. Drain and divide among 4 bowls. Ladle the chili over the pasta, top with the beans, and sprinkle with the cheese.

**Makes 4 servings**

---

**Per serving:** 306 calories, 22 g protein, 29 g carbohydrates, 13 g fat, 3 g saturated fat, 66 mg cholesterol, 519 mg sodium, 7 g fiber

**Diet Exchanges:** 0 milk, 1 vegetable, 0 fruit, 1½ bread, 2 meat, 1 fat

## Time-Saver

*Make this chili ahead of time. The meat portion keeps well in a covered container in the refrigerator for up to 5 days or in the freezer for up to 2 months. Cook the pasta and heat the beans right before serving. To reheat the meat, thaw in the refrigerator for 12 hours if frozen. Place in a saucepan set over low heat and cook, stirring frequently, until heated through, about 15 minutes.*

Cincinnati-Style Turkey Chili

Slivered Pork with *Vegetables and Pasta*

# SLIVERED PORK WITH VEGETABLES AND PASTA
*340 calories, 27 g carbs*

- **1½** cups (5 ounces) whole wheat ziti, rotelle, or other short pasta
- **1** teaspoon + 2 tablespoons olive oil
- **1** pound boneless pork loin, fat trimmed, halved lengthwise, then sliced crosswise into ¼" strips
- **1** large red bell pepper, chopped
- **1** small onion, chopped
- **6** large mushrooms (6 ounces), coarsely chopped
- **3** garlic cloves, minced
- **1** teaspoon dried oregano
- **½** teaspoon dried thyme
- **1** can (15 ounces) crushed tomatoes
- **¼** teaspoon salt
- **¼** teaspoon ground black pepper
- **1** large ripe tomato, chopped or thinly sliced, slices cut in half (optional)
- **¾** cup (3 ounces) shredded mozzarella cheese

Preheat the oven to 375°F.

Cook the pasta according to package directions. Drain and return to the pot. Add 1 teaspoon of the oil and toss to coat.

Heat the remaining 2 tablespoons oil in a large skillet over medium heat. Add the pork and cook until browned, 3 to 5 minutes. Add the bell pepper, onion, mushrooms, garlic, oregano, and thyme. Cook until the onion is almost soft, 6 to 7 minutes, stirring occasionally. Stir in the crushed tomatoes and cook for 5 minutes. Season with the salt and black pepper.

Add to the pasta, tossing to combine. Pour into a shallow 2½- or 3-quart baking dish. Top with the fresh tomato (if using), only around the edges if desired, and sprinkle with the cheese. Bake until heated through and the cheese is melted and slightly browned, 20 to 25 minutes.

**Makes 4 servings**

**Per serving:** 340 calories, 26 g protein, 27 g carbohydrates, 15 g fat, 5 g saturated fat, 60 mg cholesterol, 293 mg sodium, 5 g fiber

**Diet Exchanges:** 0 milk, 2 vegetable, 0 fruit, 1 bread, 3 meat, 2½ fat

▶**Flavor Tip**
*Replace the pork with chicken, the bell pepper with zucchini, and the mozzarella with ½ cup grated Parmesan or Romano cheese. Add ¼ cup heavy cream to the pork and vegetable mixture along with the tomatoes.*

# SAUSAGE, EGG, AND VEGETABLE CASSEROLE

*352 calories, 7 g carbs*

- 1 pound sweet Italian sausage, casing removed and meat cut into 1" pieces
- 1 tablespoon + 1½ teaspoons olive oil
- ½ small head (4 ounces total) escarole, chopped
- 2 zucchini (8 ounces), thinly sliced
- 1 red bell pepper, chopped
- 1 small red onion, thinly sliced
- ¼ teaspoon salt
- ¼ teaspoon ground black pepper
- 7 large eggs, at room temperature
- ½ cup 2% milk, at room temperature
- ¼ cup (1 ounce) grated Parmesan cheese

Preheat the oven to 350°F. Coat an 8" × 8" baking dish with cooking spray.

Cook the sausage in a large skillet over medium-high heat until half-cooked, 6 to 8 minutes, stirring occasionally. Spread over the bottom of the prepared dish. Discard the fat in the skillet. Pour the oil into the same skillet and stir in the escarole, zucchini, bell pepper, onion, salt, and ⅛ tea-spoon of the black pepper. Reduce the heat to medium. Cook, stirring occasionally, until the vegetables are tender and the liquid evaporates, 8 to 10 minutes. Let cool for 10 minutes and arrange over the sausage.

Meanwhile, in a large bowl, combine the eggs, milk, cheese, and remaining ⅛ teaspoon black pepper. Pour over the vegetables. Bake until the eggs are set, 40 to 45 minutes. Cut into squares to serve.

**Makes 6 servings**

**Per serving:** 352 calories, 23 g protein, 7 g carbohydrates, 26 g fat, 7 g saturated fat, 308 mg cholesterol, 657 mg sodium, 2 g fiber

**Diet Exchanges:** 0 milk, 1 vegetable, 0 fruit, 0 bread, 3 meat, 3½ fat

## ▶Flavor Tips

*Substitute kale, broccoli rabe, or broccoli for the escarole. Replace the pork sausage with chicken or turkey sausage.*

Sausage, Egg, and Vegetable Casserole

# Pork Chops Baked with Cabbage and Cream

*463 calories, 12 g carbs*

| | |
|---|---|
| 1 | **small head (1½ pounds) green cabbage, cored and finely shredded** |
| 4 | **boneless pork chops (6 ounces each), each ¾" thick** |
| ½ | **teaspoon salt** |
| ¼ | **teaspoon ground black pepper** |
| 2 | **teaspoons olive oil** |
| ½ | **cup half-and-half** |
| 1 | **teaspoon caraway seeds** |
| ½ | **teaspoon sweet Hungarian paprika** |
| 1 | **teaspoon dried marjoram or thyme** |
| ½ | **cup (2 ounces) shredded Swiss cheese** |

Preheat the oven to 350°F.

Bring a large pot of salted water to a boil over high heat. Add the cabbage and cook until soft, 4 to 5 minutes. Drain in a colander and dry it well with paper towels.

Season the meat with ¼ teaspoon of the salt and the pepper. Heat the oil in an oven-safe, large, heavy skillet over high heat. Add the meat and cook just until browned, 1 to 2 minutes. Remove to a plate.

Discard any fat in the skillet and heat over low heat. Stir in the cabbage, half-and-half, caraway seeds, paprika, marjoram or thyme, and the remaining ¼ teaspoon salt. Cook and stir until heated through, about 1 minute. Remove from the heat and arrange the pork over the cabbage, adding any juices accumulated on the plate. Sprinkle with the cheese. Bake until a meat thermometer registers 160°F for medium-well, about 25 minutes.

**Makes 4 servings**

**Per serving:** 463 calories, 53 g protein, 12 g carbohydrates, 20 g fat, 9 g saturated fat, 165 mg cholesterol, 460 mg sodium, 4 g fiber

**Diet Exchanges:** 0 milk, 2½ vegetable, 0 fruit, 0 bread, 7 meat, 3½ fat

Flavor Tip

Substitute bone-in chops for the boneless.

# WHITE BEANS WITH HAM AND SAUSAGE
*513 calories, 31 g carbs*

¾ **cup (6 ounces) dried great Northern or cannellini beans, soaked in 3 cups water overnight**

2 **whole cloves**

1 **large onion, peeled**

4 **smoked ham hocks (about 8 ounces each)**

2 **large celery ribs, halved, or ¼ fennel bulb**

1 **bay leaf**

1 **tablespoon olive oil**

¾ **pound sweet or hot Italian sausage, casing removed and meat cut into 1" pieces**

3 **garlic cloves, minced**

½ **teaspoon dried rosemary, crumbled**

½ **cup canned crushed tomatoes**

¼ **teaspoon ground black pepper**

¼ **cup (1 ounce) grated Parmesan cheese**

Drain the beans. Insert the cloves into the onion. In a large pot, combine the beans, onion, ham, celery or fennel, and bay leaf. Add enough water to cover the ingredients by 3". Bring to a boil, reduce the heat to low, and skim the froth from the surface. Cover, and cook until the beans are tender but not mushy, 1¼ to 1½ hours. Remove the ham to a plate and let cool. Discard the onion, celery, and bay leaf. Drain the beans, reserving 2 cups cooking liquid.

Remove the meat from the bones and cut into bite-size pieces. Discard the skin, fat, and bone. Rinse out the pot and add the oil. Heat over medium-high heat and add the sausage. Cook, stirring occasionally, until browned, 2 to 3 minutes. Stir in the ham, garlic, and rosemary, and cook for 1 minute. Stir in the tomatoes and cook, stirring occasionally, for 2 minutes. Add the beans and ¾ cup of the reserved cooking liquid (refrigerate any remaining liquid and use it to reheat leftovers). Cook, stirring occasionally, until thickened, 10 to 12 minutes. Season with the pepper.

Preheat the oven to 425°F. Spoon the mixture into a shallow 2½-quart baking dish coated with cooking spray and sprinkle with the cheese. Bake until lightly browned, 15 to 20 minutes.

**Makes 4 servings**

---

**Per serving:** 513 calories, 35 g protein, 31 g carbohydrates, 28 g fat, 10 g saturated fat, 90 mg cholesterol, 719 mg sodium, 9 g fiber

**Diet Exchanges:** 0 milk, 1 vegetable, 0 fruit, 1½ bread, 3½ meat, 3½ fat

# HAM AND LENTIL CASSEROLE

*282 calories, 26 g carbs*

| | |
|---|---|
| 2 | tablespoons olive oil |
| 1 | large onion, chopped |
| 2 | celery ribs, thinly sliced |
| 1 | large green bell pepper, chopped |
| 2 | garlic cloves, minced |
| 1 | pound boneless smoked or cured ham, cut into 1½" cubes |
| 2 | cans (14½ ounces each) reduced-sodium chicken broth |
| 1 | cup dried lentils, rinsed and drained |
| ½ | cup canned crushed tomatoes |
| 1½ | teaspoons Hungarian paprika |
| 1 | teaspoon dried oregano or thyme |
| 1 | bay leaf |
| ¼ | teaspoon ground black pepper |

Preheat the oven to 350°F.

Heat the oil in a large pot with oven-safe handles over medium-high heat. Add the onion, celery, bell pepper, and garlic. Cook, stirring occasionally, just until softened, about 5 minutes. Add the ham and cook, stirring occasionally, for 2 minutes. Reduce the heat to medium-low and stir in 2½ cups of the broth, the lentils, tomatoes, paprika, oregano or thyme, bay leaf, and black pepper. Bring to a simmer. Cover, and bake until the lentils are tender and almost all of the liquid has been absorbed, 30 to 40 minutes, adding up to ¼ cup more broth if the mixture becomes dry. Remove the bay leaf before serving.

**Makes 6 servings**

---

**Per serving:** 282 calories, 25 g protein, 26 g carbohydrates, 9 g fat, 2 g saturated fat, 35 mg cholesterol, 881 mg sodium, 7 g fiber

**Diet Exchanges:** 0 milk, 1 vegetable, 0 fruit, 1½ bread, 2½ meat, 1½ fat

▶ ## Flavor Tips

Substitute Italian sausage or Polish kielbasa for the ham. Stir in a large handful of coarsely chopped fresh parsley. Top with ⅓ cup (1½ ounces) crumbled feta or goat cheese before serving.

# EGGPLANT PARMESAN
*224 calories, 16 g carbs*

| | |
|---|---|
| 2 | **eggplants (32 ounces), peeled and sliced lengthwise into slabs ¼" thick** |
| 3 | **tablespoons olive oil** |
| ½ | **teaspoon salt** |
| I | **can (15½ ounces) crushed or chopped tomatoes (with juice)** |
| I | **tablespoon + 1½ teaspoons tomato paste** |
| I | **teaspoon dried basil or 3 large fresh leaves, chopped** |
| ½ | **teaspoon dried rosemary, crumbled** |
| ¼ | **teaspoon ground black pepper** |
| I | **cup (4 ounces) shredded mozzarella or Fontina cheese** |
| ½ | **cup (2 ounces) grated Parmesan cheese** |

Preheat the broiler.

Place the eggplant on a large baking sheet and brush both sides with the oil (work in batches if necessary). Sprinkle with ¼ teaspoon of the salt. Broil 5" from the heat until just beginning to brown, 2 to 3 minutes per side.

Set the oven temperature to 375°F.

In a saucepan, combine the tomatoes (with juice), tomato paste, basil, and rosemary. Cook over medium-low heat, stirring occasionally, until slightly thickened, about 15 minutes. Season with the remaining ¼ teaspoon salt and the pepper.

Spread a layer of the tomato mixture over the bottom of a 1½-quart baking dish. Add a layer of eggplant and top with another layer of the tomato mixture. Sprinkle with a thin layer of the mozzarella or Fontina and the Parmesan. Continue making 2 more layers with the remaining eggplant, tomato mixture, and cheeses, ending with a thick layer of cheeses. Bake until bubbling, 25 to 30 minutes. Let rest for 10 minutes before cutting.

**Makes 6 servings**

---

**Per serving:** 224 calories, 11 g protein, 16 g carbohydrates, 14 g fat, 5 g saturated fat, 22 mg cholesterol, 628 mg sodium, 5 g fiber

**Diet Exchanges:** 0 milk, 3 vegetable, 0 fruit, 0 bread, 1 meat, 2 fat

## ▶Flavor Tips

Substitute ½ cup (2 ounces) shredded Swiss for ½ cup mozzarella cheese. For a smooth sauce, puree the tomatoes in a food mill or food processor. Use the eggplant peeled or unpeeled.

# I D⭐id It!

## Janet Lasky

When a 6-year-old boy came into Janet's life, she turned herself around, made a commitment to health, and lost 155 pounds.

"I had a compulsive eating disorder from the age of 5. I constantly ate foods high in fat and sugar. It's no surprise that I was overweight for most of my life. I topped the scales at over 300 pounds before I turned my life around.

"It wasn't until I adopted a 6-year-old boy that I started down the road to recovery. He came into my life and taught me about love. My desire to live long enough to raise my son pushed me to seek help. The answer to my prayers came from an outpatient eating disorder program at a nearby hospital. During the 4 years that I participated in the program, I developed the important foundations of self-love and responsibility that are still a part of my life today. I also became more aware of myself and my eating disorder.

before

**Weight lost:** 155 pounds
**Time kept off:** 8 years
**Weight-loss strategies:**
Avoided sugar, wheat, yeast, milk, and fermented foods; controlled food sensitivities

**Weight-maintenance strategies:** Maintains low-sugar diet, avoids sensitive foods, walks, takes spinning and aerobics classes several days a week

"When I left the outpatient program, I wanted to do all that I could to be as healthy as possible. With the assistance of a nutritionist, I was able to identify which foods

*casseroles and one-dish dinners*

were best for me. I discovered that I felt best when I avoided wheat, sugar, yeast, milk, fermented products, nuts, dried fruit, corn, and a few other foods. Instead, I focused on eating vegetables, lean protein-based foods, beans, and occasionally fresh fruit.

"In 8 years, I lost 155 pounds and I now feel wonderful. My doctor discontinued my blood pressure medication; my blood sugars are within normal range despite my being diagnosed with diabetes years ago; and unlike the results of earlier readings, my cholesterol now stays well below 200. I owe much of my good health to my new eating habits, but I also exercise about 5 days a week. I take nutritional supplements, get enough sleep, drink plenty of pure water, and I play as often as I can. I have a rich spiritual life, too, which helps me to overcome life's challenges in a positive and healthy way.

"What I like best about this new lifestyle is that I don't ever feel deprived. I enjoy preparing and eating a wide variety of foods. I've discovered delicious substitutes for the foods I used to eat. And now I can truly enjoy myself with my son."

# JANET'S ROASTED EGGPLANT AND CHICKPEAS
*227 calories, 25 g carbs*

- **3–4 tablespoons olive oil**
- **1 garlic clove, minced**
- **3 tablespoons marinara sauce**
- **1 teaspoon ground cumin**
- **¼ teaspoon salt**
- **¼ teaspoon ground black pepper**
- **1 eggplant (16 ounces), cubed**
- **1 can (15 ounces) chickpeas, rinsed and drained**
- **1 onion, cut into 1" chunks**
- **1 red or yellow bell pepper, cut into 1" chunks**

Preheat the oven to 350°F.

In a large resealable plastic bag, combine 3 tablespoons of the oil, garlic, marinara sauce, cumin, salt, and pepper. Add the eggplant, chickpeas, onion, and bell pepper. Toss to coat evenly. Pour into a large baking dish and bake, stirring occasionally, until the eggplant is soft and the onions are browned, about 45 minutes. If the mixture becomes dry, add 1 tablespoon more oil. Serve warm or at room temperature.

**Makes 4 servings**

---

**Per serving:** 227 calories, 5 g protein, 25 g carbohydrates, 13 g fat, 1 g saturated fat, 0 mg cholesterol, 387 mg sodium, 8 g fiber

**Diet Exchanges:** 0 milk, 2 vegetable, 0 fruit, 1 bread, 0 meat, 2 fat

*casseroles and one-dish dinners*

Old-Fashioned Lamb Stew

# OLD-FASHIONED LAMB STEW
*356 calories, 13 g carbs*

| | |
|---|---|
| 1 | tablespoon + 1½ teaspoons olive oil |
| 1 | large onion, chopped |
| 1½ | pounds boneless lamb shoulder or neck, trimmed of fat, cut into 1½" cubes |
| ¼ | teaspoon salt |
| ¼ | teaspoon ground black pepper |
| 2 | tablespoons whole wheat flour |
| 1 | garlic clove, finely chopped |
| 2½–3 | cups chicken broth |
| 1 | tablespoon tomato paste |
| 1 | teaspoon dried thyme |
| 1 | teaspoon dried rosemary |
| 1 | bay leaf |
| 3 | carrots, quartered lengthwise where thick, and then into 1" lengths |

Preheat the oven to 350°F.

Heat 1 tablespoon of the oil in a large, heavy pot over medium heat. Add the onion and cook, stirring occasionally, until slightly browned, about 5 minutes. Scrape the onion onto a plate and remove the pot from the heat.

Season the lamb with the salt and pepper. Return the pot to the burner and heat the remaining 1½ teaspoons oil over medium-high heat. Add the lamb and cook until browned on all sides, 8 to 10 minutes.

Return the onion to the pot and sprinkle with the flour and garlic. Cook, stirring, for 2 minutes. Stir in 2½ cups of the broth and the tomato paste, adding more broth as necessary. Bring to a boil and stir in the thyme, rosemary, and bay leaf.

Cover, and bake for 1 hour. Stir in the carrots. Cover and cook until the meat and vegetables are tender, 30 to 40 minutes. If the sauce seems thick, thin it with 2 to 4 tablespoons hot chicken broth. Remove the bay leaf and serve.

## Makes 4 servings

**Per serving:** 356 calories, 32 g protein, 13 g carbohydrates, 19 g fat, 6 g saturated fat, 101 mg cholesterol, 889 mg sodium, 4 g fiber

**Diet Exchanges:** 0 milk, 1½ vegetable, 0 fruit, 0 bread, 4½ meat, 1½ fat

## ▶Flavor Tips

*Substitute parsnips or chopped turnips for the carrots. Substitute ½ cup dry Marsala or Madeira for ½ cup of the broth. Add ¾ cup peas (thawed if frozen) or shelled raw soybeans during the last 3 to 5 minutes of cooking. Serve sprinkled with 1 tablespoon chopped fresh parsley or dill.*

# LAMB SHANKS WITH RED BEANS
*574 calories, 23 g carbs*

| | |
|---|---|
| 1 | cup dry red wine or beef broth |
| 2 | tablespoons tomato paste |
| ½ | cup hot water |
| 4 | lamb shanks (1 pound each) |
| ½ | teaspoon salt |
| ¼ | teaspoon ground black pepper |
| 2 | tablespoons olive oil |
| 1 | large onion, chopped |
| 3 | garlic cloves, minced |
| 2 | teaspoons chopped fresh thyme or 1 teaspoon dried |
| 2 | bay leaves |
| ½ | cup (4 ounces) dried red kidney beans, soaked overnight in 2 cups water |
| 3 | cups water |

Preheat the oven to 325°F.

In a small saucepan, bring the wine or broth to a boil over medium heat. Cook until reduced to ¼ cup, 8 to 10 minutes. Stir in the tomato paste and water.

Season the lamb with the salt and pepper. Heat 1 tablespoon of the oil in a large, heavy pot with oven-safe handles over high heat. Working in batches, add the meat and cook until browned, 2 to 3 minutes per batch or 10 to 12 minutes total.

Remove to a plate as cooking is done. Pour off the fat and add the remaining 1 tablespoon oil. Reduce the heat to medium and stir in the onion and garlic. Cook, stirring occasionally, just until the onion begins to turn translucent, about 5 minutes.

Return the lamb to the pot. Stir in the wine mixture, thyme, and 1 of the bay leaves. Bring to a simmer, cover, and roast, turning the lamb once or twice, until tender, 1½ to 1¾ hours.

Meanwhile, drain the beans, place them in a small saucepan, and add the water and the remaining bay leaf. Bring to a boil, reduce the heat, cover, and cook just until tender, about 1 hour.

Remove the lamb from the pot. Skim and discard the fat from the surface of the liquid in the pot and discard the bay leaf. Return the lamb to the pot. Drain the beans, remove the bay leaf, and add the beans to the meat. Cover and cook 5 minutes more.

**Makes 4 servings**

---

**Per serving:** 574 calories, 67 g protein, 23 g carbohydrates, 18 g fat, 5 g saturated fat, 198 mg cholesterol, 448 mg sodium, 8 g fiber

**Diet Exchanges:** 0 milk, 1 vegetable, 0 fruit, 1 bread, 8½ meat, 3½ fat

# Spicy Curried Vegetables

*180 calories, 26 g carbs*

| | |
|---|---|
| **2** | **tablespoons vegetable oil** |
| **1** | **onion, chopped** |
| **2** | **garlic cloves, minced** |
| **1** | **tablespoon minced fresh ginger** |
| **¼–½** | **teaspoon hot-pepper flakes** |
| **2** | **teaspoons curry powder** |
| **½** | **teaspoon ground cumin** |
| **½** | **teaspoon ground coriander seeds (optional)** |
| **1–1½** | **cups vegetable broth** |
| **1** | **small cauliflower (24 ounces), cut into 1½" florets** |
| **2** | **small red potatoes (3 ounces each), cut into 1" cubes** |
| **6** | **ounces string beans, halved** |
| **½** | **cup canned crushed tomatoes** |
| **½** | **cup plain yogurt (optional)** |

Heat the oil in a deep, large skillet or pot over low to medium heat. Stir in the onion, garlic, ginger, and pepper flakes. Cook the mixture, stirring occasionally, until the onion is slightly softened, 2 to 3 minutes. Add the curry powder, cumin, and coriander (if using). Cook, stirring, for 30 seconds. Stir in 1 cup of the broth, the cauliflower, potatoes, beans, and tomatoes. Cover, and cook over medium heat until the vegetables are tender, stirring occasionally and adding up to ½ cup broth as needed, 20 to 25 minutes. There should be 2 to 3 tablespoons of thin sauce in the pan. Remove the pan from the heat and gently stir in the yogurt (if using).

**Makes 4 servings**

---

**Per serving:** 180 calories, 7 g protein, 26 g carbohydrates, 7 g fat, 1 g saturated fat, 0 mg cholesterol, 448 mg sodium, 8 g fiber

**Diet Exchanges:** 0 milk, 3½ vegetable, 0 fruit, ½ bread, 0 meat, 1½ fat

## ▶Flavor Tips

*Top each serving with 1 tablespoon chopped fresh cilantro. Add ½ cup of frozen peas during the last 5 minutes of cooking time. Substitute turnips for the potatoes. Serve with brown rice.*

# MOUSSAKA
*373 calories, 14 g carbs*

| | |
|---|---|
| I | tablespoon olive oil |
| I | large onion, chopped |
| 2–3 | garlic cloves, minced |
| 1¾ | pounds ground lamb |
| I | can (15 ounces) crushed tomatoes |
| 1½ | teaspoons dried oregano |
| I | teaspoon ground allspice |
| I | teaspoon salt |
| ½ | teaspoon ground black pepper |
| 2 | eggplants (32 ounces), peeled and sliced lengthwise into slabs ¼" thick |
| 3 | large eggs, at room temperature |
| I | cup half-and-half, at room temperature |
| ½ | cup (2 ounces) finely crumbled feta cheese |
| ⅓ | cup (about 1½ ounces) grated Parmesan cheese |
| ⅛ | teaspoon ground nutmeg (optional) |

Heat the oil in a large skillet over medium heat. Add the onion and cook, stirring occasionally, until softened and lightly browned, 6 to 8 minutes. Stir in the garlic and lamb. Increase the heat to medium-high and cook, stirring to crumble, just until no longer pink, 7 to 8 minutes. Drain the excess fat. Stir in the tomatoes, oregano, allspice, ½ teaspoon of the salt, and ¼ teaspoon of the pepper. Reduce the heat to very low. Partially cover and cook until very thick, 25 to 30 minutes.

Meanwhile, preheat the broiler. Place the eggplant on a large baking sheet and generously coat both sides with cooking spray (work in batches if necessary). Sprinkle with the remaining ½ teaspoon salt and ⅛ teaspoon of the remaining pepper. Broil 5" from the heat until just beginning to brown, 2 to 3 minutes per side.

In a bowl, lightly beat the eggs and half-and-half. Stir in the feta, Parmesan, nutmeg (if using), and remaining ⅛ teaspoon pepper.

Reduce the oven temperature to 350°F. Arrange a layer of eggplant in a shallow 2½-quart baking dish. Top with a layer of the meat mixture. Add another layer of eggplant, another layer of the meat mixture, and top with a layer of eggplant. Poke several holes through the layers with a fork. Pour the cream mixture evenly over the top. Bake until the egg is set and lightly browned, 30 to 35 minutes. Let stand 15 to 20 minutes before cutting and serving.

**Makes 8 servings**

**Per serving:** 373 calories, 25 g protein, 14 g carbohydrates, 23 g fat, 10 g saturated fat, 170 mg cholesterol, 699 mg sodium, 4 g fiber

**Diet Exchanges:** 0 milk, 3 vegetable, 0 fruit, 0 bread, 3 meat, 3 fat

## Time-Saver

This Greek-style dish keeps well. Make it ahead or store extra portions in a covered container in the refrigerator for up to 2 days. To reheat, place in a baking dish, cover, and bake at 350°F until heated through, about 25 minutes.

# Shepherd's Pie
*407 calories, 26 g carbs*

| | |
|---|---|
| 4–5 | potatoes (16 ounces), peeled and chopped |
| 2–3 | small turnips (8 ounces), peeled and chopped |
| 2 | tablespoons olive oil |
| 1 | large onion, chopped |
| 2 | large garlic cloves, minced |
| 1½ | pounds ground lamb |
| 1 | can (15 ounces) tomato puree |
| ½ | cup chicken broth |
| 1½ | teaspoons dried thyme or oregano |
| 1 | bay leaf |
| ½ | teaspoon salt |
| ½ | teaspoon ground black pepper |
| ⅓ | cup 2% milk |
| 2 | tablespoons butter |
| ¼ | cup (1 ounce) grated Pecorino Romano cheese (optional) |

Fill a large pot with salted water. Add the potatoes and turnips and bring to a boil over high heat. Reduce the heat to medium-low, cover, and cook until tender, 15 to 20 minutes.

Meanwhile, heat the oil in a large, oven-safe heavy skillet over medium heat. Add the onion and cook, stirring occasionally, until translucent and slightly browned, 5 to 6 minutes. Add the garlic and lamb, and cook, stirring to crumble, just until the lamb is no longer pink, 3 to 4 minutes. Drain off and discard the fat from the pan. Stir in the tomato puree, broth, thyme, bay leaf, salt, and ¼ teaspoon of the pepper. Reduce the heat to low, and cook, stirring occasionally, until very thick, 25 to 30 minutes. Keep warm.

In a small saucepan, combine the milk and butter. Heat over low heat until the butter is melted. Drain the potato-turnip mixture and return it to the pot. Mash, gradually adding the milk mixture, until smooth and fluffy. Season with the remaining ¼ teaspoon pepper.

Discard the bay leaf from the meat mixture. Spread the mashed potatoes over the meat to within 1" of the skillet sides, and serve. Or sprinkle with the cheese (if using) and broil 4" from the heat source until lightly browned, 2 to 3 minutes, before serving.

**Makes 6 servings**

**Per serving:** 407 calories, 22 g protein, 26 g carbohydrates, 24 g fat, 10 g saturated fat, 86 mg cholesterol, 675 mg sodium, 4 g fiber

**Diet Exchanges:** 0 milk, 2 vegetable, 0 fruit, 1 bread, 2½ meat, 3 fat

## ▶Flavor Tips
*Substitute ground beef for the lamb. Add thawed frozen peas (10 ounces) to the meat mixture during the last 5 minutes of cooking.*

Shepherd's Pie

# vegetables & side dishes

# ZUCCHINI AND RED PEPPERS IN LEMON-HERB BUTTER

*107 calories, 7 g carbs*

**6**    small zucchini (24 ounces), sliced ½" thick

**½**    red bell pepper, chopped

**3**    tablespoons butter

**2**    tablespoons chicken broth

**¼**    teaspoon salt

**⅛**    teaspoon ground black pepper

**2**    teaspoons grated lemon peel

**1**    tablespoon lemon juice

**2**    tablespoons finely chopped parsley

In a large skillet, combine the zucchini, bell pepper, butter, broth, salt, and black pepper. Cover and cook, over medium heat, until steam comes from the skillet, about 3 minutes. Uncover and raise the heat to medium-high. Cook, stirring occasionally, until the vegetables are tender but intact and practically no liquid remains in the pan, 8 to 10 minutes. Stir in the lemon peel and juice. Remove from the heat and stir in the parsley.

**Makes 4 servings**

**Per serving:** 107 calories, 2 g protein, 7 g carbohydrates, 9 g fat, 5 g saturated fat, 23 mg cholesterol, 271 mg sodium, 3 g fiber

**Diet Exchanges:** 0 milk, 1 vegetable, 0 fruit, 0 bread, 0 meat, 2 fat

## ▶Flavor Tips

*Substitute yellow squash for the zucchini, or use half yellow squash and half zucchini. Stir in 2 teaspoons chopped fresh basil with the parsley. Or add a pinch of hot-pepper flakes.*

# MUSHROOMS PROVENÇALE

*114 calories, 5 g carbs*

| | |
|---|---|
| 20 | mushrooms, thickly sliced |
| 2 | tablespoons olive oil |
| 1 | tablespoon butter |
| 4 | scallions, white part only, finely chopped |
| 2 | garlic cloves, minced |
| 2–3 | teaspoons lemon juice |
| ¼ | teaspoon salt |
| ⅛ | teaspoon ground black pepper |
| 2 | tablespoons finely chopped parsley |

Place the mushrooms in a large skillet. Cover and cook over medium-high heat until the mushrooms start to give off moisture, 5 to 6 minutes. Uncover and cook until they begin to stick to the pan. Reduce the heat to low and stir in the oil, butter, scallions, garlic, and lemon juice. Cook for 30 seconds, season with the salt and pepper, and serve sprinkled with the parsley.

**Makes 4 servings**

---

**Per serving:** 114 calories, 3 g protein, 5 g carbohydrates, 10 g fat, 3 g saturated fat, 8 mg cholesterol, 179 mg sodium, 2 g fiber

**Diet Exchanges:** 0 milk, 1 vegetable, 0 fruit, 0 bread, 0 meat, 2 fat

# SAVORY LIMA BEANS WITH BACON

*155 calories, 18 g carbs*

| | |
|---|---|
| **2** | **strips bacon** |
| **1** | **small onion, thinly sliced** |
| **1** | **carrot, finely chopped** |
| **1** | **package (10 ounces) Fordhook lima beans, thawed** |
| **¼** | **cup water** |
| **½** | **teaspoon dried marjoram or thyme** |
| **⅛** | **teaspoon salt** |
| | **Pinch of ground black pepper** |

Cook the bacon in a skillet over medium-low heat, turning the strips occasionally, until browned and crisp, 6 to 8 minutes. Drain on a paper towel-lined plate and cover with foil to keep warm. Reserve the bacon fat in the skillet.

Add the onion and carrot to the skillet. Cover and cook, stirring occasionally, until the onion is lightly golden and almost tender, 6 to 8 minutes. Stir in the lima beans, water, marjoram or thyme, salt, and pepper. Cover and cook until the beans are tender, 8 to 10 minutes. Uncover, and if any water remains in the skillet, increase the heat to medium and cook until evaporated, 1 to 2 minutes, stirring once or twice. Serve with the bacon crumbled over top.

**Makes 4 servings**

---

**Per serving:** 155 calories, 6 g protein, 18 g carbohydrates, 7 g fat, 2 g saturated fat, 8 mg cholesterol, 228 mg sodium, 5 g fiber

**Diet Exchanges:** 0 milk, ½ vegetable, 0 fruit, 1 bread, 0 meat, 1½ fat

▶Flavor Tips

Substitute 2 to 3 chopped scallions for the onion. You could also eliminate the bacon and use 2 tablespoons butter in place of the bacon fat.

# BAKED PEPPERS WITH ONION AND TOMATO

*123 calories, 8 g carbs*

| | |
|---|---|
| **2** | **large red bell peppers, halved lengthwise and seeded** |
| **1** | **large tomato, cut into 4 slices** |
| **1** | **small red onion, thinly sliced** |
| **1** | **large garlic clove, cut into 8 thin lengthwise slices** |
| **2** | **anchovy fillets, halved (optional)** |
| **½** | **teaspoon dried oregano** |
| **¼** | **teaspoon salt** |
| **⅛** | **teaspoon ground black pepper** |
| **3** | **tablespoons olive oil** |

Preheat the oven to 425°F.

Place the peppers, hollow side up, on a baking sheet. Place a tomato slice in each cavity. Top with 1 or 2 slices of onion, 2 slices of garlic, and an anchovy half (if using). Sprinkle with the oregano, salt, and black pepper. Drizzle with the oil. Roast just until tender, 25 to 30 minutes. Serve warm or at room temperature and top with any oil left in the pan.

**Makes 4 servings**

---

**Per serving:** 123 calories, 1 g protein, 8 g carbohydrates, 10 g fat, 1 g saturated fat, 0 mg cholesterol, 153 mg sodium, 2 g fiber

**Diet Exchanges:** 0 milk, 1½ vegetable, 0 fruit, 0 bread, 0 meat, 2 fat

## *Time-Saver*

*Save extras for lunch—these peppers make a nice meal with cheese and rye crisp crackers. Store leftovers in a covered container in the refrigerator for up to 3 days and serve at room temperature.*

*Asparagus with Orange-Walnut Vinaigrette*

# ASPARAGUS WITH ORANGE-WALNUT VINAIGRETTE

*111 calories, 5 g carbs*

½ + ⅛ **teaspoon salt**

1 **bunch (16 ounces) asparagus, ends trimmed**

5 **teaspoons apple cider vinegar**

2 **tablespoons walnut or olive oil**

2 **teaspoons grated orange peel**

⅛ **teaspoon ground black pepper**

2 **tablespoons walnuts, coarsely chopped**

Pour water to ½" deep in a large skillet. Add ⅛ teaspoon of the salt and bring to a boil over high heat. Add the asparagus and cook, until tender-firm, 4 to 7 minutes. Drain in a colander and cool under cold running water. Drain and lay on a paper towel-lined plate to dry.

In a small bowl, whisk the vinegar, oil, orange peel, pepper, and remaining ⅛ teaspoon salt. Remove the asparagus to a platter, spoon the vinaigrette over the top, and sprinkle with the nuts. Serve at room temperature or chilled.

**Makes 4 servings**

**Per serving:** 111 calories, 3 g protein, 5 g carbohydrates, 10 g fat, 1 g saturated fat, 0 mg cholesterol, 181 mg sodium, 2 g fiber

**Diet Exchanges:** 0 milk, 1 vegetable, 0 fruit, 0 bread, 0 meat, 2 fat

## Flavor Tip

*Lightly toast the nuts to coax out their best flavor and texture.*

# ROASTED CAULIFLOWER WITH NUTTY LEMON MUSTARD
*230 calories, 12 g carbs*

| | |
|---|---|
| I | **small head cauliflower, cut into small florets** |
| 3 | **tablespoons walnut or olive oil** |
| ⅛ | **teaspoon salt** |
| I | **tablespoon lemon juice** |
| I | **tablespoon Dijon mustard** |
| ⅓ | **cup half-and-half** |
| ⅓ | **cup toasted walnuts, coarsely chopped** |
| ⅛ | **teaspoon ground black pepper** |

Preheat the oven to 450°F.

In a roasting pan, toss the cauliflower with 2 tablespoons of the oil and the salt. Roast until tender and lightly browned, stirring once or twice, 15 to 20 minutes.

In a large bowl, whisk together the lemon juice, mustard, half-and-half, and remaining 1 tablespoon oil. Add the cauliflower, scraping any residual oil into the bowl. Add the nuts and pepper, and toss to coat. Serve warm.

**Makes 4 servings**

**Per serving:** 230 calories, 6 g protein, 12 g carbohydrates, 19 g fat, 3 g saturated fat, 10 mg cholesterol, 231 mg sodium, 5 g fiber

**Diet Exchanges:** 0 milk, 2 vegetable, 0 fruit, 0 bread, ½ meat, 3½ fat

▶Flavor Tips

*Replace the walnuts with pecans or hazelnuts. Serve topped with 1 teaspoon of chopped fresh oregano leaves. Or serve on a bed of watercress.*

# CABBAGE SALAD WITH APPLES, LIME, AND GINGER
*147 calories, 16 g carbs*

- **2**    **tablespoons rice vinegar**
- **¼**    **cup lime juice**
- **1**    **teaspoon grated, peeled fresh ginger**
- **¼**    **cup walnut or vegetable oil**
- **½**    **teaspoon celery seed**
- **¼**    **teaspoon salt**
- **⅛**    **teaspoon ground black pepper**
- **4**    **cups (about ¼ head) shredded green cabbage**
- **2**    **large sweet apples (12 ounces) such as Rome, unpeeled and cut into matchsticks**

In a large bowl, whisk the vinegar, lime juice, and ginger. Gradually whisk in the oil, celery seed, salt, and pepper. Add the cabbage and apples. Gently toss to coat. Refrigerate for 30 minutes before serving.

**Makes 6 servings**

---

**Per serving:** 147 calories, 1 g protein, 16 g carbohydrates, 9 g fat, 1 g saturated fat, 0 mg cholesterol, 106 mg sodium, 4 g fiber

**Diet Exchanges:** 0 milk, ½ vegetable, ½ fruit, 0 bread, 0 meat, 2 fat

## Smart-Carb Insider Tip

### BE WARY OF SALAD

It's not hard to go astray at a salad bar. A little of this and a little of that, and before you know it you may have piled on 30 or 40 grams of carbohydrate. Skip the prepared salads. Instead, choose fresh, plain vegetables, olives, nuts, sunflower seeds, and beans like chickpeas. Bacon bits and cheese may all be imitation and higher in carbs than you think. Choose an oil and vinegar–style dressing unless the bottles are out and you can read the labels. Remember that low-fat dressings are often higher in sugar content.

# MIDWESTERN-STYLE CREAMED CABBAGE

*112 calories, 9 g carbs*

| | |
|---|---|
| **6** | **cups (about ½ small head) shredded green cabbage** |
| **⅓** | **cup water** |
| **⅔** | **cup half-and-half** |
| **1** | **tablespoon butter** |
| **½** | **teaspoon dried dillweed** |
| **¼** | **teaspoon salt** |
| **⅛** | **teaspoon ground black pepper** |
| | **Pinch of ground nutmeg** |

Place the cabbage and water in a Dutch oven or large, deep skillet. Cook over medium-high heat, stirring occasionally, until the cabbage is somewhat softened and the water has evaporated, 12 to 13 minutes.

Reduce the heat to low, stir in the half-and-half, butter, and dill. Cover, and cook until the cabbage is tender, about 15 minutes, stirring occasionally. Season with the salt, pepper, and nutmeg.

**Makes 4 servings**

---

**Per serving:** 112 calories, 3 g protein, 9 g carbohydrates, 7 g fat, 4 g saturated fat, 28 mg cholesterol, 219 mg sodium, 3 g fiber

**Diet Exchanges:** 0 milk, 1½ vegetable, 0 fruit, 0 bread, 0 meat, 1½ fat

## *Time-Saver*

Make this dish ahead and store in a covered container in the refrigerator for up to 3 days. To reheat, place in a skillet and add 1 to 2 tablespoons water. Cover and cook over low heat, stirring occasionally, until heated through, 3 to 4 minutes.

# Red Cabbage with Apples

*122 calories, 15 g carbs*

*20 min —
350 = bubbly Ricotta*

*no salt*

...dered bacon fat

...mall head)
...bbage

...r cider

...ith or other tart
...d coarsely

...ine vinegar

...yme

...llspice

...black pepper

Heat the bacon fat or oil in a Dutch oven or large, deep skillet over medium-low heat. Stir in the cabbage and cook, stirring occasionally, until it begins to wilt, 5 to 6 min-utes. Stir in the apple juice or cider, the apple, vinegar, thyme, and allspice. Cover and cook over low heat until the cabbage is very tender, 25 to 30 minutes, stirring occasionally. Season with the salt and pepper.

**Makes 4 servings**

**Per serving:** 122 calories, 2 g protein, 15 g carbohydrates, 7 g fat, 1 g saturated fat, 0 mg cholesterol, 165 mg sodium, 4 g fiber

**Diet Exchanges:** 0 milk, 1 vegetable, ½ fruit, 0 bread, 0 meat, 1½ fat

## Time-Saver

*Make this German-style dish whenever you have a minute. It keeps in a covered container in the refrigerator for up to 5 days. To reheat, place it in a skillet and add 1 to 2 tablespoons water. Cover and cook over low heat, stirring occasionally, until heated through, 3 to 4 minutes.*

Spinach Salad with Warm Bacon Vinaigrette

# SPINACH SALAD WITH WARM BACON VINAIGRETTE
*201 calories, 6 g carbs*

| | |
|---|---|
| 3 | **strips bacon** |
| 2–3 | **tablespoons walnut or olive oil** |
| 2 | **tablespoons red wine vinegar or other vinegar** |
| 1 | **teaspoon Dijon mustard (optional)** |
| 1 | **small garlic clove, minced** |
| ⅛ | **teaspoon salt** |
| ⅛ | **teaspoon ground black pepper** |
| 1 | **bunch (10 ounces) spinach, coarse stems trimmed (about 5 cups loosely packed)** |
| 1 | **Macintosh apple (4 ounces), peeled and cut into ½" pieces** |
| 8 | **shavings (¾ ounce) Romano cheese, each about 1" × 2"** |

Cook the bacon in a skillet over medium-low heat, turning the slices occasionally until crisp and browned, 8 to 10 minutes. Drain on a paper towel-lined plate and keep warm. Measure the fat in the pan (there should be 2 to 3 tablespoons). Add enough oil to equal 5 tablespoons of total fat in the pan. Whisk the vinegar, mustard (if using), garlic, salt, and pepper into the fat in the pan. Keep warm.

In a large bowl, combine the spinach and apple. Spoon the warm bacon mixture over the spinach and apple. Toss to coat. Divide among 4 plates, crumble the bacon over the spinach, and top with the cheese.

**Makes 4 servings**

---

**Per serving:** 201 calories, 4 g protein, 6 g carbohydrates, 18 g fat, 5 g saturated fat, 17 mg cholesterol, 372 mg sodium, 2 g fiber

**Diet Exchanges:** 0 milk, ½ vegetable, ½ fruit, 0 bread, ½ meat, 3 fat

## ▶Flavor Tips

The Romano cheese on this salad tastes best when cut into shavings (thin slices) rather than grated over top. To cut a shaving of Romano cheese, drag a vegetable peeler or cheese slicer along the broad side of the block of cheese to create thin slices about 1" wide and 2" long. To make a main-dish salad, garnish each serving with 2 or 3 wedges of tomato, a few slices of hard-cooked egg, and a slice of red onion. Or add cold, cooked chicken.

# BITTER GREENS WITH GOAT CHEESE, PINE NUTS, AND PEARS

*159 calories, 7 g carbs*

| | |
|---|---|
| 3 | tablespoons (3 ounces) log-type goat cheese |
| 1 | tablespoon olive or walnut oil |
| 2–3 | tablespoons 2% milk |
| 1 | tablespoon lemon juice |
| 1/8 | teaspoon salt |
| 1/8 | teaspoon ground black pepper |
| 2 | large heads Belgian endive, leaves separated and cut into 1" diagonal slices |
| 1 | large bunch watercress, chopped |
| 2 | tablespoons toasted pine nuts |
| 1/2 | large bosc pear (4 ounces total), cut into 1/2" cubes |

**Per serving:** 159 calories, 7 g protein, 7 g carbohydrates, 12 g fat, 5 g saturated fat, 17 mg cholesterol, 214 mg sodium, 2 g fiber

**Diet Exchanges:** 0 milk, 0 vegetable, 1/2 fruit, 0 bread, 1 meat, 2 fat

## ▶Flavor Tips

*Substitute 4 cups mixed baby spring greens or 1 large bunch arugula for the Belgian endive. Substitute 2 kiwifruits for the pear. Keep the dressing refrigerated in a covered container for up to 5 days. Bring to room temperature before using.*

In a blender, combine the cheese, oil, 2 tablespoons of the milk, the lemon juice, salt, and pepper. Process until thickened and creamy, adding up to another tablespoon milk if too thick.

Place the endive and watercress in a large salad bowl, add the cheese mixture, and toss to combine. Divide among 4 plates. Sprinkle with the nuts and pear.

**Makes 4 servings**

Bitter Greens with Goat Cheese, Pine Nuts, and Pears

# I Did It!

## Norma Gates

Norma had been gaining 10 pounds a year. Before she knew it, she weighed 243 pounds and wore a size 24. When her request for gastric bypass surgery was denied, Norma became focused, ate a sensible low-carb diet, and lost 40 pounds in 8 months.

"With a steady weight gain of 10 pounds per year, I added larger- and larger-size clothes to my wardrobe each new season. Before I knew it, I was wearing a size 24. I had gained 110 pounds over the course of 12 years.

"When I had only 20 to 30 pounds to lose, I used to mentally beat up on myself for not getting hold of my problem. After gaining over 100 pounds, I desperately wanted a resolution. I went to a surgeon with hopes that a gastric bypass,

before

**Weight lost:** 44 pounds
**Time kept off:** 3½ years
**Weight-loss strategies:** Reduced carb intake, reduced portion sizes, ate more slowly, stopped eating when full, walked regularly
**Weight-maintenance strategies:** Maintains lower carb intake and smaller portion sizes, eats more slowly, stops eating when full, accepts gradual weight loss, and continues to walk 3–5 days a week

*vegetables and side dishes*

which would cause food to bypass most of my stomach, would change my life. When the doctor told me I was not a surgical candidate because I didn't have any other medical problems, I was heartbroken.

"I remember how embarrassed I was while watching a video taken of me seated on our front porch. Sadly, even that didn't motivate me enough to start watching my food intake. I was overwhelmed by cravings for food. Even when I was away from home, I would count the minutes until I could get back to my refrigerator.

"Not understanding my carb 'addiction' at that time, I could almost relate it to a person going through withdrawal from cigarette smoking.

"There came a point when I knew I'd have to do something about my eating behavior. Psychological counseling didn't help. Finally, I consulted a dietitian.

"My dietitian took a comprehensive medical and diet history and immediately placed my 243-pound body on a low-carbohydrate eating plan. As soon as I started reading food labels, I realized what massive amounts of sugars and starches I was consuming. About 90 percent of my diet was carbohydrate!

"Within 2 weeks of eating fewer carbs, I lost 11 pounds. A few weeks later—and 20 pounds lighter—I felt like I had broken my carbohydrate addiction. The food cravings finally subsided. I had more energy and I started walking five times a week for 2 to 3 miles each time.

"Over the next 5 months, I lost another 20 pounds. It is incredible how much better I felt. I can remember getting teary-eyed as I stood in front of a full-length mirror in my favorite department store admiring myself in a size 18 instead of a size 24. Extra attention from my husband and friends reinforced the excitement of being on the road to successful weight loss. Dropping below the 200-pound mark was another milestone.

"I no longer shop in the plus-size department at the stores. (I can wear sizes 16 and 18 in bottoms and extra-large tops). I can't even begin to tell someone what that feels like!

"My husband and I almost always split meals whenever we go out. It not only saves us calories (and carbs, especially in the breads and pastas that are so popular in restaurants), but it saves us money as well.

"If by chance I am not at my 150-pound goal weight as you read this, it's okay with me—as long as I have not regained the weight. I have learned to accept my body at every stage along the way to my goal. My expectations are realistic. I do not have to be in a hurry. I am eating a variety of healthy and delicious foods, I have control over my portions, I have plenty of energy, and I have newfound pleasures in life besides just food."

(continued)

vegetables and side dishes

# I Did It! (cont.)

## NORMA'S SPINACH SALAD WITH CAJUN CHICKEN

*391 calories, 10 g carbs*

- 4 **boneless, skinless chicken breast halves (6 ounces each)**
- 1 **tablespoon Cajun seasoning**
- 2 **bacon strips**
- 8 **cups (16 ounces) fresh spinach, washed and torn**
- ½ **cucumber, chopped**
- 2 **hard-cooked eggs, chopped**
- ¼ **cup crumbled feta cheese**
- ¼ **cup whole wheat croutons**
- 3 **tablespoons sliced black olives**
- 2 **tablespoons pecans, chopped, or sunflower seeds**
- ¼ **cup bottled Italian vinaigrette or other dressing**

Preheat the grill or broiler to 350°F. Coat the grill rack or broiler pan with cooking spray.

Place the chicken in a zip-top bag. Add the seasoning and shake to coat. Transfer to the prepared grill rack or broiler pan and grill or broil, turning once, until the juices run clear and the internal temperature registers 160°F, 8 to 10 minutes. Cut into strips and set aside.

Meanwhile, cook the bacon in a skillet over medium-low heat, turning the strips occasionally, until browned and crisp, 6 to 8 minutes. Drain on a paper towel-lined plate.

When cool enough to handle, crumble the bacon into a large bowl with the spinach. Add the cucumber, eggs, feta, croutons, olives, and pecans or seeds. Pour in the dressing and toss to coat. Divide among four salad plates and top with the chicken.

**Makes 4 servings**

**Per serving:** 391 calories, 48 g protein, 10 g carbohydrates, 17 g fat, 4 g saturated fat, 216 mg cholesterol, 1,241 mg sodium, 3 g fiber

**Diet Exchanges:** 0 milk, 1 vegetable, 0 fruit, ½ bread, 6 meat, 2½ fat

## Time-Savers

*If you're in a hurry to whip up this main-dish salad, you can replace the bacon with real bacon pieces (not imitation) from your grocery store. Or omit them altogether, which will reduce the sodium in this dish.*

# TOSSED SALAD WITH GREEN HERB DRESSING
*145 calories, 5 g carbs*

2   **cups baby spinach leaves**

½   **cup lightly packed parsley leaves**

⅓   **cup lightly packed fresh dill**

¼   **cup walnut or olive oil**

2   **tablespoons chicken
    or vegetable broth**

4   **teaspoons apple cider vinegar**

¼   **teaspoon salt**

⅛   **teaspoon ground black pepper**

8   **cups mixed salad greens**

Combine the spinach, parsley, dill, oil, broth, vinegar, salt, and pepper in a blender or food processor. Process, scraping the sides of the jar once or twice, until smooth and slightly thickened.

Place the salad greens in a large bowl, drizzle the spinach mixture over the top, and toss gently to coat.

**Makes 4 servings**

---

**Per serving:** 145 calories, 2 g protein, 5 g carbohydrates, 14 g fat, 2 g saturated fat, 0 mg cholesterol, 245 mg sodium, 3 g fiber

**Diet Exchanges:** 0 milk, 1 vegetable, 0 fruit, 0 bread, 0 meat, 1½ fat

## ▶Flavor Tips

*Sprinkle 1 tablespoon of chopped pecans or walnuts over the salad when serving. Garnish with slices of ripe tomato. Substitute grapeseed or flaxseed oil for the walnut or olive oil. The dressing will keep in a covered container in the refrigerator for up to 3 days.*

# Tomato-Onion Salad with Walnut Vinaigrette
*164 calories, 5 g carbs*

| | |
|---|---|
| ¼ | cup walnut oil |
| 1–1½ | tablespoons lemon juice |
| 1 | small garlic clove, minced |
| 2 | teaspoons chopped fresh tarragon or ½ teaspoon dried |
| ⅛ | teaspoon salt |
| ⅛ | teaspoon ground black pepper |
| 4 | tomatoes (4 ounces each), sliced |
| 1 | red onion, sliced |
| 2 | tablespoons chopped walnuts |

**Per serving:** 164 calories, 1 g protein, 5 g carbohydrates, 16 g fat, 1 g saturated fat, 0 mg cholesterol, 97 mg sodium, 1 g fiber

**Diet Exchanges:** 0 milk, 1 vegetable, 0 fruit, 0 bread, 0 meat, 3 fat

## Time-Saver

Make the dressing ahead; it stores well in a covered container in the refrigerator for up to 3 days.

In a small bowl, whisk the oil, lemon juice, garlic, tarragon, salt, and pepper.

On individual plates or a serving platter, overlap the tomato and onion slices in an alternating pattern until all the slices have been used. Drizzle with the tarragon-garlic mixture. Top with the walnuts.

**Makes 4 servings**

## HIDDEN ROADBLOCK to weight loss

### TRIGGER FOODS

If you eat many of the same foods day after day, there is a good chance that these are your trigger foods. Do you eat cereal every morning? Lots of pasta for dinner? The foods you eat most frequently are usually the foods that can trigger you to overeat. To manage your trigger foods, be sure to eat a wide variety of foods. Break out of old eating habits by making it a point to try something new every day. To find out more about identifying and managing your trigger foods, see page 31.

# CUCUMBER AND RADISH SALAD WITH SESAME-SOY DRESSING
*106 calories, 13 g carbs*

| | |
|---|---|
| 3 | tablespoons rice vinegar |
| 2 | tablespoons reduced-sodium soy sauce |
| 1½ | tablespoons orange juice |
| 1 | tablespoon toasted sesame oil |
| 1 | teaspoon grated, peeled, fresh ginger or ½ teaspoon ground |
| 1 | garlic clove, crushed |
| ⅛ | teaspoon hot-pepper sauce (optional) |
| 4 | small or 1 seedless cucumber (12 ounces), peeled and thinly sliced |
| 8 | radishes (about 1 cup), thinly sliced |
| ½ | small red onion, halved and thinly sliced |
| 2 | teaspoons toasted sesame seeds |

In a large bowl, whisk together the vinegar, soy sauce, juice, oil, ginger, garlic, and hot-pepper sauce (if using). Add the cucumber, radishes, onion, and sesame seeds. Toss well and serve at room temperature or chilled.

**Makes 4 servings**

---

**Per serving:** 106 calories, 2 g protein, 13 g carbohydrates, 5 g fat, 1 g saturated fat, 0 mg cholesterol, 312 mg sodium, 2 g fiber

**Diet Exchanges:** 0 milk, 2 vegetable, 0 fruit, 0 bread, 0 meat, 1½ fat

## ▶Flavor Tip

*Top with 1 tablespoon chopped fresh cilantro before serving.*

# SPANISH-STYLE GREEN BEANS
*162 calories, 13 g carbs*

| | |
|---|---|
| 16 | ounces green beans, trimmed and cut into 2" lengths |
| 3 | tablespoons olive oil |
| 1 | onion, chopped |
| 1 | small green bell pepper, chopped |
| 1 | tomato (4 ounces), peeled, seeded, and coarsely chopped |
| 2 | garlic cloves, minced |
| ¼ | teaspoon salt |
| ⅛ | teaspoon ground black pepper |
| 2–3 | tablespoons coarsely chopped, pitted kalamata olives |
| 2 | teaspoons drained capers (optional) |

Combine the beans, oil, onion, bell pepper, tomato, garlic, salt, and black pepper in a saucepan over medium heat. Cook, stirring, until the vegetables start to sizzle, 2 to 3 minutes. Reduce the heat to low, cover, and cook, stirring occasionally, until the beans are very tender but not falling apart, 20 to 25 minutes. Stir in the olives and capers (if using) and heat 1 minute. Serve warm, at room temperature, or chilled.

**Makes 4 servings**

---

**Per serving:** 162 calories, 2 g protein, 13 g carbohydrates, 12 g fat, 2 g saturated fat, 0 mg cholesterol, 230 mg sodium, 6 g fiber

**Diet Exchanges:** 0 milk, 2½ vegetable, 0 fruit, 0 bread, 0 meat, 2½ fat

# GREEN SOYBEANS WITH SESAME OIL AND GINGER
*148 calories, 9 g carbs*

| | |
|---|---|
| 1 | **bag (12 ounces) shelled green soybeans** |
| ½ | **cup water** |
| 1 | **tablespoon soy sauce** |
| 2–3 | **teaspoons minced, peeled fresh ginger** |
| 2 | **teaspoons sesame oil** |
| | **Pinch of ground red pepper (optional)** |
| | **Pinch of salt (optional)** |

In a saucepan, combine the soybeans, water, soy sauce, and ginger. Bring to a boil over high heat, stirring once or twice. Reduce the heat to low, cover, and cook for 6 minutes. Uncover and cook until the beans are tender and the liquid evaporates, 6 to 8 minutes more.

Remove from the heat, stir in the oil, pepper (if using), and salt (if using). Serve hot.

**Makes 4 servings**

**Per serving:** 148 calories, 12 g protein, 9 g carbohydrates, 8 g fat, 1 g saturated fat, 0 mg cholesterol, 244 mg sodium, 4 g fiber

**Diet Exchanges:** 0 milk, 2 vegetable, 0 fruit, 0 bread, 1 meat, 1 fat

## ▶Flavor Tips

Green soybeans (also called by their Japanese name, edamame) have a wonderful fresh flavor. They are picked before they are fully mature and are often sold in bags in Asian markets, health food stores, and large supermarkets. You might find them left in their fuzzy green pods (in which case you can simply remove them from the pods). To add a mild pepper flavor, sprinkle cracked peppercorns over the beans just before serving. Consider cracking whole peppercorns at home rather than using prepared cracked black pepper. Freshly cracked peppercorns have much more flavor. To crush peppercorns, use the bottom of a heavy skillet.

# COUSCOUS SALAD WITH LIME-CUMIN DRESSING

*214 calories, 32 g carbs*

| | |
|---|---|
| **3** | **tablespoons peanut or olive oil** |
| **½** | **large red bell pepper, chopped** |
| **1** | **cup whole wheat couscous** |
| **1¼** | **cups hot vegetable broth or chicken broth** |
| **3** | **tablespoons lime juice** |
| **1** | **teaspoon ground cumin** |
| **3–4** | **drops hot-pepper sauce** |
| **⅓** | **cup pine nuts (optional)** |
| **1** | **scallion, finely chopped** |

Heat 1 tablespoon of the oil in a small saucepan over medium-high heat. Add the bell pepper and cook, stirring occasionally, until tender-firm, 3 to 4 minutes. Add the couscous and stir for 30 seconds. Add the broth. Bring to a boil and stir once. Cover tightly, remove from the heat, and let sit for 5 minutes.

Meanwhile, in a bowl, whisk the lime juice, the remaining 2 tablespoons oil, cumin, and hot-pepper sauce.

Fluff the couscous with a fork and add it to the lime dressing. Toss to combine. Add the pine nuts (if using) and scallion and toss. Serve warm or at room temperature.

**Makes 6 servings**

---

**Per serving:** 214 calories, 6 g protein, 32 g carbohydrates, 8 g fat, 1 g saturated fat, 0 mg cholesterol, 220 mg sodium, 5 g fiber

**Diet Exchanges:** 0 milk, 0 vegetable, 0 fruit, 2 bread, 0 meat, 1½ fat

## Time-Savers

Use 1½ finely chopped jarred roasted peppers instead of the fresh bell peppers. Also, this dish stores well for later meals—and improves with age. Keep it in a covered container in the refrigerator for up to 3 days and serve at room temperature.

*Couscous Salad with Lime-Cumin Dressing*

# HOMINY GRITS, CHEESE, AND CHILE CASSEROLE

*229 calories, 20 g carbs*

3 cups water

2 cups 2% milk

½ teaspoon salt

I cup hominy grits

¼ cup butter

I cup shredded sharp **Cheddar or Monterey Jack cheese (4 ounces)**

2 large eggs, lightly beaten

2–4 tablespoons canned, roasted, chopped Mexican chiles

⅛ teaspoon ground black pepper

Preheat the oven to 350°F. Grease a shallow 1½-quart baking dish.

In a large saucepan, combine the water, 1 cup of the milk, and the salt. Bring to a boil over high heat. Reduce the heat to medium-low, and gradually stir in the grits. Cook, stirring, until very thick, 8 to 10 minutes. Remove from the heat and stir in the butter, cheese, and the remaining 1 cup milk. Gradually stir in the eggs. Stir in the chiles and pepper. Spoon into the prepared baking dish and bake until the top is browned and a toothpick inserted in the center comes out clean, about 1 hour.

**Makes 8 servings**

**Per serving:** 229 calories, 9 g protein, 20 g carbohydrates, 13 g fat, 8 g saturated fat, 88 mg cholesterol, 355 mg sodium, 1 g fiber

**Diet Exchanges:** ½ milk, 0 vegetable, 0 fruit, 1 bread, ½ meat, 2 fat

## Time-Saver

This recipe can be halved if you'd like to make less. But extras make wonderful light suppers or lunches. Store the extras in a covered container in the refrigerator for up to 4 days. To reheat, let sit at room temperature for an hour, place in a baking dish, cover, and bake at 325°F until heated through, 30 to 35 minutes.

*vegetables and side dishes*

# QUINOA AND VEGETABLE PILAF
*133 calories, 20 g carbs*

| | |
|---|---|
| 1 | **tablespoon butter** |
| 1 | **small onion, finely chopped** |
| 1 | **small carrot, finely chopped** |
| 1 | **celery rib or ½ small fennel bulb, finely chopped** |
| ½ | **cup quinoa, rinsed until the water runs clear, and drained** |
| ¾ | **cup chicken or vegetable broth** |
| ⅛ | **teaspoon salt** |
| ⅛ | **teaspoon ground black pepper** |
| 2 | **teaspoons chopped parsley (optional)** |

Melt the butter in a saucepan over medium-low heat. Stir in the onion, carrot, and celery or fennel. Cook, stirring occasionally, until the vegetables are almost tender, 6 to 7 minutes. Stir in the quinoa, increase the heat to medium-high, and cook until lightly toasted, stirring frequently, about 3 minutes. Stir in the broth, salt, and pepper. Reduce the heat to low, cover, and cook until the grains are tender-chewy and all the liquid is absorbed, 15 minutes. Serve sprinkled with the parsley (if using).

**Makes 4 servings**

---

**Per serving:** 133 calories, 4 g protein, 20 g carbohydrates, 4 g fat, 2 g saturated fat, 8 mg cholesterol, 338 mg sodium, 3 g fiber

**Diet Exchanges:** 0 milk, 1 vegetable, 0 fruit, 1 bread, 0 meat, ½ fat

## Time-Saver

Like rice, quinoa keeps well and cooks up in 15 minutes. Make extras if you can and store them in a covered container in the refrigerator for up to 4 days. To reheat, place in a baking dish, cover, and roast at 350°F until steaming, about 15 minutes.

# Brown Rice Pilaf with Hazelnuts

*179 calories, 22 g carbs*

I½ **tablespoons butter**

3 **large mushrooms, coarsely chopped**

I **small onion, chopped**

½ **cup brown rice**

3 **tablespoons (2 ounces) coarsely chopped hazelnuts**

I¼ **cups chicken broth**

½ **teaspoon dried thyme**

½ **teaspoon grated lemon peel**

Melt the butter in a saucepan over medium heat. Stir in the mushrooms and onion. Cook, stirring occasionally, until the mushroom liquid evaporates, 8 to 10 minutes. Stir in the rice and nuts and cook, stirring frequently, for 2 minutes. Stir in the broth, thyme, and lemon peel. Bring to a simmer. Cover, reduce the heat to low, and cook until the rice is tender, about 45 minutes.

Fluff the rice with a fork before serving.

**Makes 4 servings**

---

**Per serving:** 179 calories, 4 g protein, 22 g carbohydrates, 9 g fat, 3 g saturated fat, 12 mg cholesterol, 381 mg sodium, 2 g fiber

**Diet Exchanges:** 0 milk, 1 vegetable, 0 fruit, 1 bread, 0 meat, 1½ fat

## ▶Flavor Tips

*Replace the hazelnuts with walnuts, pine nuts, or pecans. For best results, avoid stirring the rice while it cooks.*

# cookies, cakes, puddings & fruit desserts

# PEANUT BUTTER COOKIES *(photo on page 332)*
*94 calories, 7 g carbs*

| | |
|---|---|
| **6** | **tablespoons unsalted butter, softened** |
| **½** | **cup unsweetened smooth peanut butter, at room temperature** |
| **¼** | **cup packed light brown sugar** |
| **¼** | **cup Splenda** |
| **I** | **large egg, at room temperature, lightly beaten** |
| **I** | **teaspoon vanilla extract** |
| **I¼** | **cups sifted oat flour** |
| **¼** | **teaspoon baking powder** |
| **3** | **tablespoons salted peanuts, chopped** |

Place an oven rack in the middle position and preheat the oven to 350°F.

In a large bowl, beat together the butter and peanut butter until very smooth, about 1 minute. Add the brown sugar and Splenda and beat until well-combined and light in color, 1 to 2 minutes. Gradually beat in the egg and vanilla extract, beating until very smooth and a little fluffy, 1 to 2 minutes. Mix in the flour and baking powder, beating until a moist but cohesive dough forms. Stir in the peanuts.

Drop by the tablespoon about 2" apart on nonstick baking sheets. Using the tines of a fork dampened in cold water, flatten each in a cross-hatch pattern until 2" in diameter. Bake until golden brown, 22 to 25 minutes. Remove to a rack to cool.

**Makes 24**

---

**Per cookie:** 94 calories, 3 g protein, 7 g carbohydrates, 7 g fat, 2 g saturated fat, 17 mg cholesterol, 56 mg sodium, 1 g fiber

**Diet Exchanges:** 0 milk, 0 vegetable, 0 fruit, ½ bread, ½ meat, 1 fat

## ▶Flavor Tips

*Stir ¼ cup currants into the batter. Use chunky peanut butter and eliminate the peanuts. For a sweeter, more crunchy cookie, use ½ cup brown sugar and omit the Splenda (this will add about 2 grams carbohydrate per cookie). Or for fewer carbs per cookie, use ½ cup Splenda and omit the brown sugar. Store the cookies in a tightly closed container at room temperature for up to 5 days.*

# CHOCOLATE-ALMOND MERINGUE COOKIES *(photo on page 332)*

*61 calories, 9 g carbs*

½   **cup blanched almonds**

5   **tablespoons sugar**

3   **egg whites, at room temperature**

¼   **teaspoon cream of tartar**

2   **tablespoons unsweetened cocoa powder**

¼   **cup raspberry or strawberry preserves**

Preheat the oven to 250°F. Line a cookie sheet with parchment paper or aluminum foil.

In a food processor, process the almonds with 2 tablespoons of the sugar until finely ground. Set aside.

In a large, clean bowl, beat the egg whites and cream of tartar until frothy. Gradually add the remaining 3 tablespoons sugar and beat until stiff peaks form when the beaters are lifted. Gently fold in the cocoa powder and almond mixture.

Spoon the meringue into 1½" mounds on the prepared cookie sheet. Using the back of a spoon, depress the centers and build up the sides of each meringue to form a shallow cup.

Bake 1 hour. Do not open the oven door. Turn off the oven and let the meringues cool in the oven. Store in an airtight container. When ready to serve, fill each with preserves.

**Makes 16**

---

**Per cookie:** 61 calories, 2 g protein, 9 g carbohydrates, 2 g fat, 0 g saturated fat, 0 mg cholesterol, 12 mg sodium, 1 g fiber

**Diet Exchanges:** 0 milk, 0 vegetable, 0 fruit, ½ bread, 0 meat, ½ fat

Peanut Butter Cookies (p. 330), Chocolate-Almond Meringue Cookies (p. 331), and Orange-Walnut Biscotti

# ORANGE-WALNUT BISCOTTI
*76 calories, 8 g carbs*

⅔ **cup walnuts**

¼ **cup sugar**

1¼ **cups whole grain pastry flour**

¼ **cup cornmeal**

1 **teaspoon baking powder**

¼ **teaspoon salt**

¼ **cup butter, softened**

¼ **cup Splenda**

2 **eggs**

2 **teaspoons grated orange peel**

½ **teaspoon orange extract**

In a food processor, combine the walnuts and 2 tablespoons of the sugar. Process until the walnuts are coarsely ground but not made into a paste. Transfer to a large bowl and add the flour, cornmeal, baking powder, and salt. Stir until combined.

In a large bowl, using an electric mixer, beat the butter, Splenda, and remaining 2 tablespoons sugar until light and fluffy. Beat in the eggs, orange peel, and orange extract. Gradually beat in the flour mixture until smooth and thick. Divide the dough into two equal-size pieces. Refrigerate for 30 minutes, or until firm.

Preheat the oven to 350°F. Coat a baking sheet with cooking spray.

Shape each piece of dough into a 12"-long log and place both on the prepared baking sheet. Bake for 25 to 30 minutes, or until golden. Remove the logs to wire racks to cool.

Cut each log on a slight diagonal into ½"-thick slices. Place the slices, cut side down, on the baking sheet and bake for 5 minutes. Turn the slices over and bake 5 minutes more, or until dry. Remove to wire racks to cool.

**Makes 24**

**Per biscotto:** 76 calories, 2 g protein, 8 g carbohydrates, 5 g fat, 2 g saturated fat, 23 mg cholesterol, 68 mg sodium, 1 g fiber

**Diet Exchanges:** 0 milk, 0 vegetable, 0 fruit, ½ bread, 0 meat, 1 fat

## ▶ Flavor Tip

*Replace the walnuts with pine nuts and the orange peel and orange extract with lemon peel and lemon extract. For a sweeter, more crunchy cookie, use ½ cup sugar and omit the Splenda (this will add about 2 grams carbohydrate per cookie). Or for fewer carbs per cookie, omit the sugar and use ½ cup Splenda.*

# GINGERBREAD CAKE WITH PEACH WHIPPED CREAM

*238 calories, 25 g carbs*

1½    **cups sifted oat flour**

¾     **cup whole grain pastry flour**

2     **teaspoons baking powder**

1     **teaspoon ground ginger**

1     **teaspoon ground cinnamon**

½     **teaspoon ground cloves**

      **Pinch of salt**

¼     **cup light molasses**

⅓     **cup vegetable oil**

1¼    **cups hot water**

1     **teaspoon baking soda**

1     **large egg + 1 yolk, at room temperature, lightly beaten**

¼     **teaspoon liquid stevia or ¼ cup Splenda**

½     **cup heavy cream**

3     **tablespoons peach fruit spread, at room temperature**

Preheat the oven to 350°F. Coat an 8" round cake pan or 8" × 8" baking pan with cooking spray.

In a medium bowl, combine the oat flour, pastry flour, baking powder, ginger, cinnamon, cloves, and salt.

In a large bowl, combine the molasses and oil. In a 2-cup glass measure, combine the water and baking soda. Whisk into the molasses-oil mixture.

Gradually whisk the dry ingredients into the molasses mixture. Whisk in the egg, yolk, and stevia or Splenda. Pour into the prepared pan and bake until a toothpick inserted in the center comes out clean, about 30 minutes.

Cool in the pan on a rack for 10 minutes. Remove to the rack and cool completely.

In a large bowl, whip the cream and fruit spread together until firm but soft peaks form. Serve wedges of cake topped with a spoonful of the peach cream.

**Makes 10 servings**

---

**Per serving:** 238 calories, 4 g protein, 25 g carbohydrates, 14 g fat, 4 g saturated fat, 59 mg cholesterol, 262 mg sodium, 3 g fiber

**Diet Exchanges:** 0 milk, 0 vegetable, 0 fruit, 1½ bread, 0 meat, 2½ fat

## ▶Flavor Tips

*Replace the peach fruit spread with apricot, raspberry, or cherry. Stir ¼ cup fruit spread and ½ teaspoon vanilla extract into 1 cup Soft Yogurt Cheese (page 107) and use instead of the whipped cream. For a more moist cake, replace the stevia or Splenda with ¼ cup sugar (this will add about 6 grams of carbohydrate per serving). This gingerbread cake (minus the cream topping) keeps well in a zip-top bag at room temperature for 1 day or in the freezer for 1 month. The whipped cream will keep in a covered container in the refrigerator for 1 day.*

Gingerbread Cake with Peach Whipped Cream

# Strawberry Cream Cake
*273 calories, 24 g carbs*

### CAKE

| | |
|---|---|
| ¾ | **cup sifted whole wheat pastry flour** |
| ¾ | **cup sifted oat flour** |
| 1 | **tablespoon baking powder** |
| ½ | **cup butter, slightly softened** |
| ¼ | **cup packed light brown sugar** |
| ¼ | **cup Splenda** |
| 2 | **egg yolks + 3 whites, at room temperature** |
| ¾ | **cup 2% milk, at room temperature** |
| 1 | **teaspoon vanilla extract** |

### TOPPING

| | |
|---|---|
| ¾ | **cup heavy cream** |
| ¼ | **cup strawberry fruit spread** |
| 1 | **pint strawberries, hulled and sliced** |

**To make the cake:** Preheat the oven to 350°F. Butter and flour an 8" round cake pan or 8" × 8" baking pan.

In a small bowl, combine the pastry flour, oat flour, and baking powder.

In a large bowl, using an electric mixer on medium speed, beat the butter, brown sugar, and Splenda until creamy, about 2 minutes. Add the egg yolks, one at a time, beating until the mixture is somewhat fluffy, 3 to 4 minutes.

Beat in the flour mixture alternately with the milk in 3 additions. Beat in the vanilla extract.

In a clean, large bowl, beat the 3 egg whites until they form stiff but moist peaks, about 1 minute. Spoon ⅓ of the whites on top of the egg yolk mixture and gently fold in. Fold in the remaining whites. Spoon into the prepared pan and bake until a toothpick inserted in the center comes out clean, 35 to 40 minutes.

Cool in the pan on a rack for 10 to 15 minutes. Remove to the rack and cool completely.

**To make the topping:** In a clean, large bowl, whip the cream until firm but soft peaks form, and refrigerate.

Melt the fruit spread in a small skillet over very low heat, stirring, about 15 seconds. To make a layer cake, split the completely cooled cake horizontally into 2 layers. Spread ⅓ of the fruit spread over the cut side of the bottom layer. Cover with ⅓ of the whipped cream and ⅓ of the berries. Top with the remaining layer and coat with the remaining fruit spread and whipped cream. Arrange the remaining berries over the top.

**Makes 10 servings**

---

**Per serving:** 273 calories, 5 g protein, 24 g carbohydrates, 18 g fat, 10 g saturated fat, 93 mg cholesterol, 253 mg sodium, 2 g fiber

**Diet Exchanges:** 0 milk, 0 vegetable, ½ fruit, 1 bread, ½ meat, 3½ fat

Strawberry Cream Cake

# CHOCOLATE HAZELNUT FLOURLESS CAKE

*160 calories, 15 g carbs*

| | |
|---|---|
| 2 | **tablespoons unsalted butter** |
| 3 | **tablespoons unsweetened cocoa powder** |
| ½ | **cup blanched hazelnuts or almonds** |
| 8 | **tablespoons sugar, divided** |
| 3 | **ounces bittersweet chocolate** |
| ½ | **cup reduced-fat sour cream** |
| 2 | **egg yolks** |
| 1 | **tablespoon Frangelico or amaretto (optional)** |
| 1 | **teaspoon vanilla extract** |
| ½ | **teaspoon cinnamon** |
| 5 | **egg whites, at room temperature** |
| ¼ | **teaspoon salt** |
| | **Fresh sliced strawberries for serving (optional)** |

Preheat the oven to 350°F. Generously coat an 8" or 9" springform pan with 2 teaspoons of the butter and dust with 1 tablespoon of the cocoa powder (don't tap out the excess cocoa; leave it in the pan).

In a food processor, process the nuts with 1 tablespoon of the sugar until finely ground.

In the top of a double boiler over barely simmering water, melt the chocolate and the remaining 4 teaspoons butter, stirring occasionally, until smooth.

Remove from the heat. Place the chocolate mixture in a large bowl. Add the nut mixture, sour cream, egg yolks, Frangelico or amaretto (if using), vanilla extract, cinnamon, 5 tablespoons of the remaining sugar, and the remaining 2 tablespoons cocoa powder. Stir until well-blended.

In another large bowl, with an electric mixer on high speed, beat the egg whites and salt until foamy. Gradually add the remaining 2 tablespoons sugar, beating, until the whites hold stiff peaks when the beaters are lifted.

Stir ¼ of the beaten whites into the chocolate mixture to lighten it. Gently fold in the remaining whites. Spoon into the prepared pan. Gently smooth the top.

Bake for 30 minutes, or until the cake has risen, is dry on the top, and a wooden pick inserted in the center comes out with a few moist crumbs. Cool on a rack until warm. The cake will fall dramatically. Loosen the edges of the cake with a knife and remove the pan sides. Serve with the strawberries (if using).

**Makes 12 servings**

---

**Per serving:** 160 calories, 4 g protein, 15 g carbohydrates, 10 g fat, 4 g saturated fat, 46 mg cholesterol, 1 g dietary fiber, 80 mg sodium

**Diet Exchanges:** 0 milk, 0 vegetable, 0 fruit, 1 bread, 0 meat, 2 fat

Chocolate Hazelnut Flourless Cake

# Zucchini–Chocolate Chip Snack Cake

*146 calories, 18 g carbs*

| | |
|---|---|
| 1¾ | **cups whole grain pastry flour** |
| 1½ | **teaspoons baking powder** |
| ½ | **teaspoon baking soda** |
| 1½ | **teaspoons ground cinnamon** |
| ¼ | **teaspoon salt** |
| 2 | **eggs** |
| ⅓ | **cup packed brown sugar** |
| ½ | **cup plain yogurt** |
| ⅓ | **cup canola oil** |
| 2 | **teaspoons vanilla extract** |
| 1½ | **cups shredded zucchini** |
| ¾ | **cup mini semisweet chocolate chips** |

Preheat the oven to 350°F. Line an 8" × 8" baking pan with aluminum foil, leaving extra foil over 2 opposite edges to use as handles after the cake is baked. Coat the foil with cooking spray.

In a large bowl, combine the flour, baking powder, baking soda, cinnamon, and salt.

In a medium bowl, with a wire whisk, beat the eggs, brown sugar, yogurt, oil, and vanilla extract until smooth. Stir in the zucchini and chocolate chips.

Add the zucchini mixture to the flour mixture and stir just until blended. Scrape into the prepared pan. Bake for 40 minutes, or until the cake is springy to the touch and a wooden pick inserted in the center comes out clean.

Let the cake cool in the pan on a rack for 30 minutes. Remove from the pan using foil handles. Discard foil and cool completely on the rack.

**Makes 16 servings**

---

**Per serving:** 146 calories, 3 g protein, 18 g carbohydrates, 8 g fat, 2 g saturated fat, 27 mg cholesterol, 127 mg sodium, 2 g fiber

**Diet Exchanges:** 0 milk, 0 vegetable, 0 fruit, 1 bread, 0 meat, 1½ fat

## ▶Flavor Tips

*For a more spicy cake, replace ½ teaspoon of the cinnamon with ½ teaspoon ground allspice and/or cloves. For fewer carbohydrates per serving, replace the brown sugar with ⅓ cup Splenda.*

# DOUBLE CHOCOLATE PUDDING
*142 calories, 23 g carbs*

⅓ **cup packed brown sugar**

⅓ **cup Splenda**

¼ **cup unsweetened cocoa powder**

2 **tablespoons cornstarch**

2 **cups whole milk or unsweetened soy milk**

1 **ounce bittersweet chocolate**

1 **teaspoon vanilla extract**

In a medium saucepan, whisk together the brown sugar, Splenda, cocoa, and cornstarch until smooth. Whisk in the milk over medium heat. Cook until thickened and bubbly, 2 minutes. Remove from the heat and stir in the bittersweet chocolate and vanilla extract. Stir until the chocolate melts.

Pour into 4 custard cups or small serving dishes. Cover with plastic wrap and chill for 2 hours before serving.

**Makes 6 servings**

---

**Per serving:** 142 calories, 4 g protein, 23 g carbohydrates, 5 g fat, 3 g saturated fat, 11 mg cholesterol, 46 mg sodium, 2 g fiber

**Diet Exchanges:** ½ milk, 0 vegetable, 0 fruit, 1 bread, 0 meat, ½ fat

## ▶Flavor Tips

*For mocha pudding, add 1 teaspoon instant espresso or coffee granules along with the milk. Cook and stir until dissolved. For the taste of chocolate cream pie, crumble a graham cracker into the bottom of each dish, then add the pudding. If you prefer, replace the Splenda with ⅓ cup brown sugar (this will add about 12 grams carbohydrate per serving).*

## HIDDEN ROADBLOCK to weight loss

### HIGH EXPECTATIONS

Whenever you set a weight-loss goal, be realistic. Losing 20 pounds in 1 week is not very realistic. It's possible, but that sudden loss would be difficult to sustain. To minimize frustration, set goals that you know you can stick to. If everything points to the fact that you are in excellent health despite the fact that you still weigh more than you want to or you don't look as slim as you'd like to, don't sweat it. You are making progress. Accept yourself the way you are, feel good about your good health, and get on with your life. Just keep making the right choices when you face a food decision (with occasional indulgences, of course) and stay physically active. And be patient. It may take time for your body weight and shape to balance out to what is ideal for your particular physical makeup.

# I Did It!

## Gene Newman

As Gene got older, he went from weighing 185 to weighing over 215 pounds. He decided to avoid breads, sweets, and soft drinks and lost 40 pounds.

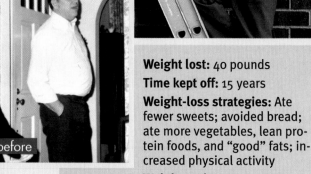

before

"Weight loss was never a real concern for me until I started getting a little older, spending more time behind a desk, and having a greater desire for ice cream and bananas as a late-night snack.

"I was on the pudgy side in my early teens. That's because my family ate a lot of fried foods—mostly chicken and pork chops—lots of biscuits, and big portions. At 13, I weighed 135 pounds and was nicknamed Butterball. But in high school, I played football, trimmed down a bit, and weighed 155 pounds. At 18, after Army basic training, I weighed 185 and had a 32-inch waist.

"I started adding pounds and inches in the mid-1970s. It became more difficult to

**Weight lost:** 40 pounds
**Time kept off:** 15 years
**Weight-loss strategies:** Ate fewer sweets; avoided bread; ate more vegetables, lean protein foods, and "good" fats; increased physical activity
**Weight-maintenance strategies:** Eats fewer sweets; avoids bread; eats more lean protein foods; eats whole grains instead of refined ones; eats sensible portions; maintains physical activity

bend over and tie my shoes and get into the size 34 pants that I had worn since my mid-twenties. By the early 1980s, I weighed over 215 pounds and had trouble buttoning a

17-inch collar. It wasn't long before I had to buy a new suit and discovered that I needed a size 38! And that *really* caused me to take a hard look at what was happening.

"I tried the grapefruit diet, a no-fat diet, a low-fat diet—I even attempted several times to just reduce the amount of food that I ate. None of these approaches worked. I kept looking for an eating style that would satisfy my hunger and be healthy enough to sustain for the rest of my life.

"Finally, I decided to cut out breads and sweets, including soft drinks and ice cream. Within 8 months, my weight had dropped back down to below 180 pounds. I was always fairly active, so all of this extra weight was due to my eating habits.

"Over the next 15 years, I tried low-fat eating plans but I immediately started to regain the pounds. Now I eat a small amount of starches, mostly in the form of high-fiber whole grains, plenty of vegetables, and lots of fish and poultry. I rarely eat cakes, candies, or soft drinks with sugar. Occasionally I eat beef, pork, and lamb in reasonable amounts. My current weight is less than 180 pounds, and I fit into size 34 pants. My cholesterol has dropped from about 190 to the 160 range. I still stay active by walking and remodeling on weekends, but I'm planning to get to the gym more often to stay fit. I feel so much better not lugging the extra weight around!"

## GENE'S LEMON GELATIN WHIP
*137 calories, 3 g carbs*

- **2 boxes sugar-free lemon gelatin**
- **2 cups boiling water**
- **1 cup cold water**
- **⅓ cup reduced-fat sour cream**
- **⅓ cup part-skim ricotta**
- **⅓ cup reduced-fat cream cheese**
- **½ teaspoon lemon extract**

Dissolve the gelatin in the boiling water. Stir in the cold water, cover, and refrigerate until firm.

In a blender, combine the sour cream, ricotta, cream cheese, and lemon extract. Blend on high speed until light and fluffy. Cut the gelatin into sections and add to the mixture in the blender. Blend on high speed until smooth and frothy like a milkshake, about 3 to 4 minutes. Pour into individual serving dishes or small containers with lids. Cover and refrigerate for at least 1 hour or overnight.

**Makes 6 servings**

**Per serving:** 137 calories, 14 g protein, 3 g carbohydrates, 5 g fat, 3 g saturated fat, 18 mg cholesterol, 537 mg sodium, 0 g fiber

**Diet Exchanges:** ½ milk, 0 vegetable, 0 fruit, 0 bread, 1½ meat, 0 fat

cookies, cakes, puddings, and fruit desserts

# CHOCOLATE PUDDING CUPS
*211 calories, 27 g carbs*

- **8**    **whole grain crepes (from recipe on page 94)**
- **1**    **cup whole milk or unsweetened soy milk**
- **1**    **package (1 ounce) sugar-free instant chocolate pudding mix**
- **4**    **ounces cream cheese, softened and cut into pieces**
- **3**    **cups strawberries, sliced, or raspberries**
- **8**    **fresh mint leaves (optional)**

Preheat the oven to 400°F. Invert eight 6-ounce custard cups or coffee mugs over a baking sheet. Coat the outside of the cups with cooking spray. Drape each crepe, browned side down, over each cup. Coat the crepes with cooking spray. Bake for 20 minutes. Turn the oven off and let the crepes sit in the oven until they are crisp, 30 minutes more. Carefully lift the crepe cups from the mold and cool on a wire rack.

Pour the milk into a food processor or blender. Add the pudding mix, cover, and process until blended. Add the cream cheese. Cover and process until smooth.

Place each crepe cup right side up on a dessert plate. Spoon a layer of berries in the bottom of each. Spoon some of the cream cheese filling over the berries. Top with additional berries and the mint leaves (if using). Serve immediately.

**Makes 8 servings**

**Per serving:** 211 calories, 7 g protein, 27 g carbohydrates, 10 g fat, 5 g saturated fat, 49 mg cholesterol, 559 mg sodium, 3 g fiber

**Diet Exchanges:** 0 milk, 0 vegetable, 1 fruit, 1 bread, ½ meat, 1½ fat

## Time-Saver

*Use store-bought crepes (they will be somewhat higher in carbohydrates). To make this dessert ahead, prepare the crepes and filling, cover each separately, and refrigerate for up to 24 hours before assembling.*

Chocolate Pudding Cups

# BREAD AND BUTTER PUDDING
*323 calories, 35 g carbs*

⅓    **cup raisins**

¼    **cup whiskey or 1 teaspoon rum extract**

2    **cups 2% milk**

⅓    **cup heavy cream**

¾    **cup peach or apricot fruit spread**

2    **teaspoons vanilla extract**

¾    **teaspoon ground cinnamon**

     **Pinch of salt**

4    **large eggs + 3 yolks, at room temperature**

8    **slices (about 1¼ ounces each) dried light whole wheat bread**

3    **tablespoons unsalted butter, softened**

1    **tablespoon confectioner's sugar (optional)**

In a microwaveable cup or mug, combine the raisins and whiskey or rum extract. Microwave on high power until hot, 15 to 20 seconds. Cover to keep warm.

In a large saucepan, combine the milk, cream, fruit spread, vanilla extract, cinnamon, and salt. Cook over low heat until tiny bubbles appear around the edge of the pan, 8 to 10 minutes, stirring occasionally to incorporate the fruit spread.

Meanwhile, in a large bowl, whisk the eggs and yolks. Gradually whisk

½ cup of the milk mixture into the eggs. Quickly whisk in the remaining milk mixture. Strain the raisin-whiskey mixture over the egg mixture, reserving the raisins.

Coat an 8" × 8" baking pan with cooking spray. Spread 1 side of each bread slice with the butter. Cut bread into cubes and arrange in the bottom of the prepared pan in an even layer. Scatter the raisins over the bread and pour the milk-egg mixture over top. Press a piece of plastic wrap directly onto the surface of the mixture and let sit until the bread is thoroughly soaked, 30 to 40 minutes, occasionally pressing down on the plastic wrap to keep the bread submerged.

Meanwhile place a rack in the middle position in the oven and preheat the oven to 350°F. Discard the plastic wrap and bake until a wooden skewer inserted in the center comes out clean, 45 to 50 minutes. Serve warm or at room temperature. Dust with the confectioner's sugar (if using).

**Makes 8 servings**

**Per serving:** 323 calories, 10 g protein, 35 g carbohydrates, 15 g fat, 7 g saturated fat, 215 mg cholesterol, 196 mg sodium, 1 g fiber

**Diet Exchanges:** ½ milk, 0 vegetable, ½ fruit, 1½ bread, ½ meat, 2½ fat

# CHOCOLATE-RASPBERRY DIP AND FRESH FRUIT

*147 calories, 24 g carbs*

| | |
|---|---|
| ⅓ | **cup raspberry fruit spread** |
| 2 | **tablespoons unsweetened cocoa powder** |
| 2 | **tablespoons milk** |
| ½ | **cup sour cream** |
| 2 | **teaspoons vanilla extract** |
| 2 | **teaspoons raspberry liqueur (optional)** |
| 6 | **drops liquid stevia** |
| 1 | **tablespoon chopped walnuts** |
| 1 | **large navel orange, peeled and segmented** |
| 1 | **pear, cut lengthwise into ½" slices** |
| 1 | **apple, cut lengthwise into ½" slices** |
| ½ | **pint strawberries, with hulls left on** |

In a small saucepan, mix the fruit spread, cocoa, and milk. Cook over low heat, stirring occasionally, until the cocoa has dissolved and the fruit spread has melted, 1 to 2 minutes. Remove to a bowl, cover, and let cool to room temperature.

Place the sour cream in a serving bowl and gradually stir in the cocoa mixture, vanilla extract, liqueur (if using), and stevia. Sprinkle with the nuts and place on a platter. Arrange the orange, pear, apple, and strawberries around the bowl.

**Makes 6 servings**

**Per serving:** 147 calories, 2 g protein, 24 g carbohydrates, 5 g fat, 3 g saturated fat, 9 mg cholesterol, 17 mg sodium, 3 g fiber

**Diet Exchanges:** ½ milk, 0 vegetable, 1 fruit, 0 bread, 0 meat, 1 fat

## ▶Flavor Tip

*The raspberry flavor in this chocolate dip becomes more pronounced after a day or two. To make the dip ahead, store in a covered container in the refrigerator for up to 5 days. Let come to room temperature before serving. To keep the dip warm, place the bowl in a larger bowl filled with boiling water and replenish the hot water as needed.*

# BAKED PANCAKE WITH BERRIES AND CINNAMON

*241 calories, 17 g carbs*

**4**    **large eggs**

**½**    **cup 2% milk**

**⅓**    **cup oat flour**

       **Pinch of salt**

**3**    **tablespoons unsalted butter, softened**

**⅛–¼**  **teaspoon ground cinnamon**

**3**    **tablespoons raspberry or blueberry fruit spread, warmed**

In a blender, combine the eggs, milk, flour, and salt. Process until smooth, about 15 seconds. Remove to a medium bowl, cover, and let rest for 45 to 60 minutes at room temperature. Meanwhile, preheat the oven to 375°F.

Heat 2 tablespoons of the butter in a 9" oven-safe skillet over medium heat and cook until frothy. Pour in the egg-flour mixture. Place in the oven and bake until puffy and set, 14 to 16 minutes.

Remove from the oven and sprinkle with the cinnamon. Spread the fruit over the pancake, and dot with the remaining 1 tablespoon butter. Using a spatula, fold the pancake in half (or roll it up) and slide it onto a platter. Slice into 4 pieces.

**Makes 4 servings**

---

**Per serving:** 241 calories, 9 g protein, 17 g carbohydrates, 15 g fat, 7 g saturated fat, 238 mg cholesterol, 83 mg sodium, 1 g fiber

**Diet Exchanges:** 0 milk, 0 vegetable, 0 fruit, 1 bread, 1 meat, 2½ fat

---

▶ Flavor Tips

*Use any fruit spread you like for this recipe. You could also arrange 1 thinly sliced banana over the fruit spread before folding. Top each serving with a dollop of unsweetened whipped cream and sprinkle with cinnamon or nutmeg.*

# CANTALOUPE SORBET
*61 calories, 15 g carbs*

| | |
|---|---|
| 4 | **cups frozen cantaloupe, slightly thawed** |
| 1 | **frozen banana, sliced** |
| ¼ | **cup Splenda** |
| 1 | **tablespoon crème de menthe liqueur (optional)** |
| 1 | **tablespoon lime juice** |
| 2 | **teaspoons grated lime peel** |
| ⅛–¼ | **teaspoon ground cinnamon** |

In a food processor, combine the cantaloupe, banana, Splenda, liqueur (if using), lime juice, lime peel, and cinnamon. Process until smooth.

Scrape into a shallow metal pan. Cover and freeze for 4 hours or overnight. Using a knife, break the mixture into chunks. Process briefly in a food processor before serving.

**Makes 6 servings**

**Per serving:** 61 calories, 1 g protein, 15 g carbohydrates, 0 g fat, 0 g saturated fat, 0 mg cholesterol, 11 mg sodium, 2 g fiber

**Diet Exchanges:** 0 milk, 0 vegetable, 1 fruit, 0 bread, 0 meat, 0 fat

## ▶Flavor Tips

*Frozen cantaloupe saves time in this recipe, but fresh will have more flavor. Use the flesh of 1 small cantaloupe, cut into chunks. For a sweeter sorbet, replace the Splenda with ¼ cup sugar (this will add about 8 grams carbohydrate per serving). Serve with toasted almonds for an extra shot of flavor—and to reduce the overall glycemic index of the dessert.*

# RASPBERRY-ALMOND TART
*138 calories, 21 g carbs*

### CRUST

| | |
|---|---|
| ⅔ | cup old-fashioned or quick-cooking rolled oats |
| ½ | cup whole grain pastry flour |
| 1 | tablespoon sugar |
| 1 | teaspoon ground cinnamon |
| ¼ | teaspoon baking soda |
| 2 | tablespoons canola oil |
| 2–3 | tablespoons plain yogurt |
| ⅓ | cup mini semisweet chocolate morsels (optional) |

### FILLING

| | |
|---|---|
| ¼ | cup raspberry all-fruit spread |
| ¾ | teaspoon almond extract |
| 2½ | cups raspberries |
| 2 | tablespoons sliced almonds |

Preheat the oven to 375°F. Coat a baking sheet with cooking spray.

In a medium bowl, combine the oats, flour, sugar, cinnamon, and baking soda. Stir in the oil and 2 tablespoons of yogurt to make a soft, slightly sticky dough. If the dough is too stiff, add the remaining 1 tablespoon yogurt.

Place the dough on the prepared baking sheet and, using lightly oiled hands, pat evenly into a 10" circle. Place a 9" cake pan right side up on the dough and trace around the bottom of the pan with a sharp knife, being careful only to score the surface of the dough. With your fingers, push up and pinch the dough around the outside of the pan to make a 9" crust with a rim ¼" high. Remove the cake pan. Bake for 12 minutes on the baking sheet. Scatter the chocolate chips (if using) evenly over the surface of the crust and bake until the chocolate is melted and the crust is firm and golden, 3 to 4 minutes more. Remove from the oven and spread the chocolate over the crust to make an even layer. Set aside to cool.

In a small, microwaveable bowl, combine the all-fruit spread and almond extract. Microwave on high power for 10 to 15 seconds, or until melted. Brush a generous tablespoon evenly over the crust. Arrange the raspberries evenly over the crust. Brush the remaining spread evenly over the berries, making sure to get some of the spread between the berries to secure them. Sprinkle with the almonds.

Refrigerate for at least 30 minutes, or until the spread has jelled.

**Makes 8 servings**

**Per serving:** 138 calories, 3 g protein, 21 g carbohydrates, 5 g fat, 0 g saturated fat, 0 mg cholesterol, 43 mg sodium, 4 g fiber

**Diet Exchanges:** 0 milk, 0 vegetable, ½ fruit, ½ bread, 0 meat, 1 fat

*Raspberry-Almond Tart*

# WARM BUTTERED FRUIT COMPOTE
*143 calories, 26 g carbs*

| | |
|---|---|
| 1⅓ | cups apple juice |
| ⅔ | cup dry white wine or white grape juice |
| 2 | teaspoons lemon juice |
| 1 | teaspoon vanilla extract |
| 6 | dried peach slices (3 ounces), cut into ¾" pieces |
| 2 | Granny Smith or other tart apples, peeled and cut into ¾"-thick wedges |
| 2 | Bosc pears, peeled and cut into 1" cubes |
| 4 | teaspoons butter |
| 4 | sprigs fresh mint (optional) |

In a wide saucepan, combine the apple juice, wine or grape juice, lemon juice, and vanilla extract. Cook over low heat for 5 minutes. Add the peaches, partially cover, and cook until tender, 8 to 10 minutes. Add the apples and pears. Partially cover, and cook until tender-firm, 5 to 6 minutes, stirring occasionally.

Remove from the heat, stir in the butter, and serve warm garnished with the mint (if using).

**Makes 6 servings**

**Per serving:** 143 calories, 1 g protein, 26 g carbohydrates, 3 g fat, 2 g saturated fat, 7 mg cholesterol, 23 mg sodium, 3 g fiber

**Diet Exchanges:** 0 milk, 0 vegetable, 1½ fruit, 0 bread, 0 meat, 1 fat

## ▶Flavor Tip

*Serve with slices of Raisin Spice Quick Bread (page 100) or with the crepes in Whole Grain Crepes with Banana and Kiwifruit (page 94). Garnish each serving with a dollop of plain yogurt instead of the butter. Or drizzle each serving with a teaspoon of heavy cream and sprinkle with a pinch of nutmeg.*

## Smart-Carb Insider Tip
### KEEP TREATS ON HAND

If you have a sweet tooth, make the cookies or desserts in this book that keep well so that they are ready when you need them. Keep sugar-free gelatin in the refrigerator and top with a couple of squirts of canned real whipped cream. Or look in your local supermarkets or health food store for low-carbohydrate chocolate snack bars, cookies, cake mixes, milkshakes, and beverages.

# DRIED APRICOT FOOL
*256 calories, 33 g carbs*

- **1**    **cup (6 ounces) dried apricots**
- **¾**    **cup orange juice**
- **1**    **teaspoon lemon juice**
- **1**    **teaspoon grated orange peel**
- **1**    **tablespoon + 1½ teaspoons rum or ½ teaspoon rum extract (optional)**
- **½**    **cup heavy cream**
- **3**    **tablespoons slivered or sliced almonds, toasted**
- **⅛**    **teaspoon ground nutmeg**

Combine the apricots and orange juice in a saucepan over low heat. Bring to a simmer, partially cover, and cook until the fruit is very tender, about 15 minutes. Pour the fruit and liquid into a food processor and process until smooth, 2 to 3 minutes. Remove to a large bowl, stir in the lemon juice, orange peel, and rum or extract (if using) and let cool.

In a large bowl, whip the cream to soft but firm peaks. Stir one-quarter of the cream into the apricot mixture. Gently fold in the rest until evenly incorporated. Remove to a serving bowl and chill for at least 3 hours or up to 3 days. Serve sprinkled with the almonds and nutmeg.

**Makes 4 servings**

---

**Per serving:** 265 calories, 3 g protein, 33 g carbohydrates, 14 g fat, 7 g saturated fat, 41 mg cholesterol, 13 mg sodium, 3 g fiber

**Diet Exchanges:** 0 milk, 0 vegetable, 2 fruit, 0 bread, 0 meat, 2 fat

Flavor Tip

*Replace the apricots with prunes, dried mangoes, or other dried fruit.*

# BROILED PINEAPPLE WITH GINGER-YOGURT SAUCE

*124 calories, 15 g carbs*

½    **cup plain yogurt**

1½    **teaspoons chopped crystallized ginger**

1    **teaspoon vanilla extract**

1    **teaspoon grated orange peel**

2    **tablespoons butter**

1    **tablespoon + 1½ teaspoons lime juice**

2    **tablespoons unsweetened peach or apricot fruit spread**

½    **cored, peeled pineapple, cut into wedges 1½" thick**

Place a broiler rack 4" from the heat source and preheat the broiler.

In a small bowl, combine the yogurt, ginger, vanilla extract, and orange peel. Cover and set aside.

In a small skillet, combine the butter, lime juice, and fruit spread. Cook over low heat until the butter and fruit spread are melted. Place the pineapple in a broiler-safe 11" × 7" baking pan. Pour the butter mixture over the wedges and toss to coat. Arrange in a single layer.

Broil, turning once, until lightly browned on both sides, 5 to 7 minutes, shaking the pan occasionally so the juices don't burn. Remove the wedges and juices to 4 bowls, and serve hot or warm topped with the yogurt sauce.

**Makes 4 servings**

---

**Per serving:** 124 calories, 1 g protein, 15 g carbohydrates, 7 g fat, 4 g saturated fat, 19 mg cholesterol, 76 mg sodium, 1 g fiber

**Diet Exchanges:** 0 milk, 0 vegetable, 1 fruit, 0 bread, 0 meat, 1½ fat

## ▶ Flavor Tip

*To grill the pineapple, toss the pineapple wedges with the butter mixture and thread onto skewers. Grill over a medium-low fire until tender, basting with the remaining butter mixture.*

# Baked Bananas with Rum Sauce
*250 calories, 35 g carbs*

**5**     **tablespoons orange juice**

**3**     **tablespoons dark rum or 1½ teaspoons rum extract**

**3**     **tablespoons plum or blueberry fruit spread**

**2**     **tablespoons butter**

**1**     **tablespoon + 1½ teaspoons lemon juice**

**⅛**     **teaspoon ground nutmeg**

**4**     **bananas (24 ounces), halved lengthwise**

**3**     **tablespoons coarsely chopped pecans**

Preheat the oven to 400°F.

In a small saucepan, combine the orange juice, rum or extract, fruit spread, butter, lemon juice, and nutmeg. Bring just to a boil over medium heat, stirring. Immediately remove from the heat.

Arrange the bananas, flat side down, in a single layer in a shallow baking dish. Pour the butter mixture over the bananas and sprinkle with the pecans. Bake until the bananas are tender and the sauce has thickened slightly, 12 to 15 minutes.

**Makes 4 servings**

---

**Per serving:** 250 calories, 2 g protein, 35 g carbohydrates, 10 g fat, 4 g saturated fat, 16 mg cholesterol, 63 mg sodium, 3 g fiber

**Diet Exchanges:** 0 milk, 0 vegetable, 2½ fruit, 0 bread, 0 meat, 2½ fat

## ▶Flavor Tips

Substitute apricot, cherry, or raspberry fruit spread for the plum or blueberry spread. Sprinkle with 1 tablespoon toasted coconut.

# Apricot-Orange Clafouti
*172 calories, 25 g carbs*

| | |
|---|---|
| ¼ | **cup granulated sugar** |
| 1⅓ | **cups 2% milk or unsweetened soy milk** |
| ¾ | **cup oat flour or whole grain pastry flour** |
| ¼ | **cup Splenda** |
| 3 | **eggs** |
| 2 | **teaspoons grated orange peel** |
| ½ | **teaspoon grated ginger** |
| ½ | **teaspoon vanilla extract** |
| 2 | **cups (about 10) pitted and sliced apricots** |
| ¼ | **teaspoon ground cinnamon** |

Preheat the oven to 400°F. Coat a 9" deep-dish pie plate or quiche pan with cooking spray and dust with 1 teaspoon of the granulated sugar.

In a large bowl, whisk together the milk, flour, remaining sugar, Splenda, eggs, orange peel, ginger, and vanilla extract.

Pour half of the batter into the prepared dish. Arrange the apricots evenly over the batter, then top with the remaining batter. Sprinkle with the cinnamon.

Bake for 40 minutes, or until puffed, browned, and firm. Cool on a rack for at least 15 minutes.

**Makes 6 servings**

---

**Per serving:** 172 calories, 8 g protein, 25 g carbohydrates, 5 g fat, 1 g saturated fat, 110 mg cholesterol, 3 g dietary fiber, 59 mg sodium

**Diet Exchanges:** ½ milk, 0 vegetable, ½ fruit, ½ bread, ½ meat, ½ fat

## Time-Saver

Replace the fresh apricots with 2 cups frozen and thawed sliced apricots or peaches. Pat the fruit dry before using. For fewer carbohydrates, replace the sugar with ¼ cup Splenda (this will reduce each serving by about 8 grams carbohydrate).

# PEACH SOUFFLÉ WITH BLUEBERRIES
*96 calories, 17 g carbs*

| | |
|---|---|
| 1½ | **cups frozen peaches, thawed and patted dry** |
| 2 | **tablespoons sugar** |
| 2 | **tablespoons Splenda** |
| 2 | **egg yolks** |
| 1 | **tablespoon lemon juice** |
| ½ | **teaspoon ground nutmeg** |
| 5 | **egg whites, at room temperature** |
| ½ | **teaspoon cream of tartar** |
| ⅛ | **teaspoon ground cinnamon** |
| ½ | **cup blueberries** |

Preheat the oven to 350°F.

In a blender or food processor, puree the peaches. Transfer to a medium bowl and stir in the sugar, Splenda, egg yolks, lemon juice, and nutmeg. Set aside.

In a large, clean bowl, using an electric mixer, beat the egg whites at medium speed until foamy. Add the cream of tartar and beat on high speed until stiff peaks form.

Stir one-quarter of the egg-white mixture into the peach mixture to lighten it. Gently fold the peach mixture back into the remaining egg white mixture.

Scrape into a 1½-quart soufflé or baking dish and sprinkle with the cinnamon. Place the dish in a larger dish or baking pan, then place on the bottom rack of the oven. Pour 1" of hot water into the large baking dish or pan. Bake for 50 to 60 minutes, or until puffed and lightly browned. Do not open the oven door during baking. Serve immediately with the blueberries. The soufflé will fall as it cools.

**Makes 4 servings**

---

**Per serving:** 96 calories, 2 g protein, 17 g carbohydrates, 3 g fat, 12 g saturated fat, 106 mg cholesterol, 5 mg sodium, 2 g fiber

**Diet Exchanges:** 0 milk, 0 vegetable, 1 fruit, 0 bread, 0 meat, ½ fat

## ▶Flavor Tips
*Replace the peaches with apricots and the cinnamon with ⅛ teaspoon ground nutmeg. For fewer carbohydrates per serving, omit the sugar and use ¼ cup Splenda instead (this will reduce each serving by about 6 grams carbohydrate).*

# index

Note: <u>Underscored</u> page references indicate boxed text. **Bold** page references indicate photographs.

# f

# g

## Conversion Chart

These equivalents have been slightly rounded to make measuring easier.

### VOLUME MEASUREMENTS

| U.S. | Imperial | Metric |
|------|----------|--------|
| ¼ tsp | – | 1 ml |
| ½ tsp | – | 2 ml |
| 1 tsp | – | 5 ml |
| 1 Tbsp | – | 15 ml |
| 2 Tbsp (1 oz) | 1 fl oz | 30 ml |
| ¼ cup (2 oz) | 2 fl oz | 60 ml |
| ⅓ cup (3 oz) | 3 fl oz | 80 ml |
| ½ cup (4 oz) | 4 fl oz | 120 ml |
| ⅔ cup (5 oz) | 5 fl oz | 160 ml |
| ¾ cup (6 oz) | 6 fl oz | 180 ml |
| 1 cup (8 oz) | 8 fl oz | 240 ml |

### WEIGHT MEASUREMENTS

| U.S. | Metric |
|------|--------|
| 1 oz | 30 g |
| 2 oz | 60 g |
| 4 oz (¼ lb) | 115 g |
| 5 oz (⅓ lb) | 145 g |
| 6 oz | 170 g |
| 7 oz | 200 g |
| 8 oz (½ lb) | 230 g |
| 10 oz | 285 g |
| 12 oz (¾ lb) | 340 g |
| 14 oz | 400 g |
| 16 oz (1 lb) | 455 g |
| 2.2 lb | 1 kg |

### LENGTH MEASUREMENTS

| U.S. | Metric |
|------|--------|
| ¼" | 0.6 cm |
| ½" | 1.25 cm |
| 1" | 2.5 cm |
| 2" | 5 cm |
| 4" | 11 cm |
| 6" | 15 cm |
| 8" | 20 cm |
| 10" | 25 cm |
| 12" (1') | 30 cm |

### PAN SIZES

| U.S. | Metric |
|------|--------|
| 8" cake pan | 20 × 4 cm sandwich or cake tin |
| 9" cake pan | 23 × 3.5 cm sandwich or cake tin |
| 11" × 7" baking pan | 28 × 18 cm baking tin |
| 13" × 9" baking pan | 32.5 × 23 cm baking tin |
| 15" × 10" baking pan | 38 × 25.5 cm baking tin (Swiss roll tin) |
| 1½ qt baking dish | 1.5 liter baking dish |
| 2 qt baking dish | 2 liter baking dish |
| 2 qt rectangular baking dish | 30 × 19 cm baking dish |
| 9" pie plate | 22 × 4 or 23 × 4 cm pie plate |
| 7" or 8" springform pan | 18 or 20 cm springform or loose-bottom cake tin |
| 9" × 5" loaf pan | 23 × 13 cm or 2 lb narrow loaf tin or pâté tin |

### TEMPERATURES

| Fahrenheit | Centigrade | Gas |
|------------|------------|-----|
| 140° | 60° | – |
| 160° | 70° | – |
| 180° | 80° | – |
| 225° | 105° | ¼ |
| 250° | 120° | ½ |
| 275° | 135° | 1 |
| 300° | 150° | 2 |
| 325° | 160° | 3 |
| 350° | 180° | 4 |
| 375° | 190° | 5 |
| 400° | 200° | 6 |
| 425° | 220° | 7 |
| 450° | 230° | 8 |
| 475° | 245° | 9 |
| 500° | 260° | – |